SUPERIOR

UNDER THE SHADOW OF THE GODS

D1403427

This printing was made possible by
Upper Lakes Group Inc.

Editor: Barbara D. Chisholm
Cover design: Silvia Molinaro
Maps: Russell Floren
Typesetting and design: Lynx Images Inc.
1st Edition, June 1998
2nd Edition, May 1999
3rd Edition, October 2001

Front cover: Lawren Harris' *Lake Superior* (1923) from the collection of K.R. Thomson. Copyright permission of Mrs. Margaret Knox.

Printed and bound in Canada by Metrolitho Inc.

Canadian Cataloguing in Publication Data

Chisholm, Barbara, 1962-
    Superior: Under the Shadow of the Gods: A Guide to
the History of the Canadian Shore of Lake Superior

Includes bibliographical references and index.

ISBN 0-9698427-7-5 Book
ISBN 0-9698427-8-3 Video
ISBN 0-9698427-9-1 Book/Video package

1. Superior, Lake Region - History. I. Gutsche, Andrea, 1964-
II. Floren, Russell, 1965- . III. Title.

FC3095.S86C44 1998   971.3'12   C98-931436-7
F1059.S9C44 1998

SUPERIOR

UNDER THE SHADOW OF THE GODS

WRITTEN BY
BARBARA CHISHOLM
ANDREA GUTSCHE

PROJECT PRODUCER
RUSSELL FLOREN

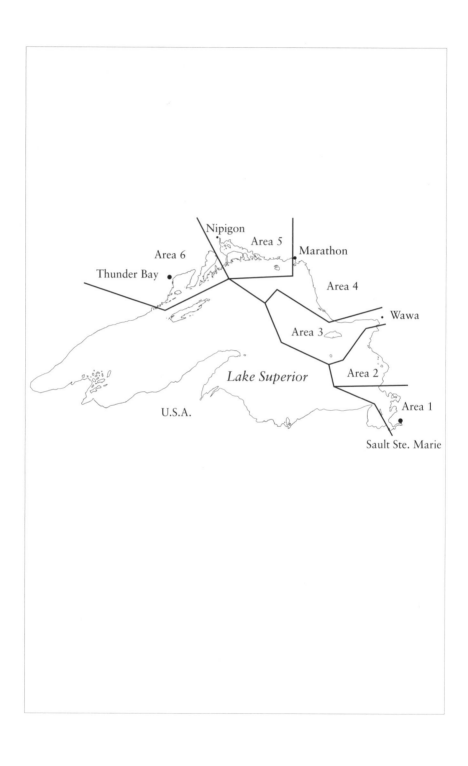

TABLE OF CONTENTS

DISCLAIMER

When trying to locate the sites in this book it is necessary to obtain proper maps and charts for the relevant areas. These will direct you to the sites and away from shoals. The maps in this book are to help the reader gain a sense of the area and are not to be used for navigation.

Every effort has been made to make this book accurate, informative, and useful. While we have scoured the area for stories and interesting information, we do not claim to be doing an exhaustive historical treatment. In condensing complex histories, we are aware of the risk of misrepresenting situations, and hope that our portrayals are found to be fair.

Exploring Lake Superior is not a simple task, it requires a thorough knowledge of boating, navigation, and, in some cases, diving. Readers should be confident they have the skills with which to safely enjoy their exploration of the area, or they are travelling with someone who does. When going to these sites you do so at your own risk. Lynx Images Inc. takes no responsibility for what might befall you. We have made every effort to note when a site is on or near private property and when permission is required in order to visit a site. Divers must be certified. And we can't stress enough that respect and common sense should always travel with you when on the lakes.

We welcome new stories, updates, information and corrections for subsequent editions. Please write: Lynx Images, P.O. Box 5961, Station A., Toronto, Ontario, M5W 1P4 or visit our web site at

http://www.lynximages.com

Assiniboia *at Port Arthur. Safe after Great Storm of November 1913*

Image depicts Hudson's Bay Company post Red Rock House on the Nipigon River

PREFACE

Lake Superior is the largest surface of freshwater in the world. It is in the Canadian psyche, yet most of us know little about it. We've heard of the *Edmund Fitzgerald*, and we know that the lake is cold. Members of the Group of Seven introduced us to the beauty of the Algoma Highlands and to the stark clarity of the North Shore. But as strong as these images are, Superior is much more.

In 1924, traveller T. Morris Longstreth recalled that an image of a grain boat in his school textbook was "all [he] knew about the lake; the terminal moraine of [his] classroom detritus." He asked why the frontier of his knowledge should have stopped at the entrance to Lake Superior; why we dismiss the greatest lake in the world, a place "suffused with the spirit of adventure and mystery," as "of great importance to trade"? So many years later, perhaps we still don't fully see the power of Superior. Our project is to help reveal the stories of this mythic lake.

In the making of this book and film we travelled by boat up the Canadian coast, through libraries and archives and many conversations. Many people living near the lake feel a deep connection to its rhythms, its moods, its wild and savage beauty. They often say, "it gets into your bones. It's part of you." They could never leave. They belong there. Next to such a giant, one feels, at the same time, small and part of a greater whole.

This deep lake has layers of meaning, layers of histories and mythologies to help make sense of it. The Ojibwe living around *Anishnaabe Chi Gaming*, the "Ojibwe Ocean," lived in a world where the manitous held sway. For those trying to use Superior for commercial gain, it could be a monstrous beast, capable of crushing them under the force of its great weight and power.

The book begins at Sault Ste. Marie on the St. Marys River and explores along Superior's Canadian shore to the American border at the Pigeon River. It is a collection of stories which together reveal the spirit of this great inland sea. We hope the book encourages respectful exploration.

Barbara Chisholm
Andrea Gutsche
Russell Floren

The first European map of Lake Superior by Jesuits Claude Allouez and Claude Dablon, from observations made on Lake Superior between 1665 and 1667

INTRODUCTION

Looking Back Across the Lake

...those who have never seen Superior get an inadequate, even inaccurate idea by hearing it spoken of as a lake... Superior is a sea. It breeds storms and rain and fog like a sea... It is cold, wild, masterful and dreaded.

—Rev. George Grant, Sandford Fleming
Expedition, 1872

Lake Superior is the largest expanse of freshwater in the world. Over 560 kms (350 miles) long, 259 kms (160 miles) wide and with a maximum depth of 405 m (1,335 ft.), it covers an astounding area of 82,100 sq. kms (31,700 sq. miles) and contains so much water that to replenish itself takes 191 years.

The largest and deepest of the Great Lakes, Superior creates its own deadly weather systems. With prevailing westerly winds and a fetch of about 440 kms (132 miles), towering waves of well over 9m (30 ft.) have been recorded. While the lake was formed more recently, its North Shore dates back to the beginnings of the earth itself.

Rock, Water, and Billions of Years

The lake is cradled in some of the oldest rock in the world. Their contours can be gently rounded, or twisted and tortured. Some of the rocks are black and menacing, others the colours of sunrise, or the purples of an evening sky. Most were born of fire, sculpted in the violence of volcanoes and earthquakes. Colliding tectonic plates, scraping ice and slow erosion did the rest.

Three billion years ago, the earth was covered with water. It was an intensely hot, grey-black world, where volcanoes spewed lava, ash, and gases. As the lava cooled, it created "islands" of rock that spread and gradually merged to become the earth's crust. Years of erosion created sedimentary rocks. Pressure became so intense 2.7 billion years ago that the rock began to fold and buckle, rising into great mountains. As the earth shuddered and heaved, magma forced its way up to the surface, creating intrusive rock like the granite of the Canadian Shield. This rock sank back into the mantle again and again, and then thrust up and cooled to become the twisted and melded formations we know today. It was during this period (the Kenoran Orogeny) that many valuable metals, like Hemlo's gold, were deposited in the region.

The flat-topped mesas of the Nipigon and Thunder Bay area were created around 1.1 billion years ago. Painting of Nipigon River by William Armstrong, 1860

The mountain ranges were steadily eroding 2.49 billion years ago, depositing layer after layer of sediment which gradually compacted and solidified into rocks such as the shale at Kakabeka Falls, limestone, dolostone, and iron-bearing taconite. The earliest forms of life started to evolve. Mats of algae and bacteria appeared in shallow waters and their rare fossil forms can still be seen in the Schreiber Channel Nature Reserve, at Kakabeka Falls, and elsewhere in the "Gunflint Formation."

The Midcontinent Rift

Sometime around 1.1 billion years ago, the North American continent ripped apart, creating one of the deepest rifts in the world, a 2,000-km (1,250-mile) trough known as the Midcontinent Rift. The core of this rift runs under what is now Lake Superior. Magma squeezed its way between the layers of early sedimentary rocks and cooled to form diabase sills, a dark rock that is highly resistant to erosion. This hard diabase provides a strong protective cap over the sedimentary layers below, causing the dramatic flat-topped mesas and cuestas of the Thunder Bay area.

Lava erupting from the rift cooled to form the black basalt rocks of Michipicoten Island, Black Bay Peninsula, and St. Ignace Island. In some places, gas bubbles were frozen into the cooling lava and these pockets later filled with minerals such as quartz and calcite. The agate on Agate Island was also created at this time. Throughout the region, rich mineral deposits were formed, including copper near Point Mamainse, silver at Silver Islet, and uranium at Theano Point.

The Ice Ages

The last major influence on the North Shore's topography came during the Great Ice Age, beginning 1.6 million years ago. Sheets of ice 2 kms (1.25 miles) thick covered the land. As the ice advanced and retreated, it scraped and scoured out the contours which are familiar today. Gradually, as the climate warmed, the last sheet of the Wisconsin Glacier melted away. Its retreat 10,000 years ago left behind deposits of gravel, sand, clay, and erratic boulders. Glacial meltwaters flooded the Superior basin creating Lake Minong, forerunner to Superior. Without the weight of the ice, the earth's crust slowly started to bounce back. At Sault Ste. Marie, a drainage outlet formed and water levels began to drop, leaving many raised cobble and gravel beaches. It is here that the earliest signs of human life around Superior's northern shore have been recorded.

Early Peoples

After the retreat of the last glacier, the first people came into the region. Known as the Plano, they hunted caribou and large game along the tundra-like northwestern shores of glacial Lake Minong, an environment that was then about 45m (150 ft.) higher than Superior today. At the north end of the Sibley peninsula, the Brohm site may be where the Plano ambushed caribou using stone-tipped spears.

The next documented culture, the Shield Archaic (c.5000-500 B.C.) was found at both the eastern and western ends of the Canadian shore. These people were miners, chipping out native copper from exposed veins, then heating and shaping the malleable ore into tools and weapons. Lake Superior copper tools from this period have been found as far away as the Atlantic seaboard. These people used bows and arrows and dugout canoes. They fished, hunted, collected wild plants and were part of an extensive trade network. It is believed they are the direct ancestors of the Ojibwe, Cree, and other Algonkians.

The Laurel culture (c. 500 B.C. to A.D. 500) introduced the use of pottery and developed seine net fishing in shallow waters. Their sites were found at the river mouths around Superior, including the Pic and Michipicoten Rivers, Sault Ste. Marie, and the Lake Superior Provincial Park region.

Evidence of the Terminal Woodland Indians, c. A.D. 900-1650, is often found on top of the Laurel culture. At the mouth of the Michipicoten, at least nine layers of encampments have been identified. These Algonkian people survived by hunting, fishing and gathering berries. They used birch bark canoes, snow shoes, and conical and domed lodges. Other sites have been uncovered at the mouths of the White, Willow, and Pic Rivers, and at Agawa Bay, and Sinclair Cove. Most of the mysterious Pukaskwa pits (see p.136) were likely made at this time.

The Ojibwe

According to tradition, law, stories and songs the Ojibwe (one of the Algonkian cultures) have long lived around this great lake they call *Anishnaabe Chi Gaming*, "the Ojibwe's Ocean." They call themselves *Giizhe Anishnaabe*, the Kind People. With the arrival of the Europeans, the Algonkians set themselves up as middlemen between other Indian nations and the French fur traders. Slowly the Ojibwe began to dominate the

Wigwams were made of bent branches covered by sheets of birch bark

region. They pushed out the Sioux and the Fox and in 1662 they faced down the mighty Iroquois at Iroquois Point just west of Sault Ste. Marie. By the mid-eighteenth century, the Ojibwe occupied all of Superior's shores.

Traditionally, the Ojibwe followed a seasonal cycle. When autumn winds began to howl, family groups travelled into the bush, where they hunted moose, caribou and small game. With the spring thaw, they returned to the sugarbush, gathering in groups to make maple sugar and to celebrate the renewal of life. During the summer they set up encampments at river mouths, where they fished and harvested berries. The largest gathering was at Bawating (now Sault Ste. Marie) for the annual whitefish run, meetings, festivities and trade.

Socially, the Ojibwe were organized into loosely-defined territorial hunting groups. Bands were linked through intermarriage, and totems, or clans. The original five totems represented the basic functions of humankind: leading, defending, providing, healing, and teaching. Their symbols were animals like Cranes, Loons and Bears. Over the years the Ojibwe developed a spiritual healing society called the Midéwiwin devoted to healing and to the development of personal spiritual powers. It involved a complex series of ceremonies, levels of initiation, and religious structures. Midé shamans recorded on sacred birch bark scrolls rituals and key cultural and historic events, laws, and beliefs. These scrolls were deposited in locations known only to the initiated. Every fifteen years, the scrolls were examined, and the decaying ones replaced.

Sleeping Giant, the figure of Nanaboozho in Thunder Bay

The Ojibwe understood their dependence on the world: on plants for nourishment and healing, on materials like birch bark for their canoes; on other creatures like beaver who gave them meat and furs for warmth. In a world where survival was a struggle, the Ojibwe had respect for animals and their keener senses. Adolescents (mostly boys) would go on vision quests, seeking a personal manitou (pronounced manido) in the form of a small animal or bird to protect them throughout life.

The Ojibwe's rich cosmology described the earth as an island cohabited by humans and other creatures lying between the sky realm and the underworld. In the sky realm were the Thunderbirds—protectors of the Anishnaabe—giant eagles living in western mountain tops and travelling in storm clouds. They flashed lightning from their eyes, and their voices were the thunder. The underworld was ruled by Mishepeshu, a great horned lynx who sometimes appeared as a horned serpent. He moved around the Great Lakes through underwater tunnels, and on a whim would whip the water into a fury. Reliant as they were on the water, the Ojibwe would try to appease this unpredictable manitou with offerings of tobacco and respect.

On the side of the Ojibwe were the Thunderbirds who nested on Thunder Mountain and Mount McKay at Thunder Bay. In Thor Conway's *Spirits on Stone*, Cockburn Island Chief Norma Fox relates the story of a woman at Agawa, who watched as the sky darkened, "and great flashes of lightning appeared. Not far away from the woman, the waters of Lake Superior swirled. She recalled seeing a silvery form being carried into the sky by a giant thunderbird. Thunderers are always protecting Indian people by hunting the giant serpents." The Ojibwe also shared their world with other manitous such as grandmother moon Nokomis and Windigo, the spectre of starvation and greed. To the powerful manitous, the Ojibwe offered gifts of tobacco, the smoke being like thoughts and prayers that one could see.

Elders told stories of Nanaboozho, half human and half manitou, sent by the Creator to teach the Ojibwe how to live well. Like all humans, Nanaboozho learns as he goes along. He was known to be foolish and silly yet he gave the Ojibwe revered gifts such as the pipe of peace and fire. Many of the impressive land formations around Superior relate to him, such as Sleeping Giant, Devil's Warehouse, and Devil's Chair. In one story, the lake is said to have been created when a beaver built a dam at Sault Ste. Marie. One time when Nanaboozho was too lazy to trap the beaver, he began pulling apart its dam so that the beaver would crawl out. In so doing, he created the St. Marys Rapids that drain the waters from Superior.

The Europeans are Lured West:
The Route to the Orient, and Castor Canadiensis, the Beaver

In the early 1600s, Etienne Brûlé reported finding a vast inland sea beyond these same rapids he called the *Sault de Gaston*. Could this lead to the sought-after route to the Pacific Ocean and China? His trip inspired others. In 1660, adventurers Pierre Esprit Radisson and Médard Chouart, Sieur des Groseilliers returned to Quebec laden with furs from around Lake Superior. But instead of receiving a hero's welcome, they were arrested and fined for trading without a license. Their furs were seized. This action was to change the course of history. The two men "turned coat" and approached the English with their idea of conducting the fur trade from Hudson Bay. In 1670, the "Company of Adventurers of England Tradeing into Hudson's Bay" was chartered by King Charles II, granting it the rights to all the lands of North America flowing into Hudson Bay.

Not prepared to stand by and watch the British take control of the northern half of the continent, the French held a pageant at Sault Ste. Marie the following year, claiming all the lands west of Montreal in the name of Louis XIV. The first French forts in the Superior region: Fort La Maune on Lake Nipigon, and a second at the mouth of the Kaministiquia River in Thunder Bay were founded in the late 1670s and early 1680s by French nobleman Daniel Greysolon, Sieur du Lhut. (His anglicized name lives on at Lake Superior's westernmost city, Duluth.)

The traders were followed by the missionaries. By 1668, Jesuit Father Jacques Marquette had established a mission at the Sault rapids, the annual gathering place of the Ojibwe and their neighbours. Father Claude

The beaver took hold of the European imagination

Dablon wrote in the *Jesuit Relations* of 1669-70, "To render [the native people] more stationary, we have fixed our abode here, where we cause the soil to be tilled, in order to induce them, by our example, to do the same; and in this several have already begun to imitate us." In fact, the mission soon burned and it would be many years before the French would again take a strong interest in the Sault.

Instead, they focussed on Hudson Bay. In 1682, the French took over four of the five Hudson's Bay Company forts. The territory and forts continued to be in dispute until the French finally relinquished Hudson Bay to Britain after the 1713 Treaty of Utrecht. Adopting a new strategy, the French were determined to stop all furs trapped in the interior from reaching Hudson Bay. Lake Superior suddenly took centre stage. In 1716, the French instituted *les postes du nord*, three posts at the mouths of the major river routes from Lake Superior to Hudson Bay: a post on Thunder Bay, a post at Nipigon, and one at Michipicoten. Then in 1731, with the help of native guides, Sieur de la Vérendrye discovered the Pigeon River route to Rainy Lake, Lake of the Woods and the Northwest.

With shifts in European powers, the late 1700s were a period of great instability in the region. The most drastic change came at the end of the Seven Years' War between Britain and France. With the 1763 Treaty of

Paris, France ceded all of its North American territories to Britain. The Algonkian nations were staunch allies of the French. To allay the Algonkians' fears that they would lose their lands and rights, the British proclaimed that the Crown alone could purchase native territories, and that it could do so only if the territories were surrendered voluntarily. The early years were difficult for British traders. The Ojibwe believed British control of the region was temporary and that with Ojibwe help, the French king would "arise from his sleep" and help drive the despised English "back into the great salt water." At times Indian resentment spilled over into violence, but eventually the British did gain the support of the Ojibwe and other Algonkian nations.

The fur trade was flourishing. Independent traders used the inland canoe route from Montreal, aggressively penetrating far into the interior of the continent. Meanwhile the Hudson's Bay Company (HBC) still insisted the Indians travel to their forts on Hudson Bay. With the HBC asleep "at the edge of a frozen sea," Montreal rivals came together around 1783 to form the competing North West Company (NWC). On Superior, the NWC had forts at Grand Portage near the Pigeon River (later moved to Fort William on the Kaministiquia), at Nipigon, the Pic River, Michipicoten, Sault Ste. Marie, and other outposts which succeeded in cutting off much of the HBC's trade.

The North West Company's coat of arms. With such fierce competition between the rival fur companies, "Perseverance" was the name of the game.

It was a three-thousand-mile water highway open only for about five months of the year. As soon as the ice was out in the spring, the "wintering partners" (who spent the hunting season in the Northwest gathering furs from native trappers) would transport the furs down to Grand Portage on Lake Superior in their *canots du nord*, compact 7-m (24-ft.) river-going birch bark canoes. At the same time, voyageurs would depart from Lachine Quebec, in their large 11-12-m (36-40-ft.) *canots de maître*, or Montreal canoes, loaded with tons of trading goods and supplies for their 7-8 week journey.

The voyageur canoe brigades followed the Ottawa River to Lake Nipissing, then the French River to Georgian Bay and onward through the North Channel to the Sault. Despite the treacherous waterways, and their fragile craft, they averaged 25 miles a day, at a gruelling 45 strokes a minute. "Express" canoes travelled at the incredible rate of sixty strokes per minute. (HBC Governor George Simpson is said to have "dined one day at the Sault, and breakfasted the next at Michipicotin, a distance of one hundred and twenty miles.")

In the words of Peter C. Newman, this "inland navy" of voyageurs had a "flowing intimacy with the millions of square miles of wilderness." As the backbone of the NWC fur trade, they adapted well to the rugged conditions, and were on familiar terms with the natives. They were fiercely proud of their strength and endurance.

Each July, the Northmen, the voyageurs and Montreal agents descended on the post at Grand Portage (after 1803 at Fort William) on Superior's North Shore for the annual Great Rendezvous—two weeks of intense business dealings, strategizing, and wild, abandoned revellry. They had much to celebrate. For almost four decades, the NWC had dominated the fur trade. But the battle was becoming increasingly difficult. The HBC were becoming more proactive and heading inland. Both the NWC and the HBC were competing more and more fiercely for a dwindling supply of furs.

The competition hurt them both, and in 1821, the two companies merged under the Hudson's Bay Company name. The heyday of the voyageurs and the NWC's Great Rendezvous was over. Lake Superior headquarters moved to Michipicoten where, until about 1863, most of the furs were sent up the river system to Hudson Bay. Supply posts on the NWC canoe route to Montreal languished, although the HBC continued to use the Lake Superior posts to protect their trading region from encroachment, especially from the American Fur Company. To strengthen their position and to undercut the competition, they traded at lower prices on this "frontier."

Copper Frenzy, Land Disputes, and Locks

One of the earliest references to Superior's copper deposits was on a map of Lake Superior belonging to Samuel de Champlain which was marked "where there is an island of copper." In 1666, Jesuit Father Claude Allouez having discovered large pieces of pure copper, commented,

> One often finds at the bottom of the water pieces of pure copper... I have seen such pieces several times in the Savages hands; and since they are superstitious, they keep them as so many divinites, or as presents which the Gods, dwelling beneath the water, have given them and on which their welfare depends... they preserve these pieces of copper, wrapped up, among their most precious possessions....

However, it wasn't until the early 1840s that the cauldrons of North America's expanding industrial revolution brought increasing demand for minerals. A giant pure copper boulder was found at Ontonagon on Superior's southern shore, setting off a flurry of prospecting along the eastern shore at places like Mamainse and Pointe aux Mines. The mines were on native land, so the mining inevitably aroused the anger of the Ojibwe. Repeated peaceful petitions to the government failed. Three Superior chiefs, including Shingwauk from Garden River and Kinebinogojing from Badjiwanung, finally made a much-publicized visit to Lord Elgin in Montreal, during the summer of 1849

Shingwauk led a raid on a copper mine at Pointe aux Mines.

where they aired their grievances (to no effect). It was to be the chiefs' last act of diplomacy.

Tensions came to a head that winter. Shingwauk and Kinebinogojing led a raid on the copper mine at Pointe aux Mines, driving the miners away and forcing the government to deal with the Ojibwe about the ore that had been taken. The following year, 1850, two treaties were signed giving some compensation, an annuity, small reserves, and continued fishing and hunt-

Silver Islet harbour in the 1870s

ing rights in exchange for Ojibwe title to vast tracts of land around Superior. (See Pointe aux Mines p.40.) There is still a point of contention as to what the treaties were about. As well, at the time of the treaties, not all the Lake Superior chiefs had been accounted for, and they did not all sign. The several problems with the treaties created disputes that remain unresolved to this day.

None of the mines turned out to be very productive, and coupled with the huge cost of transporting the ore, mining the east shore proved to be less than economical. The problems were made worse by the need to bypass the rapids on the St. Marys River. Some vessels, like the NWC's *Fur Trader* tried to run the rapids, but with predictably disastrous results. In 1845 the propeller *Independence* became the first steam-powered ship on Lake Superior but it took about seven weeks to portage the boat around the rapids. One English observer, Laurence Oliphant, wrote of the American Sault in 1854, where trucks on the tram-road "loaded with huge blocks of copper, are perpetually rumbling." A canal was needed.

As a result of increased prospecting and copper mining on Superior's southern shore and a growing number of immigrants en route to destinations further west, pressure intensified to build locks at Sault Ste. Marie. The first to be constructed was Michigan's State Lock, completed in 1855. The floodgates to Superior were opening. In 1857, writer John Disturnell enthused, a ship navigation is now opened from Montreal to half way across the continent; instead of the canoe timidly hugging the shores of the great lakes, the steamer and propeller are now seen mid-lake pursuing their course undeterred by wind or wave.

Most of the ore cargo heading down through the locks was American and most of the immigrants were heading to the American mid-west. The Canadian shore was relatively quiet. The first regular service along the Canadian side was provided by the steamer *Rescue* and in 1859, the steamer *Collingwood* began limited mail service along the North Shore.

Then, in 1868, a silver vein was found just off a tiny islet at the south end of the Sibley Peninsula, on the eastern shore of Thunder Bay. The newly-named Silver Islet became one of the richest silver mines then in existence, no thanks to Superior which seemed intent on its destruction. During the 1870s, there was a rush to exploit other ores to feed the massive industrial expansion. It was a frenzied time, exactly the right climate for hoaxes such as the Otter Head Tin Swindle (p.138). Steamers and steam barges crowded the waters alongside sailing ships, some of which had been converted to cargo barges.

As Prime Minister of a struggling new country, Sir John A. Macdonald supported the development of east-west lines of transportation, partly to help attract British Columbia into Confederation. His dream gained support when the Americans blocked one of the boats carrying troops and munitions headed for the Red River during the 1870 Northwest Rebellion. Nationalist fever rose. Macdonald pushed for the construction of a Canadian canal at the Sault and pledged to build a railway from coast to coast. Few believed that this daring and costly project was possible for such a young nation.

Two Hundred Miles of Engineering Impossibilities: Building the CPR North of Superior

To the Opposition, and even many within the governing party, the idea of building the transcontinental railway north of Superior was scandalous. They preferred the much less expensive option of using American rail lines already constructed south of the border. Besides, the route north of Superior had rock ledges sheer down to the lake, and impenetrable bog— not exactly railway terrain. Yet the Superior route won out.

The Canadian North Shore came alive. Ships full of workers and materials unloaded at railway depots set about one hundred miles apart. (Some

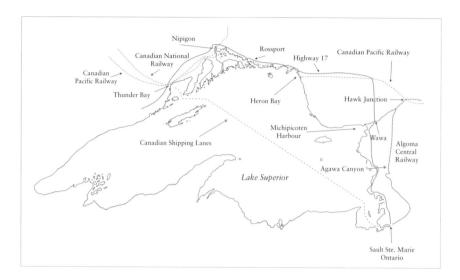

such as McKay's Harbour, now Rossport, and Peninsula Harbour, now Marathon, survive today.) They were anything but orderly communities. With twelve thousand men working on the line, gangs in Peninsula Harbour, White River, and Michipicoten had a ready market for their thriving whiskey trade. In *The Last Spike*, Pierre Berton refers to a regular Canadian Pacific Railway weapons count which revealed that "there were five thousand revolvers and three hundred shotguns and rifles, together with the same number of dirks and bowie knives, in the possession of railroad workers on the Lake Superior line."

The cost of building the rail line was enormous. Explosives to blast the right of way out of the Precambrian Shield alone cost $7.5 million. (Three factories were built in the Jackfish/Coldwell area, turning out a ton of dynamite a day.) Altogether, the men consumed twelve tons of food a day. It was hardly surprising therefore when the railway began to run out of funds. It took two very different men to save the project: Louis Riel and W. C. Van Horne, General Manager of the CPR. When the Second Riel Rebellion flared up in the brutal winter of 1885, military experts shook their heads in despair. In 1870 it had taken five months to send out an expeditionary force. Van Horne saw his opportunity: use the CPR, and he would guarantee the troops would arrive in eleven days. His real purpose, of course, was to win support for additional funds to complete the railway. Having no viable alternative, the government accepted.

It was a daring proposal. There were still four gaps in the track totalling 138 kms (86 miles) along the most rugged stretch of the North Shore

Horseshoe Trestle west of Schreiber

route. Winter gripped the land. Despite steep ledges, deep drifts, slush ice, and plummeting temperatures, the soldiers with horses and artillery managed to cross the gaps, and reach their destination on schedule. The success of the operation demonstrated the vital importance of a national railway. On May 16, 1885, the last spike of the line from Winnipeg to Montreal was driven at Noslo, near Jackfish.

Throughout the 1870s, settlers flooded west and within a few years, Canada's breadbasket was overflowing. Grain elevators were built at the Lakehead in Port Arthur and Fort William. Communities popped up all along the railway and native trappers were drawn away from fur trading posts like the Pic to the rail lines. Fishermen could even ship fresh fish via rail to distant markets.

Sail was giving way to steam and so began construction of iron and steel lake freighters. In 1883, the CPR had three steel propellers, the *Alberta*, *Algoma* and *Athabasca*, built in Scotland and brought to Canada. The ships were cut in two to get them through the locks of the St. Lawrence River and the Welland Canal. Their first season, 1884, the ships carried rail construction materials, immigrants to the prairie provinces, and tourists who were attracted by the CPR's promotion of elegant (and perfectly safe)

Whalebacks at the Sault

cruises through scenic Lake Superior on the *Algoma*. Ironically, the *Algoma* was wrecked in a gale in 1885 with the loss of about 45 lives.

At the eastern end of the lake, change was coming fast and furiously. In 1887, the CPR opened its "Soo Line" from Sudbury to Sault Ste. Marie, offering year-round access to the region for Canadian and American entrepreneurs. Construction had also begun on the long-awaited Canadian canal. When completed in 1895, it was the longest and deepest canal yet to be built, able to take the largest freighters. It also had one of the most advanced electrical systems in the world.

The real transformation followed the arrival in the Sault of financier and promoter Francis H. Clergue. Within a very few years, he took control of all power generation, set up a pulp mill, bought logging rights up the east shore, started to mine iron ore at Michipicoten, and constructed a spur line for shipments from the mine to Michipicoten Harbour. He acquired three passenger steamers and four ore cargo ships: the *Monkshaven*, *Leafield*, *Paliki*, and *Theano*. As if that were't enough, Clergue initiated construction of the Algoma Central Railway to ensure reliable year-round shipping of ore and pine saw logs to his mills. The development was not without its costs. Early in the 1900s, Clergue expropriated the Ojibwe's ancestral Whitefish Island in the St. Marys River for his railway interests, against their protests. The canals and power generating station also destroyed the Ojibwe's traditional whitefish fishery at the rapids.

The Fisheries

While the Ojibwe had fished Superior's waters for centuries, perhaps the first "commercial" fishery was the whitefish fishery in the rapids at Bawating (the St. Marys). Here, smoked and dried whitefish was traded for tobacco and other goods with other Ojibwe and natives from other nations.

Wider commercial fishing of whitefish and lake trout started with the fur trade. In 1839, the HBC began hiring Indians to fish during the summer to keep them from trading with the encroaching American Fur Company who had begun offering year-round employment. Fishing and processing—salting and barrelling—centred around the Michipicoten post. Over thirty stations were maintained from the bases at Michipicoten, the Pic, and Fort William. However, the fishing was never very lucrative, and the Company's commercial fisheries declined in the 1850s and 1860s.

Next to dominate the scene was A. Booth and Co. In the 1890s, the Chicago-based company grew into a strong "fish trust" comprised of about 10 different companies, holding a virtual monopoly on the Upper Great Lakes. Beginning with the purchase of the Wiarton-based Dominion Fish Co., Booth extended operations through Lakes Huron and Superior, including large stations at Quebec Harbour on Michipicoten Island, and Gargantua Harbour. As an employer, Booth charged high rates for the nets, but paid little for the fish. To survive, fishermen had to set many more nets than they held license for. In 1899, 95% of Canadian fish

Small fishing villages like this one at Tee Harbour sprang up along Superior's shores

caught in eastern Lake Superior was being exported, and only inferior fish was sent to Sault, Ontario... with a duty of 1 1/4 cents levied on each pound.

By the early 1900s, traffic up the east shore had become more regular once the steamers *Caribou* and *Manitou* (owned by a Booth subsidiary) began to transport fish and people between Owen Sound and Michipicoten. By this time much of the Canadian competition had been caught in Booth's wide net. Nevertheless, there were always independents. Fishermen such as the Nicoll Bros. at Port Coldwell prospered and gained a reputation for paying other fishermen a fair price. Their success was even greater after a new rail line offered access to distant markets. But the larger markets and improved tugs and nets came with a price: increased pressure on fish stocks.

Despite Superior's size, its cold waters have few nutrients to support only a relatively low density of stocks. The fish population is fragile. With the development of the Sault canals, the whitefish spawning habitat at the St. Marys rapids was destroyed and in other places, whitefish spawning grounds were destroyed by debris from logging drives. As early as 1910, whitefish was already in decline from the Michipicoten Island grounds. Commercial fishing was banned from the Lizard Island grounds, after Booth had already abandoned them due to damage caused by excessive pound-net fishing.

In 1934, James and Ivan Purvis bought the station at Quebec Harbour from the then-bankrupt Booth Co. running a successful operation until the parasitic sea lamprey invaded Superior in the 1950s, depleting whitefish and lake trout stocks. Over the years, a successful herring fishery was run out of the Thunder Bay/Black Bay areas. As well, there has been fishing for sturgeon, northern pike and walleye. Today commercial fishing is enjoying a small, controlled revitalization on the lake, but the many abandoned fish camps are reminders of the importance fishing once played along Superior's islands and shores.

Sawing Up the Shore

Some of the earliest timbering along the Canadian shore was at Point aux Pins near Sault Ste. Marie, where stands of red pine were felled for shipbuilding as early as the eighteenth century. In the late 1880s, logging sawed its way up towards Superior as Ontario's pine forests were depleted in order to build a new country.

The mixed forest of the Great Lakes-St. Lawrence stretches up the eastern shore and from Thunder Bay west. But in between, the northern Boreal

Forest covers most of the North Shore. Timbering took longer to reach this region. Instead of tall pines useful for construction, the North Shore was covered with scraggly northern conifers like the black and white spruce, balsam fir, jack pine, and tamarack. In the 1870s and 1880s, some early timbering for railway ties and trestle timbers for the new CPR line provided revenue for people at Nipigon and near Heron Bay. They would earn 25 cents for each tie.

It wasn't until the late nineteenth century that the potential of these forests was realized. An increase in publishing and literacy, combined with the use of wood fibre instead of cotton to make paper, created a demand for pulp logs and pulp and paper mills. And one of the first men to seize this opportunity was Francis Hector Clergue. He prospered, thanks to his electrical generation station at Sault Ste. Marie and his timber rights on fifty square miles of Crown lands, which he interpreted as almost half way around the Canadian shore. Clergue's successor, the Lake Superior Paper Company, also gained rights to cut on railway lands along the Algoma Central Railway in exchange for promising to bring 1,000 settlers to the district for each of ten years. Two million acres were opened for settlement, but few people were enticed to set down roots.

Pulpwood logging began to move steadily north and west from the Sault. The era of the Big Tow had begun. Tugs towing giant log booms to the Sault at one mile per hour became a common sight along the North Shore. Because the rafts were vulnerable to damage, a subsidiary industry emerged, run by locals wishing to supplement their income. They would pick up stray logs along the shore, then sell them back to the timber companies.

By the 1930s, most of the rivers capable of a log drive along the eastern shore had been timbered, including the Goulais, Batchawana, Chippewa (Harmony), Agawa, Michipicoten, Magpie, and Pukaskwa. As time passed, new operations opened along the Pic, Little Pic, Black, and White Rivers, and pulp logging was done on Superior's shores and islands. The Slate Islands were used as a place to sort the logs before they were transported to their final destinations. Pulp and paper mills sprang up around the shore at places like Port Arthur, Red Rock and Terrace Bay, providing employment and income in the region. Boom logs and driftwood still can be seen around Superior's shores. On the rivers, remnants of old dams are left from the days of the pulp logging drives.

Thanks to those who truly saw Superior in all her majesty, the idea of conservation gradually took root and large tracts have been preserved as parks, such as Sleeping Giant Provincial Park, Pukaskwa National Park, and Lake Superior Provincial Park. The opening of Highway 17 in 1960 finally made the entire north shore of Superior more accessible to all those who had only heard of this magnificent land. *More* accessible. But not *accessible*. Superior will always demand much from whomever seeks to truly know it or to carve out a living near its shores.

For thousands of years, people have gazed across Superior's great waters and seen different things. For the original inhabitants, the Ojibwe and their ancestors, this vast inland sea was the home of powerful manitous who ruled the earth and underworld. To the explorers and early settlers it was a wild land difficult to tame. Sailors, miners, railway navvies, loggers and fishermen, both from Canada and abroad, welcomed the job opportunities provided by her rich resources. To lighthouse keepers and their families the lake meant an unending battle to provide their vital services. For the Group of Seven it was a challenge to capture on canvas Superior's wild and mystical spirit. Superior's looming presence haunts all who have passed through.

Old graveyard at Batchawana

Natural Phenomena of Superior

From Sailor's Lore to Truth:

"Superior Never Gives Up Her Dead"

Superior's dynamic nature is a symphony of power. Majestic in her quiet harmony or her crashing storms, the spirit of Lake Superior rises far above an ordinary lake. Like the open sea, her rolling, heaving waves can turn mean and deadly. Her fogs can drop from nowhere, a heavy, solid curtain, choking out the sun for days. Other times they are fleeting as a breath, wafting lazily upon you. Superior's world, unpredictable and sometimes cruel, ruled the lives of sailors in the thousands. To cope with this uncertainty, these sailors often turned to superstitious rules and turns of phrase. Using myth, they tried to understand and humanize the grand lake's chaotic forces and to negotiate protection from her most volatile moods.

Richard M. Dorsin captured the world of Great Lakes superstition in his 1975 book *Bloodstoppers and Bearwalkers: Folk Traditions of the Upper Peninsula*. In an interview with Dorsin, sailor Ora Endress related two such superstitions:

> The most superstitions people is the sailors. They'll never take a boat out on Friday, on her maiden voyage. And a Friday the thirteenth is Black Friday... The 1913 blow, one of the fiercest blows ever on the Great Lakes, some twenty-odd boats lost—was on a Friday.

> In foggy weather you see little men jumping on the bow of the boat and dancing on the upper deck. They call that the loup-garou. Its caused by currents of air or a change in the atmosphere that make cold and warm spots in the air. I've heard some sailors say it's a warning; when you see that, something's going to happen. A man'll be at the wheel and he'll say, 'lots of loup-garous tonight—they'll be trouble.' For instance, if the boat runs aground they'll say, 'That's that damn loup-garou last night.'

Even with the advent of radio, gyrocompass, radar, computer and global positioning units which have brought greater security to Great Lakes ships, sailors still dabble in superstition. After all, as recently as 1975, the 218m (729-ft.) *Edmund Fitzgerald* was lost, a grave reminder that Superior will not be tamed by our technology. (On that same ill-fated day in 1975, the captain of a German ocean-going freighter snorted arrogantly "It's just a lake" when a pilot refused to take over at the Sault. After personally experiencing the momentous storm, he could only meekly comment, "Damned big lake. Damned big.")

Compare the real Superior to old lake lore and you will find threads of truth. Take the sinister phrase: "Superior never gives up her dead." Due to the extreme cold of the Lake, a corpse pulled down into the depths will decay slowly, inhibiting the release of gases that normally pull a body up to the surface. Few families have been able to bury loved ones lost to Lake Superior. Other "myths" are closely tied to fact yet they seem too bizarre to be true.

The Storm That Couldn't Be

It was a balmy summer day in 1913. The 74m (248-ft.) steamer *Leafield*, her hold full of steel rails, was making good time. Suddenly without warning and with no apparent reason, the water rose up in gale-size waves that pummelled the *Leafield* from all sides. For half an hour, the captain struggled to manoeuvre through the freak storm. Incredibly, not far away, the winds were calm and the sky was clear. The Ojibwe believed this strange phenomenon was caused by a giant sturgeon which stalked the lake. The crew of the *Leafield* never knew what hit them.

In 1933, the villages of Rossport and Port Coldwell witnessed a similar puzzling event. Four times the lake rose and heaved against the shore, ravaging docks and tossing boats on the beach. At first locals suspected an underwater earthquake or volcano. In fact what they had witnessed was a rare phenomenon called a seiche. As far back as 1789, fur trader Alexander Mackenzie documented this strange characteristic of Superior: "the water withdrew, leaving the ground dry which had never before been visible, and

then rushing back with great velocity above the common mark." John Disturnell also witnessed an upheaval in August of 1860: "the water was observed to fall some three or four feet, then rise about a half an hour, as suddenly again to recede and rise several times."

Leafield *survived freak storm*

Ruthless Ice and the Terror of the "Little Ice Devils"

Not all of Superior's behavioural patterns are so erratic; some strike dread in all who sail her waters precisely because of their predictability. Even with the inevitability of autumn storms, owners and captains dared them in order to squeeze every last ton of grain and ore through the Sault locks before ice claimed the waterways, and their boats became prisoners for the winter. As the ice began closing in Whitefish Bay, an observer once described "billowing black smoke, the evidence of panic all along the horizon."

Pushing the limits of the season again in the spring, sailors again fear the ice. Floe or raft ice catches the wind and rides the waves in chunks and sheets. A steady wind can turn this icy armada into a battering ram. Dwight Boyer in his book *Great Stories of the Great Lakes* elaborates:

> Hundreds of sailing ships have been wrecked or shredded, reduced to kindling while they lay helpless in its grasp. Yet today's steamer, though it has the ability to claw its way from encroached ice fields rapidly, is an even more subservient victim once it is surrounded. Lacking the resilience of the old wooden hulls, the plates crack and the frames bend. And they do not spring back in place when shifting winds ease the pressure.

Slush ice can also seize a ship, bending propellers and rudders below the waterline. If the wind blows unabated, a ship can be held prisoner for weeks on end.

A third even more terrifying form of ice, sailors blame on the "little ice

After the "Big Push" to cut through the harbour ice at the opening of navigation, a long line of ships leaves Port Arthur, 1912.

"Little Ice devils" can sink a ship

devils" that come out to play when late autumn gales pound freezing waves against a vessel. The fortunate survivors of these "devils" can be seen limping into the Soo locks, gleaming white like ghost ships entombed in ice. There is a saying among old sailors: "What the little ice devils pull down in Superior never comes up again." Their terror was aptly described by James Oliver Curwood in his 1909 article, "The Perils of Late Navigation on the Great Lakes":

> The waves break over her, and the spray dashes high over her spars and rigging. There it freezes, and its this freezing that makes the "little ice devils." The deckhouses, the boats at their davits and every plank above water quickly become coated with ice. Every minute it grows thicker. A ton of water plunges over the bow, but only half goes off again. Every man and boy in the crew is set to work with picks and axes, each of them is give a flask of whiskey. Inch by inch the vessel is weighted down, and with each inch she settles the sea has greater play over her. Like millions of little fiends the "ice devils" pull down, until she grows "logy," founders, and sinks like a piece of lead.

The true tale of the *Queen of the West* illustrates the drama of the "little ice devils." In 1903, the beleaguered ship, weighed down with ice, was spotted by the steamer *Cordurus* which immediately signalled for the Queen to lay to.

Instead she started to veer away. Certain the Captain of the floundering vessel had lost his mind, the *Cordurus* took chase. Her aggravated Captain shouted, "You're sinking, you idiot! Why don't you heave to?" The *Queen of the West's* Captain replied, "I know it—but I can't. We're almost gone and if we stop our engines for a second, we'll go down." In a courageous move, the *Cordurus* drew alongside as the *Queen of the West* stopped her engines. Miraculously her crew jumped safely to the *Cordurus* seconds before the ship plunged into the icy waters.

Storms and the Deadly Three Sisters

Estimations vary widely of the number of ships wrecked and abandoned on the Great Lakes but marine researcher Patrick Folkes believes the figure is about 4,000; four thousand vessels lost to fire, collision, scuttling, fog, compass deviations and of course, to storms. The "Great Storms" raged throughout the Lakes: in 1905 (70 vessels foundered, 70 lives lost); 1913 (21 ships wrecked, 52 damaged and over 248 sailors killed); and 1942 (50 ships lost and 50 seamen dead). Yet Superior has mustered many a fury that belong solely to her private legacy.

The waves seamen fear most are called the "Three Sisters," an anomalous formation of three large waves marching in lethal unison. The ship is already battling a storm when the first sister tosses tons of water across the deck. Before the backwash can pour off, the second sister lunges aboard. With two sisters already weighing down the ship, the third sister pounces. Thousands of tons of water push the ship's bow under before the crew can even launch a lifeboat. Rarely are there survivors to tell the tale.

Lethal waves known as the "Three Sisters"

Surviving Peril

Many a sailor reminisces about his ship: its unique character, its foibles, its specific sounds all dictated how she was handled and understood. Dave Thomas, a porter on the ships in the 1930s, recalls how he found it hard to sleep on land after getting accustomed to the soothing hum and vibration of travelling on the lake. Of course some ships, nicknamed Black Cats or Hoodoos (see the *Crescent City* p.8), were considered bad luck and rarely kept a crew. The reputation of these ships was either marred by an unfortunate history, or by owners who neglected maintenance, making disaster seem inevitable. Sailors followed a clue that signaled trouble: the behaviour of rats. For example, half the crew of the steamer *Sault Ste. Marie* deserted when they saw rats filing down a breast line to the shore. It was basic intelligence. Any ship unsuitable for rats was unsuitable for men. The *Sault Ste. Marie* foundered the very next day just outside Grand Marais.

For the most part, history has concentrated on the stories of ocean-faring sailors, paying little or no attention to those gallant men who have sailed the Great Lakes. In fact, before lighthouses and more advanced navigation technology, some of the most difficult and challenging sailing was done on shoal-ridden inland seas. And acts of extraordinary courage and dedication are legendary.

When the Great Storm of November 1905 erupted the retired freighter *Madeira* was under tow by the *William Edenborn*. Afraid the *Madeira* would pull them down, the *Edenborn*'s Captain decided to set the freighter loose, even though he knew he was condemning her crew to an unimaginable nightmare. Within hours the *Madeira* struck the sheer face of Golden Rock Cliff with such force the crew was thrown to the floor. Again and again the 131m (436-ft.) freighter was bashed against the rock. Someone tossed a rope hoping it would attach to something—anything! No luck. They were doomed.

Then suddenly sailor Fred Benson shocked everyone by grabbing the rope and jumping as the *Madeira* heaved away from the rock. Timing was crucial. If he misjudged, he would be crushed to death by the hurtling ship. Benson landed and managed to scramble out of the way just as the ship struck again, the loud scream of crushing steel rising above the thundering crash of the waves. Pounded by the spray shooting up more than 30m (100 ft.), he finally made the summit, weighted the rope and threw it back to the ship. With this they passed him a heavier line which provided a lifeline for the crew. Shortly afterwards, the freighter broke up. After tramping through waist deep snow in freezing temperatures, the crew made it to a fisherman's cabin and was found forty hours later. All but one of the crew survived—thanks to the heroism of Fred Benson.

Other crews have shown an incredible attachment to their ships. When the Canadian vessel, the *Maplehurst*, was breaking up, only ten of her twenty-one crew chose to jump ship to the safety of the rescue vessel. The shredded *Maplehurst* was discovered the following day, only her smoke-stacks above the water. None aboard had survived.

The tug Energy

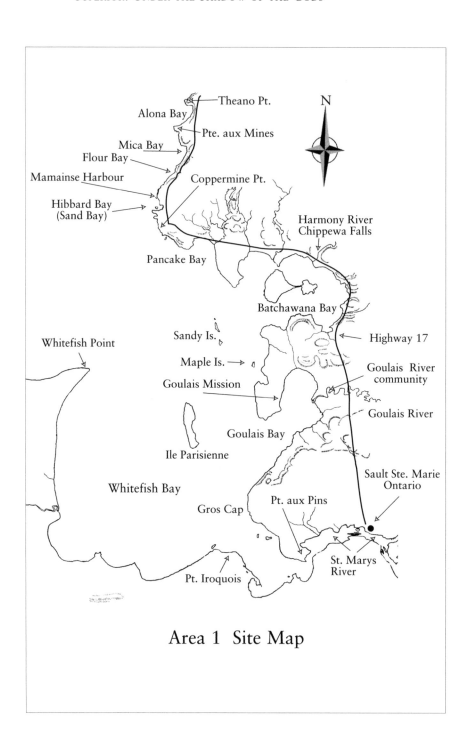

Area 1 Site Map

1

SAULT STE. MARIE TO THEANO POINT

SAULT STE. MARIE

Bawating —The Ancestral Gathering Place

Today two cities bearing the same name face each other across an international border. But three hundred years ago, the Sault rapids area was a gathering place for Ojibwe peoples living along the shores of Lake Superior and Lake Huron. They called this place Bawating, "shallow water rushing over stones."

The group who settled around the rapids or *sault* (known to the French as the Saulteurs) had been attracted by the plentiful whitefish, "caribou of the water," whose sweet-tasting flesh, dried and smoked, sustained them through the long, bitter winter. The Saulteurs (or people from *Badjiwanung* in Ojibwe) were superb fishermen. Standing upright in a canoe, the stern-paddler would skillfully wedge the canoe between some rocks while the bowman dipped a large hooped net into the eddies, scooping out large quantities of fish.

Bawating's regular population was 150-200 but in the summer and autumn, it swelled to around 2,000, many coming from the shores of *Chi Gaming*, Lake Superior. They came for the social activities and to renew friendships, to hold important ceremonies, to fish, and to trade. Because they lacked the fishing skills of the Saulteurs, they often traded for whitefish. A Sulpician missionary once commented, "This fish is so cheap that they give ten or twelve of them for four fingers of tobacco."

Bawating fishermen using dips nets for whitefish in St. Marys Rapids

The first European known have to visited Bawating was explorer, Etienne Brûlé. In 1619-22, he described a massive inland sea beyond the *Sault* drawing other French explorers and missionaries to this unknown territory. In 1641, the site was renamed Sault Ste. Marie by two Jesuits, Charles Raymbault and Isaac Jogues. By 1668, a Jesuit mission was established on the south shore, "that we may more conveniently instruct" "the great concourse of people" who gathered here each year. Three years later, France extended its rule over all the upper lakes and adjacent territory in a declaration full of pomp and ceremony.

The Declaration at Bawating

It was June, 1671. Simon-François Daumont, Sieur de St. Lusson had been sent on a "modest" mission—to claim for King, Louis XIV, possession of the upper country. Land was important, but the French were really after copper and furs. More specifically, they were determined to keep furs out of the hands of the Hudson's Bay Company, newly-created by the English. St. Lusson looked out the window of the Jesuit mission fronting the south shore of the St. Marys River. For weeks, hundreds of canoes had been arriving carrying Ojibwe and other natives from five hundred miles around. The area was a sea of wigwams. These leaders would carry St. Lusson's message far beyond the Sault to places he knew only as names on Jesuit maps. The King would be pleased.

The ceremony was a blend of Christian pageantry, political pomp and spectacle. Black-robed Jesuit priests led the procession holding their crosses high and chanting in Latin. St. Lusson, ramrod-straight in his military finery, his sword gleaming and the royal fleur-de-lis flashing on his helmet, walked behind with great dignity. Two thousand natives representing 14 nations were brilliant in their ceremonial garb. They watched as the procession made its way up the hill (now Government Park) to a spot where an enormous wooden cross and a cedar pole bearing the escutcheon of the King of France had been ceremoniously erected and sanctified.

Raising high a piece of sod, St. Lusson took formal possession of the territory of Lakes Huron and Superior, and all the land bounded by the northern, western, and southern seas. Accompanied by cries of *Vive le Roy*, and the discharge of muskets, he promised the King would take the Indians under his protection. Jesuit Father Claude Allouez described the French king's power:

> When he attacks, he is more terrible than thunder: the earth trembles, the air and sea are set on fire by the discharges of his cannon; while he has been seen amid his squadrons all covered with the blood of his foes, of whom he has slain so many with his sword that he does not count the scalps, but the rivers of blood he sets flowing.

"No one dares make war on him," he continued, "all nations beyond the sea having most submissively sued for peace.... He alone decides all the affairs of the world." Having extolled Louis' military power, Allouez added:

> You count yourselves rich when you have ten or twelve sacks of corn, some hatchets, glass beads, kettles.... He has towns of his own, more in number than you have people in all these countries five hundred leagues around. In each town are warehouses containing enough hatchets to cut down all your forests, kettles to cook all your moose, and glass beads to fill all your cabins.

The festivities concluded with an enormous bonfire, and a final Te Deum to thank God "on behalf of those poor peoples, that they were now the subjects of so great and powerful a monarch" (as written in the *Jesuit Relations*). The reaction of the assembled natives was not recorded but some were later observed ripping the King's escutcheon off the cedar pole.

Years of Turbulence and the Move to the North Bank

Despite the declaration, French interest in the area cooled, perhaps influenced by Louis XIV's late-century ban on fur trading due to over-supply. It wasn't until 1750-51 that the first French fort at Sault Ste. Marie was built by Sieurs de Repentigny and de Miselle who were granted exclusive trading privileges and land along the south shore of the river. This renewed interest would prove to be too little, too late.

James Wolfe's 1759 victory on the Plains of Abraham and the Treaty of Paris four years later led to the total withdrawal of French forces from the continent, leaving Britain in control. The British preferred Fort Michilimackinac as a base and left the Sault to independent fur traders. The Ojibwe were strongly allied with the French, and resented British incursion in the region. For many years, the region was unsafe for British fur traders like Alexander Henry, because the Ojibwe believed the French withdrawal was only temporary, and that the French would soon "arise from their sleep" and help drive the British from the region.

Other rivalries were developing. The North West Company, launched and managed by Montreal merchants to better compete with the Hudson's Bay Company, established a fur-trading post at the Sault. However, the situation took another turn after the American Revolution, and the drawing of the international boundary along the St. Marys River. The south shore was awarded to the United States, forcing British merchants to retreat to the less-attractive north shore, thick with marshland in 1796. The Nor'Westers bought 100 square miles from the Ojibwe paying two pounds, some goods and "valuable considerations." By 1798 they had constructed a sawmill, canal, tow path, wharf and storehouse. For the next twenty years the fort struggled to survive. In 1821, the two fur-trading rivals amalgamated. Most of the pelts were now being sent north to the Hudson's Bay posts on Hudson Bay, rather than through the Great Lakes water route, further diminishing the Sault's importance.

The Canadian Sault remained the lesser of the two Saults for many years. This speaks volumes, considering the description of the American Sault in 1848 by a member of Louis Agassiz' zoological expedition:

> The most striking feature of the place is the number of dram-shops and bowling-alleys. ...I counted seven buildings where liquor was sold, besides the larger stores.... Nobody seems to be at home, but all out on a spree, or going a fishing or bowling. There are no symptoms of agriculture or manufactures; traders enough, but they

are chatting at their doors or walking about from one shop to another. The wide platforms in front of the two large taverns are occupied by leisurely people, with their chairs tilted back and cigars in their mouths. Nobody is busy but the barkeepers....

However, the increased demand for shipping between Lakes Huron and Superior would soon cause the pace of life at the two Saults to pick up steam.

SAULT STE. MARIE CANAL

The 6.4-m (19-21ft.) drop of the St. Marys Rapids had long been an encumbrance for navigation between Lake Superior and the rest of the Great Lakes. In 1798, The North West Company constructed a canal for bateaux but larger craft had to portage either around the rapids—an incredibly laborious and time-consuming process—or be sent over the rapids, a decidedly risky operation.

With the explosion of copper mining and prospecting on Superior's southern shore in the 1840s, pressure grew for a canal to be constructed capable of transporting cargo ships. The State of Michigan responded by building the first canal in 1855.

Although the canal was open to both American and Canadian traffic, many wanted an all-Canadian shipping route from the St. Lawrence to Superior. Their arguments were given weight during Louis Riel's 1870 Red River Rebellion, when the Americans refused to permit transit through their canal to the British vessel, the *Chicora*, carrying Colonel Garnet Wolseley's forces west. This was an intolerable situation for Canadian nationalists. The *St. Catharines Constitutional* was outraged:

> Of all Governments within the pale of civilization, the Yankee Republic is one of the most uncertain to deal with, and is the most devoid of dignity in its administration.... It was this one idea of shameless desire to rob us of the north west that dictated this policy in preventing the *Chicora* from going through their canal.... Their conduct in this matter should teach us another lesson of not expecting favours at their hands and it also tells us that we should have a canal of our own at Sault Ste. Marie built this season.

The pressure continued to mount as production rose at Lake Superior mines and the Prairies began to ship east increasingly larger

Constructing the Sault Ste. Marie Canal, 1893

quantities of grain. 1887 was a crucial year for the Canadian Sault. The CPR's "Soo Line", a spur line from Sudbury, was completed and construction on a canal was finally started. Slavs, Irish, Ukrainians, and Finns were brought in, along with Cornish miners, to cut the sandstone removed in the excavation. At any one time, there might have been 600 men working at the canal site and fully 200 more working the stone quarries.

When they were finished in 1895, the engineers and labourers had succeeded in constructing the world's longest lock 274m (900 ft.), one capable of holding one upper laker and two smaller vessels. They had used the finest materials, including metre-thick lock gates made of Douglas fir, and had been innovative in their use of concrete in canal-building. They had also introduced a new, sophisticated lock-chamber design which allowed the water to empty and fill through the floor, causing the boats less stress.

This lock was the first in the world to be illuminated and operated by electricity, and its power plant had one of the most advanced electrical systems in the world. Perhaps most surprisingly, the project came in under budget. According to Brian S. Osborne and Donald Swainson, authors of *The Sault Ste. Marie Canal*, the government was so proud of the achievement that in 1900, it put the "Soo" canal's image on the

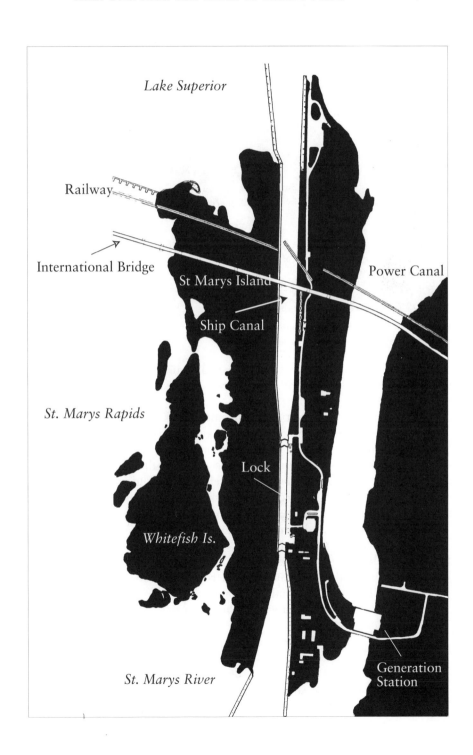

Water rushing through the Canadian lock after freighter Perry Walker *smashed through the lower lock gate, June 1909.*

Canadian $4 bills. There was only one problem. The image depicted one of the American locks! The mistake was corrected when the bill was reissued in 1902.

In the early years of the twentieth century, lake traffic increased considerably. Use of the Canadian canal peaked in 1913, then declined after the larger American Davis lock was completed a year later. The big cargo carriers used the new lock, while the Canadian lock was mainly for passenger and smaller regional vessels. During the two World Wars, the locks were closely guarded. No unauthorized persons could enter the area for fear of sabotage which would have cut the Allies off from Lake Superior's iron and other strategic materials.

Today the Sault Ste. Marie Canal is a fascinating national historical site with its lovely grounds and its red sandstone buildings constructed of rock excavated during canal construction. Inside the Powerhouse and the Motorhouses, the original lock-operating machinery has been preserved. The canal itself is now open only to recreational traffic.

The Wild Ride Through the Sault Locks

Her captain, Fred Rice, once described the 128m (426-ft.) lake freighter, *Crescent City*, as a slow-witted hound: "[She] could get herself into such a mess of trouble," he said with a chuckle, "why, you almost didn't dare lower your eyes to put an entry in the log without having her go off on some frolic of her own." On an otherwise balmy June afternoon in 1909 at the Canadian Sault locks, his words proved prophetic.

It was a busy afternoon for the locks. All morning, ships upbound were raised from the St. Marys River to Superior's level; downbound vessels loaded with ore, fish, pulp and lumber were lowered to Lake Huron's level. There was also the Canadian Pacific's *Assiniboia*, its 300 passengers on their way to Owen Sound. They lined the rails to watch as the ship passed into the locks. Behind the *Assiniboia*, the *Crescent City* was just entering. Below the closed lower lock gates, the freighter *Perry Walker* was approaching from the other direction at a "high rate of speed." Her captain ordered the engines slowed. Nothing happened. The vessel was fast closing on the lower gate. Again he commanded the engine room to slow. No response. He threw the chadburn lever to "Reverse" and sent a runner down to the engine room, ordering the reverse of the *Walker's* props. They did, but much too late.

With a grinding roar the ship's bow crushed the lower gates releasing the water from the lock. The *Assiniboia*, the half-in and half-out *Crescent City* and ultimately much of Lake Superior itself, thundered down the 6.4-m (20-ft.) drop into the river. It was like riding a roller coaster. As reported by the *Crescent City's* captain, Frank Rice, "The stern of the *Assiniboia* leapt through the air like the sail of a flying fish. Her nose pointed down for that inevitable plunge into the furious waterfall." Rice continued,

> without a single means of control to save life or ship... we were a little boy's toy boat floating unguided into a sewer hole.... We were over-taking the Assiniboia... about to ram into her stern when, with a thun-dering bolt, she crashed down over the cataract.

(Some passengers aboard the *Assiniboia* whooped and laughed, believing the sudden rush of water to be normal procedure.)

The *Assiniboia* smashed into the broken gates, and swept out of the lock, striking the *Perry Walker* before coming to rest in the lower channel. Behind her, the *Crescent City* crashed against the lock sill, poked a hole in her hull with the *Assiniboia's* anchor, struck the *Assiniboia's* stern, and finally began to sink.

Although the passengers aboard the *Assiniboia* were frozen with fright, amazingly no one was injured. A brief inspection revealed only superficial damage, and the ship continued on to Owen Sound. No

Francis Hector Clergue

doubt, there was no shortage of conversation that night. (The *Crescent City* and the *Perry Walker* did not fare as well, requiring extensive repairs.)

Behind them lay devastation. Traffic was diverted to the U.S. system. The questions on everyone's lips were: How could the facilities ever be restored and how long would it take? The answers were surprising. First the emergency swing-dam was positioned to stem the flow of water. Then with a flurry of activity, repairs were made and new gates installed. The locks re-opened to traffic late on June 22, less than two weeks after the incident.

The last of its type in the world, the swing dam can still be seen today.

Francis Hector Clergue and the Transformation of the Sault

For most of his life, Francis Hector Clergue seemed to be in transit. Born in Maine, Clergue originally planned to become a lawyer. He was called to the bar in 1876, but his real skills lay in promotion and financial matters, not in questions of law. In his home state he became involved with pulp milling and launched an electric street railway in Bangor. Although his ventures were not always successful, he spent much of his life roaming the world in search of new opportunities. By the time he was 38, he had promoted dry-docking in Alabama, and tried to launch a project to build a railway in Persia, along with a waterworks system for the city of Tehran.

In 1894, Clergue came to investigate a small Canadian community, called Sault Ste. Marie, which was said to be in deep financial trouble. The town had over-extended itself and had no way to pay its bills. To local citizens, this represented a crisis. To the American financier, it was a golden opportunity. Addressing the city council, Clergue stated he would assume the town's debts if the community would grant him exclusive rights to electric power generation at the Sault rapids. The offer was too good to resist. Clergue's smooth tongue and valuable connections won him support from American financial interests. He was on his way—and so was the industrialization of Sault Ste. Marie, Ontario.

Clergue's entrepreneurial abilities unleashed as much energy as the rapids. Having launched the Consolidated Lake Superior Company in 1898, he found it was producing more power than local companies could absorb. Clergue looked around for ways to use the power himself. He eyed the vast stands of spruce along Superior's shores that could be floated down to the Sault—and built his own pulp mill. He recognized that the pulp being shipped to paper mills was wet, and therefore heavy and expensive. His solution: pioneer a dry-pulp process to lower transportation costs.

To produce a good product required large quantities of sulphur, which Clergue knew was a by-product of Sudbury's nickel smelters. Why not purchase a nickel mine, name it Gertrude in honour of one of his sisters, then encourage his laboratory technicians to search for a method of extracting sulphur from its operations? When they succeeded, Clergue discovered to his delight that the Gertrude Mine was now producing a valuable nickel-iron alloy that happened to be in great demand by various munitions manufacturers—including the German firm, Krupp.

Told of an iron ore discovery at Michipicoten (he needed iron for the Krupp contract), he bought the site and founded the Helen Mine (named after another sister). Clergue wasn't finished. Since iron ore production demanded a reliable transportation system, in 1899 Clergue launched the Algoma Central Railway, running from Sault Ste. Marie to join up with the CPR main line. He also had a 12-mile spur line constructed from the Helen Mine to Michipicoten Harbour. Not content to relax and enjoy his success, Clergue had another inspiration. What to do with a surplus of iron? Process it into steel of course. This idea led to the founding of the Algoma Iron, Nickel and Steel Company of Canada and the first production of steel in Ontario's history. Eight years after Clergue first set foot in Sault Ste. Marie, it had been transformed from a town with a fiscal problem into a booming community. It was a wonderful moment for the brash bachelor.

Unfortunately, like many entrepreneurs, Clergue had one major weakness—management. He was superb at launching new ventures, but less talented at running them. He was also something of a spendthrift. To celebrate the opening of a new power canal, he spent over $50,000 in fireworks, brass bands and chartered trains to carry celebrants to the Sault from New York, Philadelphia, Detroit, Montreal and Toronto.

Overextended, Clergue's Lake Superior Corporation collapsed in 1903. Riots broke out among unpaid workers, and after they stormed the company offices, troops had to be sent from Toronto. His companies were reorganized under new management. Clergue moved on. He was next heard of negotiating a contract for Americans to provide Czarist Russia with military equipment.

Clergue spent the last years of his life in Montreal, returning briefly to a hero's welcome at the Sault in 1937. Two years later, he died at age eighty-three. He left the town of Sault Ste. Marie a vastly different place from the town where he planned to make an overnight stop forty years earlier. The changes were more than commercial and industrial. Clergue had encouraged an influx of Italian immigrants, together with Slavs and Finns, whom he saw as cheap labour for his mills and his railroad, and the city grew more cosmopolitan as a result.

THE CLERGUE BLOCKHOUSE & THE ERMATINGER OLD STONE HOUSE

The two oldest stone structures west of Toronto are both found on the same site at the Sault. One intriguing building combines Clergue's history with the city's earlier fur-trading heritage. In his early years at the Sault, Clergue had acquired the stone ruins of the powder magazine/fur storage building from the old North West Company post. Adding a windowed second story of peeled cedar logs, he used it as a dwelling. One can imagine Clergue staring out from "the Blockhouse," his mind drifting back to Persia, perhaps ahead to Russia, while all around him the eastern corner of Lake Superior underwent its metamorphosis.

The Ermatinger Old Stone House was built in 1814 for Charles Oakes Ermatinger. Ermatinger's marriage to Mananowe, the daughter of a prominent Indian Chief, helped to advance his career. In 1800 he became a clerk for the North West Company, and in 1805 a partner. Only three years later he broke away to become an independent fur trader. His home became the social centre for communities on both sides of the river, and invitations to his annual caribou dinner were eagerly sought. For museum information call (705) 759-5443.

Clergue's Blockhouse, note the two pet bears

POINT AUX PINS

With the 1785 launching of the 45-ton *Beaver* in Detroit, the North West Company was now the owner of the largest craft on Lake Superior, capable of hauling provisions to Grand Portage at the far end and returning with rich harvests of furs. With a 4m (13-ft). beam and 10m (34-ft. keel), she was neither pretty nor a particularly good sailer. But for the Company, practicality was all that counted.

Unfortunately, one critical detail was overlooked. How was the boat going to get into Lake Superior? Every effort to haul her up the St. Marys rapids failed. Finally, all efforts were abandoned in frustration and the homely *Beaver* was dispatched to do service on Lake Huron and Lake Erie.

The following year, the North West Company took delivery of the *Athabasca*. Having learned their lesson, the company had the new boat shipped to the Sault in pieces and assembled at Point aux Pins. It was both an early demonstration of prefabrication and a tardy acknowledgement of the wisdom of French commandant Louis Denis, Sieur de la Ronde. Fifty years earlier in 1735, his decision to build a barque at Point aux Pins (the first decked vessel on Lake Superior), helped to establish the local shipbuilding tradition. Fur trader Alexander Henry had also chosen this site to build a barge and later a sloop. Both men were intent on exploiting newly discovered copper sites on Superior's

Left) Gros Cap Light Ship was a harrowing place to be in a storm, 1927. Right) Building Gros Cap Lighthouse, 1953. Pat Johnston recalls hanging over the sides to paint it.

southern shore. Henry also attempted (unsuccessfully) to develop mining on the eastern shore at Point Mamainse, Pointe aux Mines, and Michipicoten Island. He even built the lake's first smelting furnace at Point aux Pins in 1769.

Taking advantage of the surrounding stands of red and white pine, the North West Company constructed several more sailing vessels including the *Otter*, *Mink*, *Fur-Trader* and *Discovery*. It is not surprising then, that when Dr. John Bigsby passed through in 1823, he found the Point only thinly clad with pines.

GROS CAP LIGHTHOUSE

After a rough voyage on Superior, many a navigator has given thanks at the sight of the Gros Cap light marking the bottom of Whitefish Bay and the entrance to the more protected waters of the St. Marys River. It stands on the dangerous submerged Gros Cap Reefs close to the shipping lanes. Originally just a light ship anchored to the shoal, it was replaced in 1952-3 by a permanent lighthouse with reinforced concrete cribs that had to be built in drydock at Sault Ste. Marie and towed to the reef. The building's distinctive design resembles the bow of a freighter, the better to break up winter's advancing ice.

Inside, the lower windows were shuttered against the pounding waves making the lighthouse seem cramped, cold and dank. Mirrors in front of the upper windows angled upward so that keepers could check the light's operation from inside without having to disturb their cribbage game or *Reader's Digest* stories. Outside and poised for action, a lifeboat was ready to be lowered at a moment's notice.

The lightkeeping season began in April, as soon as the tenders could break their way through the ice. If the ship delivering keepers was unable to pull alongside, the men had to pole through floating pans of ice and then climb a ladder onto their water-encircled post. (As with all Great Lakes lighthouses, Gros Cap has been "destaffed." Periodic checks are made by maintenance staff who arrive by helicopter onto the roof-top helicopter pad.)

GROS CAP AND THE MASSACRE AT IROQUOIS POINT

Throughout the Great Lakes, there are places imbued with a dark, unsettling presence. Iroquois Point is just such a place. Still, from the giant towering headland of Gros Cap, the view of the open water is spectacular. Canadian Gros Cap and American Point Iroquois face each other across the dramatic southern entrance to Whitefish Bay (sometimes called the "Pillars of Hercules"). It was here that a critical battle was fought between the Iroquois and the Ojibwe during the bloody Iroquois wars of the 1600s.

In 1662, having learned that Iroquois had invaded the North Channel and were heading towards Superior, Ojibwe from around the Great Lakes joined together at Gros Cap to halt their advance. Below the St. Marys rapids, Ojibwe scouts grimly watched as the Iroquois tortured prisoners, their screams melding with the loud sound of rushing water. Finished with their grizzly task, the invading band carried the bodies west along Superior's south shore and set up an encampment directly across the water from the Ojibwe. Their feasting and all night celebrations drifted across Whitefish Bay providing a beacon for the Ojibwe as they stealthily advanced in their war canoes.

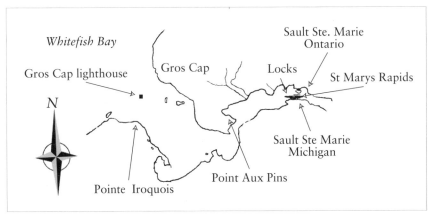

At dawn, as the Iroquois were sleeping heavily, the Ojibwe beached their canoes and stormed the encampment. The Iroquois had no chance. Within minutes, all but two lay dead or dying. These captives had their noses and ears ceremoniously cut off and were sent east in a canoe with instructions to convey a warning: the Ojibwe would tolerate no further invasions of their land. The strategy worked. Never again did the Iroquois venture into the Ojibwe's Lake Superior territory. The site of this battle, recorded by French trader Perrot and early Jesuit missionaries, is still known as Iroquois Point.

Gros Cap marks the end of Highway 550. From the parking lot a trail climbs to the top of the headland offering a panoramic view of Whitefish Bay.

ILE PARISIENNE LIGHTHOUSE

In response to the growth of east-west shipping in the years following the opening of the Canadian Sault lock, a lighthouse and fog alarm building were constructed in 1911 on the southernmost tip of Ile Parisienne. From the lanternroom of the tower which was made of reinforced concrete (an innovative building material at the time), the keeper was charged with ensuring the safe passage of a stream of ore, timber and grain boats carrying a nation's resources to world markets.

On crisp, clear days, the elegant white tower still gleams, its beaver weathervane perky atop the crimson lanternroom. The modern solar-powered light functions automatically, but hints remain of a time when this lightstation was inhabited. A lilac tree blooms in front of the two-storey keeper's house and phlox is mixed among the wild grasses. Inside, an ironing board is covered with an old Lake of the Woods Milling Co. sack bearing the words, "100 pounds when packed" Laying Mash.

The west beach is scattered with driftwood and rimmed with large smooth cobblestones, shiny and dark like the skin of an amphibian. Shallow turquoise waters and a sand beach are protected by a concrete wharf—once busy, now silent.

WHITEFISH BAY: GRAVEYARD OF THE GREAT LAKES

Coming upbound through the Sault locks for the first time, one is filled with trepidation. Lake Superior's reputation is intimidating. At first, the pastoral shores are reassuring, fringed with cottages, manicured lawns and gentle light green-blue waters. But as Gros Cap light-house becomes a speck on the horizon and the shore grows more and more distant, wariness returns. As Whitefish Bay opens up, the large waves take on a sinister, mottled blue and black, and Superior's dark folkloric stories begin to play on the imagination. It is hard not to think of the twisted freighters and the waterlogged bones of smashed schooners lying somewhere, deep under one's hull. Whitefish Bay is lit-tered with wrecks and many believe these waters are haunted by their ghosts.

To enter either the locks or Superior itself, all up-and-downbound shipping must pass through the massive funnel of Whitefish Bay. The weather is a challenge in every season: clogging ice in winter; fog so thick in spring and early summer that a sailor joked he once carved his initials in it; late autumn snow so dense that another old sea dog recalled opening his mouth and having it fill instantly with heavy wet mush. Most terrifying to seagoers are the storms. Driven by fierce winds, waves gather momentum as they cross the clean sweep of the lake. At their peak, they are forced into the confines of Whitefish Bay where they have been described as "marching gray beards, soldiers of death", towering up to 9m (30 ft).

This bay is called the graveyard of the Great Lakes for a good reason.

Whitefish Bay, The Graveyard of the Great Lakes

Shipwrecks on the Canadian Shore of Lake Superior

1. AURANIA: Jan. 1909, steel prop sank in 50 m, abreast of S end of Parisienne I., crew walked over ice pack to J.H. Bartou, L.352'.

2. V.H. KETCHUM: Sept. 1905, schooner, burned and sank off S end of Parisienne I., 2 lost, L 223'.

3. SERVIA: Apr. 1898, schooner allegedly burned and sank 15 miles off Whitefish Pt, L 242'.

4. BATCHAWANNA: June 1907, Cdn. prop beached and burned off Coppermine Pt, L 209'.

5. CHARLES HEBARD: Nov. 1902, prop lost her tow and was blown aground, S of Point Mamainse, crew was rescued by Oscar Carlson who had a cabin nearby, L 184'. A.C. KEATING: Nov. 1900, schooner-barge broke from towing vessel *New York*, 20 miles W of Whitefish Pt, driven E by storm and beached above Coppermine Pt, L 138'.

6. W. O. BROWN: Nov. 1872, schooner aground slightly N of Pt Mamainse Lt, 6 lost.

7. EDMUND FITZGERALD: Nov. 1975, steel bulk ore carrier, disappeared 17 miles off Whitefish Pt. found on bottom in two pieces, all 29 crew lost, L 729'.

8. MISSOULA: Nov. 1895, prop broke shaft 30 miles off Whitefish Pt., ship disappeared, L 272'.

9. ORINOCO: May 1924, prop lost 6 miles off Agawa Bay, vessel broke up and disappeared, 5 lost, L 295'.

10. GOLSPIE: Dec. 1906, Cdn. prop stranded on rock, S side entrance of Brule Harbour, L 183'.

11. ACADIA: Nov. 1896, Cdn. composite prop stranded on Brule Pt., L 177'.

12. HIRAM R. DIXON: Aug. 1903, Cdn. composite prop burned at Michipicoten Harbour, L 149'.

18. CERISOLES & INKERMAN: Nov. 1918, two French minesweepers disappeared in storm, 76 French officers and men as well as two Cdn. pilots lost, L 143'.

19. BARGE 115 (whaleback): Dec. 18, 1899 was stranded, L 256'.

20. JUDGE HART: Nov. 28, 1942 was stranded, L 250'.

21. RAPPAHANNOCK: July 1911, prop stranded on W side of NE corner of Jackfish Bay, struck shore and slid back, L 308'.

22. GUNILDA: Aug. 1911, prop struck McGarvey's Shoal NW of Copper I., in Schreiber Channel, slipped off into deep water, ship in excellent condition at 273'.

23. ONTARIO: July 1899, Cdn. prop driven ashore S end of small I. S of Salter I., 1 1/2 miles NE of Battle I., L 181'.

24. MARY ANN HULBERT: Dec. 1883, 2-masted schooner capsized off St. Ignace I., took water and slid under, 20 crew and passengers lost.

25. ST. ANDREW: Sept. 1900, Cdn. prop stranded S side of Bachand I., at mouth of Nipigon Strait, machinery recovered, L 193'. SOVEREIGN: Oct. 1891, Cdn. prop sank, 1/2 mile SW of Lamb I. Lt. Nipigon Strait, valuable cargo reported.

26. NEEBING: Sept. 1937, Cdn. prop capsized and sank at Eagle Nest Pt. while towing barge *Coteau* from Paradise I. to Red Rock, boiler exploded, 5 crew lost, 9 rescued by barge, L 193'.

27. THEANO: Nov. 1906, Cdn. steel prop sank 3 miles E of Thunder Cape Lt, struck Trowbridge I. rocks, slid off, and broke up, L 255'.

28. MAGGIE MC RAE: Cdn. bark lost 3 miles off Thunder Cape Lt, cargo 300 t copper ore and spirits, L 139'. SCOTIADOC: June 1953, Cdn. prop sank in 30 mins after collision with *Burlington* out of Thunder Bay at Trowbridge I. 1 lost, 29 saved, L 416'.

29. LEAFIELD: Nov. 1913, Cdn. prop grounded on Angus I., slid off into deep water, 18 crew lost, L 249'.

30. MARTIAN: Dec. 1927, Cdn. prop stranded at Hare I., 15 miles off Port Arthur.

13. *CHICAGO*: Oct. 1929, downbound prop struck reef of westerly Michipicoten, crew reached shore, L 324'.

14. *STRATHMORE*: Nov. 1924, Cdn. prop struck rocks at NW tip of Michipicoten I., slid off into deep water, 13 crew reached shore, L 205'.

15. *ANNIE SHERWOOD*: Oct. 1893, schooner abandoned in waterlogged condition S of Caribou I., reported sunk, 2 crew lost, L 184'.

16. *ARLINGTON*: Apr. 1940, Cdn. prop lost 12 miles S of Superior Shoal, 18 members of crew in boats rescued by *Collingwood*, Captain Burke went down with his ship, L 244'.

17. *JAMES GAYLEY*: Aug. 1912, steel prop collision with *Rensselaer*, 43 miles E of Manitou, sank in 16 mins, crew rescued, L 416'.

Shipwrecks on the U.S. Side of Whitefish Bay

A *SAGAMORE*: July 1901, steel whaleback, barge struck by *Northern Queen*, sank 1 mile off Gros Cap Reefs, 3 lost, L 308'.

B *CHARLES C. GRISWOLD*: Nov. 1872, Schooner lost 3 miles W of Gros Cap I., mast above water, 8 lost.

C *SAMUEL MATHER*: Nov. 1892, Prop lost after collision with *Brazil*, 8 m N of Pt Iroquois, 4-year-old vessel, intact, masts standing in 100', 1 mile inside American waters, L 246'.

D *PANTHER*: June 1916, prop run down by upbound *J.J. Hill* sank 4 miles off *Le Parisienne* S Lt, L 147'.

E *JOHN B. COWLE*: July 1909, steel prop in collision with *Isaac M. Scott*, 2 miles off Whitefish Pt, cut in two and sank in 3 mins, 14 crew lost, L 440'.

MYRON: Nov. 1919, prop, lumber hooker, waterlogged and sank in 4 mins, 2 miles W of Whitefish Pt, 1.5 miles offshore, stern broke off and drifted to Cdn. shore. Captain survived by clinging to pilot house and was picked up 24 hrs later by *W C Franz*, 16 crew in yawl perished, L 186'.

F *MIZTEC*: May 1921, 3-masted schooner-barge, stranded 5 miles NW of Whitefish Pt, 15 miles offshore, broke up and hull slid back into deeper water, wreck scattered in 45', 5 lost, L 194'.

In the early days, traffic was heavier and communication more difficult. Many of the tragedies resulted from collisions due to either poor visibility or human error. For the fated *John B. Cowle* and the *Isaac M. Scott*, it was a lethal combination of both.

The Collision of the John B. Cowle *and the* Isaac M. Scott

It was July 1909. The steel steamer, *John B. Cowle*, was travelling at a brisk pace through thick fog when out of nowhere appeared the 151m (504-ft.) *Isaac M. Scott*. With the deafening sound of screaming metal, a 6m (20-ft.) hole opened up along the *Cowle*. Six sleeping men were crushed to death.

The 126 m (420-ft.) *Cowle* sank so rapidly that another fourteen men were drowned. One sailor reached the upper deck just as the ship slipped beneath the water. Though he was dragged under, his desperate kicking enabled him to break free of the suction, shooting to the surface where he clung to a piece of wreckage. Floating aimlessly in the dense fog, he was surrounded by moans and screams coming from all directions. He whistled loudly to attract attention and was eventually rescued. An inquiry into the disaster resulted in charges against the the two captains for operating their ships at excessive speed in adverse fog conditions.

The Hosford: *A Nightmare in Fog*

One of the few vessels fortunate enough to survive a collision on Whitefish Bay was the *Hosford*. In an accident similar to the *Cowle/Scott* disaster, the *Hosford's* captain and crew demonstrated a professionalism exhibited by many Great Lakes' sailors. Caught in a pea-soup fog, the Captain ordered the anchor to be dropped. No sooner was the chain rattling down when a ship loomed up. Sailor Fred Dutton recalled, "My feet rooted, I watched a great black ship coming toward us with deadly, irresistible momentum. A terrible cry from the other ship then the crash. Steel tortured steel."

The captain yelled for his men to stuff the gash with mattresses, but they could not stop the rushing waters. It was then that Captain Jacobsen made a bizarre decision. Checking their co-ordinates, he told the engineer they were going to try to beach her. The crew hovered around the lifeboats while the firemen and engineers worked frantically below, shovelling coal to maintain steam and manning the straining pumps. Wordlessly, the men watched the water rise within inches of the deck. Dutton recalled the Captain's "face showed nothing. It was as though he were steering the ship in the open lake without a care in the world."

When waves started to roll over the deck, each man was aware he was within minutes of being sucked to his death. Yet no one moved. Everyone waited for the Captain's command before launching the lifeboats. Suddenly the vessel shuddered with a huge tremor. She had beached. They were safe.

Pumped dry and temporarily patched, she limped to the Canadian Sault, where the American boat was fined $100 for landing without clearance in a foreign port!

Myron *and* Miztec: *Brutal Choices of Death and Survival*

While poor visibility caused the most havoc on busy Whitefish Bay, it was Superior's infamous storms that struck the deepest terror into the hearts of sailors. In some of these exhausting battles, captains had to choose between saving one ship and its crew or another.

November 22, 1919... the 55m (186-ft.) hooker, *Myron,* weighed down with 700,000 board feet of lumber, was towing the schooner barge *Miztec,* also overburdened with timber, through a terrifying storm. Looking back at the defenseless *Miztec,* Captain Neal knew it would eventually founder and take his ship with it. He ordered the towline cut. Everyone watched in horror as the powerless *Miztec* and its crew were abandoned.

Then within minutes, the *Myron* itself was overwhelmed and began to sink. As the lifeboats were launched, the crew looked back and saw the small figure of the captain in the pilothouse. He had refused to leave. After some time, a passing freighter unsuccessfully attempted to rescue the crew, who were too numb to grab hold of the rescue lines. Later, in the pitch dark, the Vermilion Point lifesaving crew arrived but failed to find the lifeboats or the drifting *Mitzec.* Tossed by waves and battered by the *Myron's* floating cargo, they retreated, frozen and exhausted to the Whitefish Point lighthouse.

A full twenty hours after the *Myron* went down, the captain from the *W.C. Franz* spied movement on a floating object. Evidently when the ship sank, the pilothouse had been ripped off, taking Captain Neal with it. There he was now, clinging to the roof, barely able to withstand the freezing waves washing over him. As for the *Myron's* sixteen-member crew, all drowned or froze to death. That spring, one of the lifeboats was discovered at Salt Point, Michigan. The bodies had to be chopped out of the ice. A local mill built coffins for the sailors to be buried in an old Indian cemetery.

Today the *Myron* rests in 19m (65 ft.) of water. Her anchor is displayed at the Valley Camp Museum in Sault, Michigan. Amazingly, the helpless *Mitzec* which had been cut free by the *Myron* was pushed by the waves to safe harbour.

Tales of Whitefish Bay shipwrecks are legendary. However, one in particular has come to symbolize all that is brutal and horrifying about Lake Superior—the S.S. *Edmund Fitzgerald*, lost November 1975 above Whitefish Bay.

The Devastating Loss of the S.S. Edmund Fitzgerald

"We are holding our own." Those final words, uttered by the captain of the *Edmund Fitzgerald*, still haunt all who sail Superior. It was the last transmission sent by an experienced captain aboard a legendary ship, minutes before it was torn apart during one of the worst storms in Superior's long history of killer gales. "We are holding our own,"— then 218m (729 ft.) of iron and steel disappeared from the radar screen like a stone dropped into a lake.

Sunday, November 9, 1975 it was a glorious day as the *Edmund Fitzgerald* sailed out of Superior, Wisconsin on the final voyage of her seventeenth season. At the helm was Ernest McSorley, a veteran of over 44 years. With him was an experienced crew of 28 and a ship that could carry more than 26,000 tons of iron ore pellets in her hold. The *Fitz* was scheduled to reach Detroit late Tuesday afternoon. Just another routine voyage.

Underway, Capt. McSorley learned that a cold front was marching down from the north-west and was expected to collide with two other weather fronts: a low-pressure area moving in from the American Rockies and warm moist air rushing up from the Gulf of Mexico. The news did not faze the Captain who had complete faith in his ship—a legend on the Great Lakes for safety, reliability and comfort—and in his skill and that of his crew.

As it turned out, the collision of the three weather fronts late that day was catastrophic. By Sunday evening, the sky was leaden and the rising winds had beat the waters into a frenzy. All through the night the storm worsened. Devastation spread throughout the Upper Great Lakes. Docks were destroyed; bridges swept away. Some foolish curiosity seekers were sucked into the waves and drowned. Residents along the shores stared out their windows, thankful they were not on the water and anxious for those who were.

Around 3:20 p.m., Captain Cooper of the *Arthur M. Anderson*, a 230m (767-ft.) vessel sailing 27 kms (17 miles) behind the *Fitz*, suggested that she was dangerously close to Six Fathom Shoal. Shortly afterward, Captain McSorley seized the radio transmitter and called the *Anderson*, "I have sustained some topside damage. I have a fence rail laid down, two vents lost or damaged, and have taken a list." Would Cooper stay with him as a safety precaution? By now the *Fitzgerald's* two ballast pumps were spewing out 14,000 gallons per minute.

The Edmund Fitzgerald *dropped off the radar screens, November 10, 1975.*

The two ships plowed onward, hoping to reach Whitefish Bay by nightfall. The winds lessened, then strangely rose even more strongly to 42 knots. Waves measured 4.8m (16 ft.) and growing. The *Fitzgerald's* main radar failed. By late afternoon, vessels were reporting waves of 7.5m (25 ft.) and the Sault locks clocked the wind at 144 kph (90 mph).

The *Fitz* and its 26,000 tons of cargo was reported to be leaning 15 degrees to starboard and with both radar systems now gone, it was travelling blindly. At 7:10, the First Mate aboard the *Arthur M. Anderson* contacted the *Fitzgerald*, now less than 16 kms (10 miles) ahead. After warning about an approaching ship coming out of Whitefish Bay, the *Anderson's* First Mate asked, "How are you making out with your problems?" The ever-calm McSorley replied, "We are holding our own." Barely 10 minutes later, the *Anderson's* First Mate stared in disbelief at his radar screen. The *Edmund Fitzgerald* had vanished from sight.

The wreckage from Superior's most infamous disaster rests in Canadian waters about 23 kms (17 miles) northwest of Whitefish Point at a depth of 159m (530 ft.). As a measure of the *Fitzgerald's* size, it would tower nearly 52m (173 ft.) above the surface if it were to be stood upright on the lake bottom.

Despite an extensive official inquiry, the cause of the disaster is full of speculation. The U.S. Coast Guard Marine Board of Investigation suggested the *Fitz* sank because of ineffective or incorrectly closed hatch covers which allowed the holds to be flooded, causing instability and loss of buoyancy. Some believe the vessel hit the shoals off Caribou Island (one of which was not charted until six months after the ship foundered). Others say there is evidence the distressed ship snapped in two on the surface. Whatever the cause, the *Edmund Fitzgerald* now rests in two pieces on the bottom of Lake Superior.

Each year on November 10, relatives gather at the Great Lakes Shipwreck Museum at Whitefish Point for a ceremony and vigil. The ship's original bell, recovered in 1995, tolls for each of the 29 dead and a thirtieth time for all sailors lost on the Great Lakes. The museum is part of the restored Whitefish Point Lighthouse and Coast Guard Rescue Station complex that features dramatic exhibits on Lake Superior shipwrecks and the lightkeeping service. For more information call (906)635-1742.

GOULAIS BAY: THE HORROR OF WINDIGO

During the winter of 1767, a severe famine gripped the area. One evening at Goulais Bay, fur trader and explorer Alexander Henry, his Indian guides and their families faced a bizarre and unsettling incident.

Huddling around a campfire in the Goulais forest, Henry's group turned their heads as a shudder of wind passed through the trees. To their surprise, a stranger stood nearby. Moonlight carved deep shadows in his gaunt face and the glow of the flames cast a red hue on the matted fur draped about his shoulders. Warily extending the visitor a piece of fish, Henry maintained his distance. The man's stench was unbearable. The emaciated Indian only grunted and turned his face away. The group froze. Such a reaction could mean only one thing—he was possessed by Windigo.

For the Ojibwe, no spirit was more terrifying than Windigo, a giant skeletal being with sunken eyes and rotting lips tattered by the gnashing of teeth, whose bones pushed through ash-grey flesh. On the verge of perpetual starvation, he craved human flesh and blood. This spirit strides through native legend like a nightmare come to life. Victims who died of fright were fortunate to avoid the agony of being ripped apart limb by limb. The madness of Windigo was never ending, and its appetite was never sated. For the Ojibwe, Windigo represented both the

During the famine in 1767, fur trader and entrepreneur Alexander Henry witnessed the horror of cannibalism.

horror of starvation and the spectre of greed. The more it ate, the taller it grew, the more frenzied its need to seek out and devour humans especially those guilty of greed. The cold wind that followed the spirit invoked a kind of insanity that could drive a man to unspeakable deeds. Because of this, Henry's guides feared the stranger.

Several of the group tracked the stranger's footsteps through the woods until they came to a smouldering campfire... and a half-baked hand. Back at the camp, Henry confronted the man who admitted his crime. Driven by hunger, he had devoured his uncle and then his four children, one by one. Henry again offered him fish, but the stranger refused, his hollow eyes fixed on the children in the group. "How fat they are," he whispered. Henry later wrote that in order to protect the youngsters, the stranger was killed by the blow of a sharp axe. Ojibwe knew, that when possessed by Windigo, a man who had tasted human flesh would never be satisfied.

GOULAIS MISSION

Atop a rise on the west side of Goulais Bay stands the white Our Lady of Sorrows church, built in 1862 under the charge of the Eastern European Roman Catholic missionary, Frederick Baraga. As Bishop, he was responsible for missions from Bruce Mines to Fort William and during his tenure he created an Ojibwe grammar dictionary. One of the colourful surviving traditions at Goulais is the Corpus Christi procession which began as early as 1863. The old schoolhouse near the Church has also survived.

Frederick Baraga created an Ojibwe grammar dictionary

GOULAIS RIVER

The community of Goulais River was developed first as a fishing station. In fact, the old French name for the bay was *Anse de la pêche*, "Fish Cove." Later settlers came to farm and to log the surrounding hills. For those who settled along the lowlands near the river mouth, the vagaries of the Goulais River presented a real challenge. Even today, spring ice jams can cause the river to back up and flood four to five feet—enough that canoes have to be used to get in and out of homes. As if that weren't enough, the river is continually seeking new courses through the soft, sandy soil, and embankments regularly give way. One resident claims: "a house can be on a corner one year, and not on the next." An early settler, Mrs. Tilley, often spoke with amusement of the particularly bad flood when her cows took refuge on frozen manure piles. She had to row out in a boat to milk them!

TRAGEDY AT MAPLE ISLAND

A late summer storm exploded over Superior's eastern shore on that August day in 1816. It was to have marked Lord Selkirk's revenge, but instead it ended in tragedy and recrimination. Selkirk, a Hudson's Bay Company shareholder, had been given an enormous land grant in the area of present-day Winnipeg to establish his Red River Colony. But earlier that summer his colonists had been attacked by a group of Manitoba Métis... and North West Company partners were accused of having aided and abetted them (see p 242). Seeking retribution, Selkirk, along with Swiss mercenaries and soldiers, occupied the North West Company's fur-trading post at Fort William, arresting

The death of prisoners on Maple Island in 1816, destroyed Lord Selkirk's reputation.

several of the partners. Among them were explorer Simon Fraser and a director of the North West Company, William McGillivray, after whom Fort William was named. Selkirk's plan was to have the Nor'Westers escorted to Montreal where they would be tried in connection with the massacre.

When the storm broke, everyone instinctively turned to the most experienced canoeist for guidance. That was the "prisoner", McGillivray, who immediately instructed the brigade of canoes to head for Maple Island. They made it there but to everyone's horror, one of the canoes broke up on a shoal, and its 21 passengers were tossed into the surging waters. Nine aboard the doomed canoe drowned. Among them, Kenneth Mackenzie, a North West Company partner. His body was returned to Sault Ste. Marie for burial while the others, including a British sergeant, one of the Swiss mercenaries and six natives guides were buried on the island.

Selkirk was charged with responsibility for the deaths. Already ill with consumption, he was finally broken by the scandal and the ongoing fight with the NWC. He retreated to England and died soon after

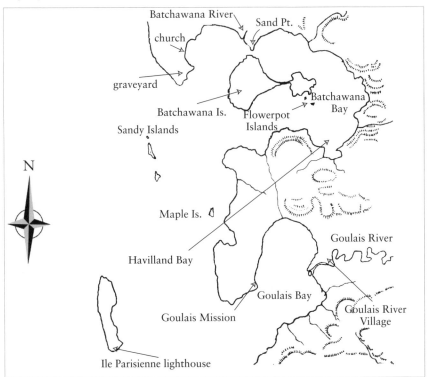

in 1820. A year after his death, the Hudson's Bay Company and the North West Company amalgamated, bringing to an end the fur-trading wars between these two ambitious groups. Selkirk would have rolled over in his grave.

NORTH AND SOUTH SANDY ISLANDS

On a windless August morning when the giant lake is like glass, North Sandy Island looks like a penny lying flat on the water. However the lake is rarely like glass and so there are fishing camps on the Islands where boxes of macaroni are consumed and hands of cards dealt by fishermen waiting for rough conditions to subside. On North Sandy's west side, ribs of a wrecked steamer stick up just below the water's surface. Its boiler rests on a shoal around which the fishermen lay their nets. According to Peter Robinson, if the seas get so rough you can't see the boiler, "you know you're in trouble". His grandson Kevin still ekes out a living fishing from a small aluminium outboard with a 45hp motor, although he did give it up for a time after two frightening incidents in which his boat was swamped to the gunwales, and he had to slowly make his way in from the high open seas.

HAVILLAND BAY

Along a cliff face near the marina at Havilland Bay, there is what appears to be a boarded up mine shaft, but it has no connection with mining. Rather, it was supposed to have been an elevator which would take boaters to a restaurant on a bluff overlooking Superior. The dream died, leaving behind a 30-foot-deep cooler.

BATCHAWANA BAY

Years of fishing and travelling over Superior's waters have given the Ojibwe of *Badjiwanung* an intimate knowledge of her character. *Badjiwanung* is said to refer to water that bubbles up, as if it were boiling. Where this occurs, between Batchawana Island and Sand Point, it is believed that the underwater spirit who travels through subterranean tunnels is about to surface.

This expansive bay and the entire coast from Batchawana Bay down to about Gros Cap is termed *Badjiwanung* (referring to the constant undertow). When the local Ojibwe set their nets, and mysteriously felt them pull, they would wonder what or who was doing the pulling.

Traditionally, the people from Badjiwanung are said to have fished as widely as Pigeon Point along the north shore of Superior, and what is now Collingwood in southern Georgian Bay. They were also the expert rapids fishermen at Bawating (see p.1). Because of their exposure to other groups, the Ojibwe of Badjiwanung learned the languages and customs of other groups, and developed skills in diplomacy.

But it was the good fishing (and experienced fishermen) that attracted the North West Company. The Hudson's Bay next kept an outpost and fishing station at the mouth of the Batchawana River. Years later, the Booth Fish Co. built a large ice house to store fish before having it delivered to the Sault. Around 1900, one commentator observed of the steamboat landing/fishing station at Batchawana, "The village is not a savory one, since the offal of fish is dumped not far off, forming a perpetual attraction to gulls and crows; and the idle horses of the lumbermen

St. Isaac Jogues Church (named after the 17th-century Jesuit missionary and martyr who came to Sault Ste. Marie). In the 40s, it was moved on log skids to its current location along the shore. The old graveyard can still be found at its former site on "Church Hill."

roam the point at will." In the early 1920s, Frank Lapoint caught the largest fish ever recorded on the Great Lakes here, a 140-kg (310-lb.) sturgeon, reputed to have been 90 years old and 2.25-m (7.5-ft.) long.

BATCHAWANA ISLAND AND FLOWERPOT ISLANDS

Low, flat, Batchawana Island is the focal point of beautiful Batchawana Bay. Spirit houses, or elevated graves are said to be on the Island, and throughout the region. These were possibly erected after disease swept through a community thought to have once been based near the river mouth. The island is designated an Environmentally Sensitive Area, since its interior marshlands provide an important autumn stopover for migratory birds.

Just off the south-east tip of the island are a group of tiny, peaceful islands, the Flowerpots. Dead tree branches provide an eerie, Dr. Seuss-like home for colonies of Great Blue Herons and Herring Gulls.

HARMONY RIVER/CHIPPEWA FALLS

Stand at the highway near the Harmony River and you are at the exact centre of the Trans-Canada Highway. From here the road stretches 3,888 kms (2,430 miles) in each direction to Canada's eastern and western coasts. The nearby picnic area is a perfect place to view the 6-7-m (20-23-ft.) drop of the lower Chippewa Falls. Near their base round depressions up to 1.5m (5 ft.) in diameter, known as potholes can be seen. Over time, hard round rocks, carried by strong, eddying currents, have ground out depressions in the volcanic rock and granite. A short, rough trail leads up from the highway to the picturesque upper Falls.

PANCAKE BAY

There are competing stories about how this bay got its name. In one version, it was the voyageurs. Weary after their long trip from Fort William, they feasted on a hearty batch of pancakes. In another version,

Voyageurs at Dawn *by Frances Hopkins*

it was local trappers who came down the Pancake River and cooked up the pancakes in question. The whole mystery may be more simply explained. The beach-lined bay looks flat and round... like a pancake.

Over the years, pancakes continued to play a part in local legend. Commercial fisherman, Charlie Carlson is reputed to have eaten up to 24.. 42... or was it 54?! flapjacks at one sitting, earning the nickname "Pancake Charlie," "Pan" for short. According to Wayne Pickard, he was also noted for smoking a pipe for a week or two until he got a heel on it, then carving this out and chewing it. "But he put a little Copenhagen in to make it stronger," his son, Oscar added.

The two-mile-long sand beach and bay are now part of Pancake Bay Provincial Park, designed for recreational use with campsites, a picnic area and a short nature trail. For information, contact: (705) 882-2209.

COPPERMINE POINT: *GARGANTUA* AND *GRAY*

The Harrowing Tug Life of the "Big Tow"

North shore lumbering boomed when entrepreneur Francis Clergue constructed his pulp mill in the Sault in the late 1800s. The industry created hundreds of jobs for loggers and mill workers. One demanding job was working on the tugs of the "big tow," in which tugs hauled huge rafts containing up to 12,000 cords of pulpwood from the river mouths to the mill at the Sault.

The tugs, known as "workhorses" or "beavers," worked in concert. At the river mouths smaller tugs gathered the logs that had been driven down river and filled the booms formed by large white pine or British Columbian spruce logs chained together. Larger tugs then took them in tow and hauled them at the excruciating pace of one mile an hour. Conditions on the tugs were Spartan to say the least. The captain slept in the wheelhouse while the crew bunked in the forepeak. Hygiene was non-existent as they did without lockers and showers, taking turns bathing on deck in a washtub. Some vessels even lacked toilet facilities. In the early years, workers were paid a flat wage to work from early morning well into the night.

In pleasant weather tug work was tolerable, but during storms, it was hellish at best. Everyone feared being dragged backwards for miles by the weight of the boom or worse being dragged onto rocks. Then

The Gargantua *and other workhorses of the Big Tow. The* Gargantua *and the* Gray
nearly met their ends off Coppermine Point in 1937

there was the terror of towing a massive boom through the heavily-traf-
ficked Whitefish Bay under a curtain of fog. A bad situation could
quickly turn into a nightmare as it did in September 1937 for the tugs,
Gargantua and *Gray*.

Caught in a classic Superior gale while pulling an 8,000-cord pulpwood raft, the tugs rounded Coppermine Point in heavy seas. The *Gray*
was hammered so hard she began to roll over. When the vessel righted,
the crew breathed a collective sigh of relief... until they realized the tug
had lost its steering! The *Gray*'s funnel had torn off flush with the cabin
roof, breaking the auxiliary line to the steering cable and taking with it
the steam-line to the whistle. The tug was adrift in a cloud of billowing
steam with no way to signal her partner. Bucking wildly in massive
combers, the *Gray* drove straight for the unsuspecting *Gargantua*. Just
missing her, it ripped through the towline, abandoning the gigantic raft
to the storm. The *Gargantua* worked quickly to toss the *Gray* a line,
dangerous work with the untethered boom so treacherously near.

With the line secured, the *Gargantua* towed the crippled tug to
Batchawana Bay. The following day she headed back out into the gale
in an unsuccessful attempt to find the raft. It was later located drifting
outside Goulais Point—with almost no loss of wood! And so ended
another day in the life of "the big tow."

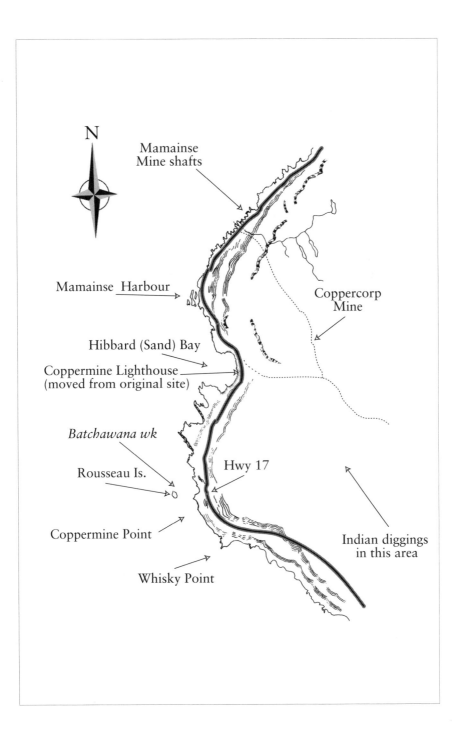

N

Mamainse
Mine shafts

Mamainse Harbour

Coppercorp
Mine

Hibbard (Sand) Bay

Coppermine Lighthouse
(moved from original site)

Batchawana wk

Rousseau Is.

Hwy 17

Coppermine Point

Indian diggings
in this area

Whisky Point

The 1901 Coppermine Point lighthouse was moved to Hibbard Bay

COPPERMINE POINT AND THE WRECK OF THE *BATCHAWANA*

The Coppermine Point lighthouse marked the northeast entrance to Whitefish Bay. The sight of its beacon must have been a glad sight in a night storm for sailors yearning for the protection of the bay. But on June 26, 1907 it failed to protect the *Batchawana*, heading down to the Algoma Steel plant with a cargo of iron ore. The 63m (209-ft.) wooden steamer caught fire. Efforts to control the blaze failed and the entire crew took to the lifeboats just before the steamer was engulfed. The vessel sank just off Rousseau Island north of Coppermine Point in 9m (30 ft.) of water. According to Chris Kohl, much of its hull can still be found along with the propeller and drive shaft. The 1901 lighthouse was moved (see Hibbard Bay) and replaced by a modern metal beacon.

HIBBARD BAY

When the Coppermine Point lighthouse was deemed obsolete in the 1960s, local resident Ernie Demers bid for the right to dismantle it for scrap. Combining a respect for history with an entrepreneur's sense of promotion, he reconstructed the lighthouse a few miles north along the Trans-Canada Highway at Hibbard (Sand) Bay. He added the Lighthouse Restaurant and Tavern and eventually a campground. He and friends also raised the propeller from the wrecked *Charles Hebard*, (see p.37) and brought it to the site. Today the lighthouse building has lost some of its lustre and is little noticed by motorists speeding past on Highway 17.

Copper Creek Mine, Sand Bay, one of the early copper mines.

COPPERCORP MINE

Unearthed in 1936 during construction of Highway 17, a copper nugget weighing 67 kgs (147 lbs.) was sent to Toronto to be displayed at the Canadian National Exhibition, providing dramatic evidence of the mineral riches awaiting exploitation along Superior's Canadian shores. However, such easy retrieval was not the norm for the copper near Sand (Hibbard) Bay. Until the mid-1950s, various mining ventures staked claims in the area but it was Coppercorp Ltd. that had the most success, stockpiling an estimated 600,000 tons of ore. After new owners took over in the 1960s, a mill was constructed and a townsite built on the shore at Sand Bay for the mine's more than 100 employees. Ore was hauled through 14,000 feet of underground tunnels along an electric railway before being crushed into copper concentrate (a fine black sand) for shipment as far away as Spain.

MAMAINSE POINT

Ancient Copper Diggings

"How far?" David Thompson asked the Ojibwe guides. It was 1798, and the explorer was anxious to see the legendary copper deposits at this place called "Mahmaize." Indians had told him their ancestors had come to a spot near here seeking pure copper to make heads for their lances, arrows, axes and knives: "by their description the place was about five miles in the interior. I requested to be shown the place, but they said they did not exactly know it, and dreaded the Musquitoes...."

Jack Roussain (l) and "Pancake" Charlie Carlson (r). Carlson and others lived on the island at Mamainse Harbour. Former fisherman Lloyd Morden recalled that Carlson's sons had to cross from the island on cakes of ice in the spring to go to school.

Strange and magical powers were associated with copper sites. Copper was said to be the property of the feared underworld manitou, Mishepeshu. Ojibwe feared that if they revealed the locations they would die within a year. They only used copper found on the surface, refusing to dig into Mother Earth. They considered copper sacred, and used it only for medicinal rites and for ornament.

Earlier native peoples, however, used the copper extensively. Evidence of ancient "Indian diggings," likely from Shield Archaic Indians (c.5,000-500 B.C.) can still be found on Mamainse Island, and inland from Hibbard Bay. Along exposed copper veins are a series of shallow holes. It is believed the surface was heated, then water thrown on it to make it crack. Miners would gouge out the ore with stone or copper wedges and chisels, and then heat the metal in order to shape it into tools.

Although Thompson never located the source, sporadic copper mining attempts continued for many years. About 3 kms (2 miles) north of Mamainse Harbour, the Mamainse Mine operated between 1879 and 1884. The settlement consisted of 30 buildings, including compressor buildings, a boarding house, powder house, stamp mill and dwellings for about 400 people. Five years later the ore ran out. Stone foundations, three shafts and anchor bolts indicating where the ships once tied up can still be found at the site.

FISHING FROM MAMAINSE HARBOUR

As early as the 1850s, a fishing station was set up at Mamainse Harbour, a sheltered channel between Mamainse Island and Mamainse Point. Various outfits operated here over the years, including the Gauthier fishery, and more recently, Ferroclad Fisheries. The catch was mostly whitefish, although herring was fished for a stretch between the 1950-70s.

As related in Don Steer's *Superior's East Shore*, stories of the fishermen are legendary. Although they usually stopped fishing around the first of February, some like Charlie Carlson, Jack Roussain, G.A. Jones and Olie Bjornaa continued through March with the help of dog teams. They would cut a hole in the ice and insert a device called a "creeper" which would pull a line about 100 yards distant. Following the creeper by sound, they would cut another hole at the far end, attach a net to the line and pull it back through to the first hole. Sometimes fishermen failed to notice deteriorating ice conditions. One couple, Shane and Dorothy MacWilliam, recall being on the ice when their sled dogs sat down and refused to go any further. They turned back just as the ice began breaking up. They were lucky to reach shore.

Getting into Mamainse Harbour can be tricky at the best of times but in a gale with 128 kph (80 mph) winds, it is a miracle. According to Art Bodley, Olie Bjornaa performed just that: "That channel was bare between each sea. He checked her down until he hit the crown of a wave when he gave her the gun and tied up at the dock just as neat as could be. I never saw anything like that in all my life."

POINT MAMAINSE: VALIANT RESCUE OF THE *HEBARD'S* CREW

It was late November 1902. Oscar Carlson stared out his cabin window at Superior, which was being whipped into a froth like eggs in a bowl. "Get the boys," he urged his wife. Above the roar of the waves and wind, he thought he heard shouting. His ears were not playing tricks. The lumber hooker, *Charles Hebard*, and three barges were in imminent danger of being smashed against the rocky headlands.

Sailing from Superior, Wisconsin, her decks piled high with hardwood, the 763-ton, 14 crew *Hebard* had been towing three large barges, each with its own crew and lumber cargo. But in the gale, the lines separated, releasing the barges. It was a fortunate accident as it turned out, for within no time the *Hebard* was driven onto rocks at Point Mamainse and began to break up. Carlson was slipping into his oilskins when he shook his head in disbelief at the sight through his window. Rowing towards shore, disappearing at times in the swells, came two men in a small yawl, trailing a lifeline behind them. "They're either fools or heroes," he muttered, as he and his sons raced to their aid.

They rigged a bosun's chair to carry eleven men and Jennie Barns, the cook, to safety. The last to leave the *Hebard* was Captain George Ryan who was not so fortunate. He was trapped between the deck and cargo. On shore the lines became so tangled, the chair was useless. Captain

Ryan had to make the journey hand over hand along the line, half the time his body dragging through freezing surf.

When all were safe, they gathered in the warmth of the Carlson home, waiting for a rescue tug from the Soo. There was little rejoicing, however, as the three barges and their crews were nowhere to be seen. Yet, in one of those quirks of fate, the barges were pushed safely into shore. A century later, the rusting boiler and other machinery still mark the *Hebard* wreck. The propeller was salvaged, and is at the site of the former Lighthouse Restaurant on Highway 17 at Hibbard Bay.

POINT MAMAINSE

The aircraft made another pass along the shore, its engine humming smoothly. It was a beautiful clear sunny day in 1953. A perfect day for flying, until.... A series of sharp reports exploded from among the trees. The aircraft shuddered. A portion of wing broke away, then most of the tail. Shattered by anti-aircraft fire, the plane plummeted like a stricken bird. Then a parachute billowed out. A cheer echoed through the trees.

War along the eastern shore? Not really. Just the U.S. military practising its anti-aircraft skills. The aircraft, a radio-controlled model with a 14-foot wingspan was painted brilliant red—the better to see it against the sky. For about a decade after World War II, U.S. Army personnel trained here each summer. When they weren't sharpening their anti-aircraft skills, the soldiers would target practise with 45-gallon drums lashed to rafts floating on the water.

The R-CATs, as the radio-controlled targets were called, were expensive but relatively safe. When hit, the models deployed a parachute to permit recovery. The alternative to the radio-controlled models was a drone plane, pulled by cable behind a DC-3 transport aircraft, like a trailer behind a tractor. Unfortunately, on at least one occasion the anti-aircraft teams took better aim at the tractor than the trailer, almost bringing down the DC-3 and its frightened yet infuriated pilot.

During these years, aircraft engines, anti-aircraft guns, machine guns and the usual boisterous adventures of young men far from home sometimes disturbed the tranquillity of the eastern shore, but there were benefits to having the U.S. Army as temporary neighbours. Often the regiment was oversupplied with food such as canned bacon which the residents would exchange for local specialties such as fried whitefish livers and fillets. During a brewery strike, friends of the soldiers were the envy of other thirsty Ontarians as they enjoyed the refreshing taste of cold American beer.

Gun crews left, and Point Mamainse safety tower, right.

FLOUR BAY

Word spread up and down the shore like wildfire. "Just south of Mica Bay," everyone was told. "Get down there!" Those who arrived early couldn't believe their eyes. The water in and around the cove was dotted with hundreds of smooth shapes, like the backs of small humpback whales. Dinghies, yawls, rafts, anything that could float was rowed, paddled, sailed and otherwise propelled toward the strange objects.

It took a strong man to hoist the grey shapes out of the water and into a small boat. The efforts of the growing crowd went on throughout the day until each carcass-like shape had been retrieved and stacked on shore like... well, like damp sacks of flour. That was precisely what a down bound boat had been carrying when she went aground in the cove. In order to break free, the crew had to jettison much of her cargo.

Locals hauled away as many sacks as they could, ensuring a steady supply of pancakes, pies and pastries for the coming winter. Since then, the little cove has sported the name Flour Bay.

MICA BAY PICTOGRAPHS

In the 1960s, a noted scholar of Indian rock art wrote about some badly faded pictographs found twenty feet above the water on a rugged granite headland at Mica Bay:

l. to r. William Robinson, Chiefs Shingwauk and Kinebonegojing

They seem to have been painted in an oil medium, laid on so thick that brush marks were still visible in a few places.... Crude and acculturated, they could neither be accepted as authentically aboriginal nor dismissed as coming from a frivolous hand. It was rather as if they had been the work of a canoe-man of mixed origins from a passing fur brigade, forced to lay over till a storm blew itself out, who had painted it as a simple gesture to half-remembered deities for luck on his current voyage.

This critique surprised everyone, especially the artist Ken MacDougall who had painted them in 1959. Ken had been on a painting trip with a friend and began to record events from their trip on the rocks. "I just drew some stick figures about a foot high, walking along and carrying paint boxes.... I even made a sun because it was a sunny day." Little did he think they would be mistaken for art of a by-gone era.

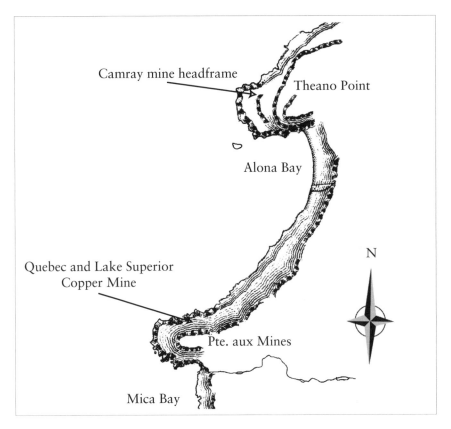

Camray mine headframe

Theano Point

Alona Bay

Quebec and Lake Superior
Copper Mine

N

Pte. aux Mines

Mica Bay

THE RAID AT POINTE AUX MINES

While legends of copper had abounded for centuries, in the early 1840s, publicity about a 3,708-lb. copper boulder at Ontonagon on Superior's southern shore set off a staking rush up the eastern shore. Prospectors and mining companies poured in and mines, such as Pointe aux Mines, sprang up. In 1849, the Quebec and Lake Superior Mining Company's operation was in full swing, complete with smelting works, crushing mills, railroads, scow, bunkhouses, storehouses, offices and repair shops. Amid all this frantic activity, there was one major oversight, although it had been brought to the government's attention years before. In 1840, Chief Peau de Chat from Fort William protested:

The miners burn the land and drive away the animals.... Much timber is destroyed and I am very sorry for it. When they find mineral, they cover it over with clay so that the Indians may not see it, and now I begin to think that they wish to take away and to steal my land....

In the following years, the situation worsened: mining machinery rumbled and smoke belched from the smelter at Pointe aux Mines. As a final diplomatic act, in the summer of 1849, Chief Shingwauk (White Pine) from Garden River and Chief Kinebonegojing from Badjiwanung along with another chief and a priest had travelled to Montreal to air their grievances directly to the Governor General, Lord Elgin. While the visit was much publicized and created quite a stir in Montreal, it had no effect. Shingwauk and Kinebonegojing had had enough. Along with two English adventurers and a group of native men—and, legend has it, a cannon—they made a lightning raid on the Pointe aux Mines mining site and drove the miners away. It was too late in the season for the government to send troops but the two chiefs were arrested, brought to Toronto and jailed. There was only one problem. They had done nothing wrong. The land belonged to them.

The incident did spark a general recognition of the need to address land claims. The well-connected William B. Robinson was appointed to negotiate on behalf of the government. As a member of the Board of Directors of the mining company that had just been attacked, he definitely had a vested interest in the result. His sympathies and ambitions lay in securing as favourable an agreement as possible for the mining industry.

William Robinson

The following year, Robinson signed two documents with the Indian chiefs: the Robinson-Huron Treaty and the Robinson-Superior Treaty. The Robinson-Superior Treaty covered the territory that included the northern shore of Superior from Batchawana Bay to the Pigeon River inland to the height of land, plus the islands. In return for surrendering these vast tracts of land, the Ojibwe bands would receive a lump-sum cash payment and annuity payments in perpetuity. The annuity amounts would increase in proportion to any profits earned from the land. In addition, the Ojibwe would be awarded small reservations and could keep their hunting and fishing rights, but only on lands the government did not subsequently sell or lease.

Some chiefs signed the document as they wanted some compensation for the ore that was being taken. Some did not know about it (at least one of the Lake Superior chiefs was off hunting at the time). Others had not been identified and did not sign. The Pic Mobert, Pic Heron Bay, Pays Plat and Long Lake bands continue to claim lands from the Pukaskwa River west to Lake Nipigon and from the Superior islands and shore north to the height of land.

Two years after the treaty, the Indians of Fort William complained to Lord Elgin, Governor of Canada, that the paper treaties were different from their oral agreement with Robinson:

> We thought that what was written on your paper came out of your heart, like the words that we heard come out of your mouth. Since your paper has been explained to us, we see how much difference there is between your words and your writing.

During negotiations, Robinson had argued that the land was "notoriously barren and sterile." Yet, around the same time, an annual report of the Montreal Mining Co. described this 500 miles of Lake Superior shoreline as "a region abounding in mineral treasures requiring only the hand of the miner to convert it into a source of perhaps inexhaustible wealth." Several problems with the treaties created disputes that remain unresolved to this day.

Ironically, the Pointe aux Mines operation closed within the year as did others along these shores. Today, mining historian Ted Leahy reports having found the mine's smelter, along with bits of slag in which specks of metallic copper can be seen. A brick foundation corner, three large depressions—likely former shafts—what appears to be a small forge, square nails, and even a miner's pickhead are reminders of this historical venture.

ALONA BAY/THEANO POINT: URANIUM FEVER

Lake Superior had already tried to protect her treasure from Robert Campbell once that year, but he was not about to let her do it again. In early September 1948, the prospector pitched a tent within sight of the place where he and two assistants had watched Superior's waves tear their wooden boat, the *Theano*, to pieces in front of their eyes.

Derelict headframe from uranium mine, active at Theano Point in 1949.

"We lost the boat on July 23," Bob recalled twenty-five years later, "...couldn't get it away from the rock in increasing ground swell conditions—we abandoned it. The next day the boat was spread all along the Alona Bay beach, the largest piece being about 3 by 3 feet." Campbell and the other two had to walk out through the woods hauling their heavy gear and Geiger counters with them. For all their weeks of trekking up and down the shoreline, they had found nothing.

But Campbell was not easily discouraged. Just 33 years old, his life had already been filled with enough adventure and accomplishments for an entire lifetime. He had mined in California, discovered a major gold deposit in the Missinaibi Range, spent six months aboard a Norwegian tanker and served in the Canadian army during World War II. After the atomic bomb was dropped, he became intrigued with stories of pitchblende (a lustrous black mineral which is a major source of uranium) being found along this shore a hundred years earlier. He had failed to find it the first time but he was back to try again, this time alone.

On September 8, barely a mile from the spot where his boat had been destroyed, he began looking for a place to have lunch. Ahead of him lay a narrow gorge, its steep cliffsides showing some green rock. He clambered up the sides of the gorge to the location of the rock and switched on his Geiger counter.

Bob Campbell had located the source of uranium first reported in 1847 (probably Canada's first uranium discovery). By the time he had staked 30 claims, including all of Theano Point (named after his wrecked boat) and Ossifrage Island, word had spread. The rush was on. By November, prospectors' tents lined Highway 17 at Alona Bay and airplanes with Geiger counters were conducting fly-overs. In less than three years, about 5,000 claims had been staked in the area.

Campbell's Camray Mine consisted of a headframe over a shaft against a sheer cliff face on Theano Point's north side and a mining camp located atop the 75-m (250-ft) high cliff. Camray did not live up to expectations, however. The operation proved unprofitable and was abandoned before having gone into full production. Instead, attention shifted to the Elliot Lake discoveries east of Sault Ste. Marie, which were proving far more rewarding. Today, the weathered, wooden timbers of Camray's headframe still cling stubbornly to the towering rock facing Superior. It is a uniquely beautiful setting, with the pink granite of Theano Point set against shoal-filled turquoise waters.

And Bob Campbell? He was a prospector to the end, dying of a heart attack in 1980 at age 65, somewhere in the northern bush, searching for one more claim to stake.

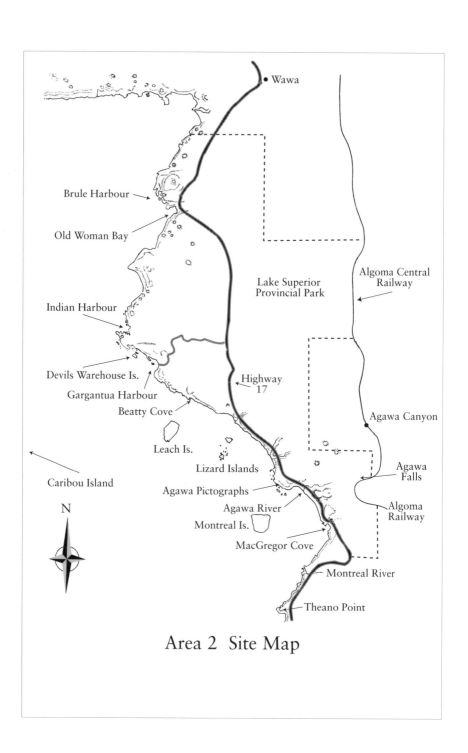

Area 2 Site Map

2

AREA TWO: MONTREAL RIVER TO BRÛLÉ HARBOUR

TRAGEDY AT MONTREAL RIVER

Maybe it was exhaustion caused by walking the long trap lines and hauling back the furs to their canoe above the falls on the Montreal River. Maybe it was just bad luck. Whatever it was, the events of that April day in 1921 would haunt Fred Coutu forever. Fighting winter's icy runoff, Coutu and his trapping partner, Joe Rivers, had set off across the Montreal River. Halfway, their canoe overturned. Clinging to the craft, they found themselves being swept towards the falls. Fred was tempted to try to make shore but Joe couldn't swim. So instead Fred tried desperately to steer the canoe towards the nearest riverbank. Struggling only made them sink further beneath the rushing water. The lip of the falls was already in sight; the roar was deafening. Joe was panicking. There was nothing they could do, except.... Fred kicked away from the canoe and swam against the current toward the shore. Exhausted, he touched land just above the falls. As he pulled himself up, he heard above the angry roar, "Don't let me drown!" Just as Fred turned, he saw the canoe tipping over the falls, beginning its long drop to the rocks below.

Fred suffered through a stormy night, making it to the Bussineaus at the mouth of the Agawa River around noon the following day. As soon as possible he led a search party back to look for his friend. But there was no trace of Joe or the canoe to be found.

1930s precarious log bridge over the Montreal River Canyon. Instead of trucks driving fully-loaded across the bridge, they would stop, supplies would be unloaded and carried over, then reloaded on the other side.

TWILIGHT LODGE ON HIGHWAY 17

Depression Era Work/Conscientious Objectors

In the early 1930s, the road north from Sault Ste. Marie was a single-lane track, with its shoulders often touching both sides of the car. A trip from the Sault to Montreal River could take eight hours. Oncoming traffic meant one party had to go into the ditch, and getting over hills often took several tries. A highway was needed, and during the Depression, building one seemed to be a good way to provide employment.

The work was painfully slow as there were only picks, shovels and wheelbarrows, no machinery or horses. They lived in tent camps set up every five miles. In Don Steer's *Superior's East Shore*, Don MacMillan relates that each camp had its own ethnic makeup and personality. Flour Bay was predominantly Italian; Mica Bay had many French speakers; Alona Bay seemed to attract the Finns; and the Mamainse camp, within driving distance of Sault Ste. Marie was filled with stable, married men who returned to the Sault on weekends.

In 1935, a camp was built at the mouth of the Montreal River where the Twilight Resort sits today. A cross-shaped building had three wings which functioned as bunkrooms (the longer you had been at the camp, the closer your bed was to the stove). The fourth wing served as a kitchen and dining area. Washrooms were in the centre of the cross. This camp was known for its "wine gang", who were said to be trouble-makers. Raisins, other fruit—anything with sugar in it—mysteriously bypassed the kitchen and went directly into their still.

Building the highway was agonizing work. The crews encountered obstacle after obstacle. At Mica Bay alone, they tried four different routes. Alvie Thomas recalls that at Mica Bay, "one of the bunkhouses is under the present highway. All they did was build right over top of it and let it fall in." Other setbacks were political in nature. After the Liberals won the provincial election in 1934, they fired many of the workers, including foremen and supervisors, who had voted the "wrong way" and replaced them with inexperienced workers. Construction slowed to a crawl. Contractors were dismissed, replaced by new firms who had friends in high places. Even survey maps were tossed out. Everything came to a stop. It took years before construction would regain momentum.

In 1937, heavy equipment was finally brought in to complete the job. Bulldozers accomplished in weeks what had taken 100 men an entire winter to do. By 1939, the road had essentially reached Montreal River, but with the outbreak of World War II, work was suspended. In 1941,

Depression-era construction crew on the Montreal River Bridge. "You soon learned not to wear shirts with buttons because the blackflies crawled in, dropped to your waist and helped themselves. At times you found your shirt just soaked in blood."

—Roy Burnfield

Twilight Lodge camp for Conscientious Objectors during WWII

the hand picks and shovels once again appeared on the Montreal River hill. The abandoned camp was transformed into one of thirty make-work camps for Canadian conscientious objectors (COs). Many of the young men were Mennonites. For room and board plus fifty cents a day—most of which had to be "tithed" to the Red Cross—they worked six days a week, all year round. Food was adequate if not entirely appetizing. Pork and beans were a staple. The rare occasion when sausages appeared on the menu, they were often spoiled and green. Although the COs were generally treated well, they sometimes had to deal with the resentment of those whose sons were fighting overseas.

Following the war, the Montreal River site was converted into Twilight Cabins and Lodge, a tourist facility still in operation. The circular driveway replaced the cross-shaped dormitory where hundreds of bored young men waited out the war. The two log buildings are original, used over the years as church, post office, theatre, house, bunkhouse and now storage. The nearby lodge, Trails End, was literally the end of the road for the period before road contruction resumed north of Montreal River in the 1950s (see Closing the Gap, p.62).

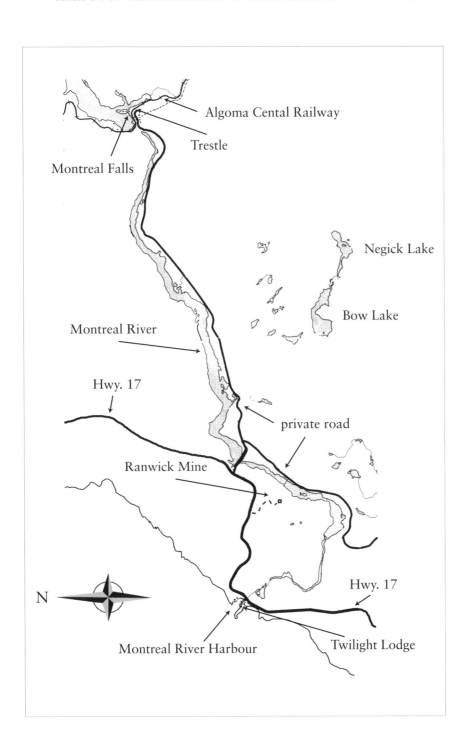

Algoma Cental Railway

Trestle

Montreal Falls

Negick Lake

Bow Lake

Montreal River

Hwy. 17

private road

Ranwick Mine

N

Hwy. 17

Montreal River Harbour

Twilight Lodge

RANWICK MINE: TOURISTS AND URANIUM

Roy Ranson was this close—this close!—to discovering the pitch-blende that made Robert Campbell a legend. And it happened 15 years before Bob Campbell's Geiger counter almost exploded from the uranium find at Theano Point.

Roy had heard tales of pitchblende being recovered ninety years earlier. Although uranium (a product of refined pitchblende) wasn't quite the better-than-gold discovery it became after World War II, there was still a ready market for it. Roy devoted the entire summer of 1933 to covering every stretch of shoreline between Batchawana Bay and Michipicoten River. Unfortunately, he lacked the two things that Bob Campbell carried in his hip pocket: a Geiger counter and good luck. When in 1948, Campbell's prospecting activity paid, Ranson immediately rushed back to stake his own claim near the Montreal River.

Within three years, the mine was played out, so Roy and his wife Dorothy switched to tourism. For seventeen summers beginning in 1961, the Ransons operated the Ranwick Mine. As many as a hundred people a day paid $1.25 to walk the trail from a gift shop (where they could buy radioactive ore samples) past a thriving beaver dam to the uranium mine. "The mine tunnel was horizontal, following a seam of pitchblende," Dorothy Ranson recalled years later. "The radioactivity of the pitchblende would be shown by a Geiger counter. We took visitors about 500 feet into the mine where we had a little room with a display of fluorescent minerals which glowed in the dark."

The mine welcomed busloads of visitors eager to learn about uranium and to cart off polished semi-precious stones and samples of radioactive—but safe—ore. In 1977 the Ransons' ill health forced them to give up their operation and a few years later the buildings were levelled. Today, the mine entrance is still visible but overgrown with weeds.

LAKE SUPERIOR PROVINCIAL PARK:

Geology

In the Lake Superior basin, the crust of the earth began forming over three billion years ago. Molten material slowly began to cool on the surface of the young earth. The weight of this new crust bore down on the

This is a beauty
of dissonance,
this resonance
of stoney strand,

This is the beauty
of strength
broken by strength
and still strong.

–A.J.M. Smith, "The Lonely Land"

more liquid interior, causing cracking and heaving. More molten material oozed to the surface, incorporating patches of the original crust. Remnants of this original crust became the the "greenstone" belts of today. Repeated cycles of cracking and heaving, and cooling and oozing of molten material resulted in the twisted and blended metamorphic rocks and granitic hills that we see today.

These stunning and diverse rock formations include the dramatic cliffs at Old Woman Bay which follow an old fault or crack in the earth's crust. At Rhyolite Cove, layer upon layer of hot volcanic ash melded together to form impressive redish beds of jointed rhyolite. Rapid cooling caused the rock to crack in a symmetrical octangonal pattern. The vertical chasms visible on the trail to Agawa Rock were created by the erosion of softer, younger rock.

More recently, beginning about 1.5 billion years ago, four separate ice ages carved and recontoured the land. The last glacier retreated no more than 9,000 year ago, leaving the landscape much as we know it today. The eroding meltwater carved the lakeside rocks, leaving behind the legacy of sand and gravels which dot the landscape. Some of this sand now sits as dunes along the shore of Katherine Cove and many other places. The glaciers also dropped huge boulders about the land as if giants had been at play. Less accessible are the potholes at Grindstone Point, formed by the power of meltwater rivers swirling hard "grindstones" around on softer sandstone. Some of the pot-shaped depressions which resulted still have the grindstone sitting in them.

Like all of nature, this strong land is always in a state of flux. Hills are eroding from the wind and water, and sand spits and beaches can change form in a single storm.

Human Response

This powerful, capricious landscape means different things to different people. For the Ojibwe, Gargantua, Devil's Warehouse, Agawa Rock, all traditionally have spiritual significance. While it is primarily the region's beauty that draws visitors to these shores today, few who come remain untouched by the region's mystical presence.

The Natural Environment Park was created in 1944 with its stunning scenery, ecological importance and remarkable geology. The region marks the transition between the more southerly Great Lakes-St. Lawrence forest and the Boreal forest to the north. The dividing line is most obvious at Old Woman Bay, where hardwoods grow on the south side of the bay and evergreens grow to the north. Moose, deer and black bear are all at home here along with Arctic plants (with wonderful names like Encrusted Saxifrage) which are relics of the last Ice Age.

Criss-crossing the park are eleven hiking trails covering over 125 kms (78 miles) and 8 canoe routes. The trails range from short, family hikes to longer, more demanding routes. One follows a former trap-line and has a floating boardwalk from which to observe wetland wildlife.

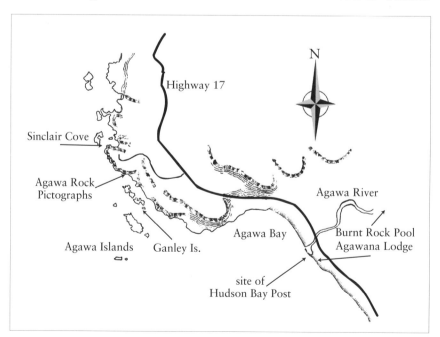

Ojibwe/Iroquois battle off Agawa, 1600s

Another passes by prehistoric Pukaskwa Pits (see p.136), while the Towab Trail leads up the Agawa River Valley to the impressive 25-m (83-ft.) Agawa Falls. The Towab Trail is named after the legendary guide and hunter, Towabanasay, whose name means "Man who travels by moonlight." Perhaps he acquired this name after an incident at Burnt Rock Pool on the Agawa River. After dinner he told the other guide he was going home to Batchawana that night as his wife was expecting a baby. He left at 6 p.m., ran cross-country to Batchawana and found his wife had had a baby girl. Then he returned in time to guide the party the following morning. (No one is quite sure how he managed to cross the Montreal River.) The longest and perhaps most challenging route in the park is the rugged 55-km (34-mile) coastal trail from Sinclair Cove in the south up to Chalfant Cove in the north.

Kayakers and canoeists who paddle the 120-km (75-mile) Lake Superior coast are in for an exhilarating wilderness experience. But be warned, the weather can vary from heavy fog, cold and high waves to warm and calm—all within minutes. Visitors often feel they have discovered the many secret coves but this has long been a well-travelled route. There are still a few signs of the early native peoples, voyageurs, fishermen, loggers and prospectors.

It wasn't until the arrival of the Algoma Central Railway in 1912 that the interior became accessible. Today, lake and river routes are available that range from relaxing day paddles to adrenaline-rushing whitewater adventures. The construction of scenic Highway 17, which skirts the shore in many places, has opened the Park even more. For information about the Park, drop by the headquarters at Red Rock, 35 kms (22 miles) south of Wawa; call (705) 856-2284; or write Box 267, Wawa, Ont. P0S 1K0.

AGAWA BAY

The Iroquois made several attempts to invade the Superior region but they never succeeded in setting foot on the North Shore. (For the decisive battle with the Iroquois on Lake Superior, see Gros Cap p.15.) One important battle with the Iroquois seems to have likely taken place some time before 1662 in the waters off Agawa. Ojibwe oral history recounts that during the years of Iroquois incursions, an Ojibwe shaman, Shingwauk, flew over the lake gathering support from Ojibwe groups. As the Iroquois paddled toward the North Shore to attack the Ojibwe at Agawa, Shingwauk sent a great fog to cover Superior. Under this cover, (and with help from the underwater manitou, Mishepeshu) the Ojibwe went out to meet the Iroquois and all of them drowned. (One panel at Agawa Rock is thought to refer to this event.) (See Agawa Rock and Myeengun p.63.)

The Agawa band lived along this eastern shore as far up as Gargantua. Small fragments of their pottery, bone tools and arrowheads suggest the existence of a settlement at the mouth of the Agawa River. Later the Hudson's Bay Company chose this spot for a small post consisting of a few log buildings, surrounded by tents and wigwams. It had to be moved three times due to spring floods. Furs were collected and shipped to the larger post at Michipicoten.

Disease and famine stalked the band. In the winter of 1879, the daughter of the post's last Hudson's Bay fur trader wrote, "there was no game in the bush, and the fish, packed in pork barrels, all rotted. The Indians ate chipmunks and squirrels, and the dogs all died. The weather was unusually severe and... the waters of the Agawa backed and threatened the post." Food was so scarce that ceremonial bear bones were boiled with fungus, bear grease and small, rotten potatos to provide sustenance. The cemetery grew that winter. By the

Early Sport Fishermen from the North Shore Club

mid-1800s most of the survivors had resettled at Goulais or Batchawana. The Agawa River site was to be rediscovered in the 1900s by another very different group.

AGAWA RIVER

Sport Fishermen Discover Superior's East Shore

American sport fishing publications had started to trumpet the wonders of the Agawa River, with its "trout in every pool and upon every rapid." The Prairie Club from Chicago set up tents near the site of the former Hudson's Bay Post south of the river mouth. Mary and Dave Bussineau had scarcely completed their log homestead in the summer of 1915 before guests began arriving. Fishermen came for the pike, brook, and rainbow and lake trout from Superior. Everyone competed for bragging rights, some even putting stones down the throats of their fish to make them weigh more!

In the autumn, hunters came for deer and moose. By 1923, the Bussineaus were hosting as many as 200 guests a year at their Agawana Lodge and adjacent cabins (one of which was known as "Camp Cold Beans"). Naturalists, photographers and painters arrived either on the steamers *Caribou* or *Manitou*, or via the Algoma Central Railway. The first of several tourist lodges in the area, the Agawana prospered in the

River drivers pose at the edge of log jam during the Agawa River drive

1920s. But by 1939, it was closed. Eventually the buildings fell into disrepair and were razed.

AGAWA RIVER DRIVE OF 1918

On May 31, 1918, in order to hold back the spring runoff a dam was in place on the main river along with smaller dams on its tributaries. They would be re-opened only when everything was in place for the annual Agawa River pulpwood drive. The tremendous rush of water would flush the logs down the river and out into Superior where tugs would collect them into giant booms ready to be towed to the pulp mill at Sault Ste Marie. Above the dam, Burnt Rock Pool was the holding pond for the logs cut that winter. Suddenly at two a.m., with the tugs still en route to Agawa Bay, the dam broke. Thirteen thousand cords of wood came rushing down on the raging waters. It was not until afternoon that the pulpwood could be retrieved; but it was a futile task, as strong winds had already scattered the logs around the bay.

Although this was one of the more hair-raising drives, none lacked excitement or danger. On the Agawa the drive was done at night to avoid the strong wind currents that rushed up the canyon during the day. Many were the simple wooden crosses found along the logging riverbanks. During the drive, "river hogs" strategically placed along the river, used pike poles and peavies to free any jammed logs to avoid serious pileups. In an interview with Rick Vosper, former logger Lee Fletcher recalls dynamiting a two-mile-long jam. Bit by bit, parts of the jam were loosened. All of a sudden, "the whole bloody thing let go, the whole channel. I've never heard anything like it or seen anything—of course you couldn't see a hell of a lot 'cos it was dark—but there was pulpwood flying in the air, there was roaring and snapping and it moved down... at least 2,000 cords." Behind the drive, shallow-draft pointer boats would clean up any stray logs and carry down the camp tents and cooks, who had somehow managed to make bread and hot beans on the turbulent ride!

THE ALGOMA CENTRAL RAILWAY AND THE AGAWA CANYON

(Information was gathered from Rick Vosper's 1984 reports on Lake Superior Provincial Park.)

The Algoma Central Railway's story centres around industrialist Francis H. Clergue. In the mid-1890s, Clergue counted among his many enterprises a pulp and paper company with logging rights on Superior's eastern shore, as well as the Helen Mine at Michipicoten. There was one problem. For much of the year—September to April—water travel was restricted. In order to unlock the potential wealth of the region, Clergue needed a dependable year-round transportation system. He initiated the building of the Algoma Central Railway. His vision did not end with the ore at Michipicoten, however. In a characteristically modest and understated move, in 1901, he renamed the railway the Algoma Central and Hudson Bay Railway Company. His plan? For the railway to reach as far as Hudson Bay so that arctic fish could be brought south to U.S. markets.

As the base for railway construction, Sault Ste. Marie was bursting with activity in 1902. The following year, however, things fell apart. Clergue ran out of money and work on the railway stopped. In 1909, British investors took over the project but it floundered again in 1914. When war became imminent, Michipicoten's iron ore and the sulphur from Nichol were suddenly deemed essential and so the government quickly completed the rail line to Hearst.

"The bright sparkling lakes we named after people we admired...; to the swampy ones, all messed up with moose tracks, we gave the names of critics who disparaged us" —A.Y. Jackson. Painting is J.E.H. MacDonald's The Solemn Land

One of the best descriptions of the dramatic scenery along this rail line was written in 1924 by T. Morris Longstreth in *The Lake Superior Country:*

> The more I saw of the Algoma Central the more I wondered at the energy of the will which had driven its course through such a territory. We had climbed 1500 feet. We shifted from side to side of one canyon after another. The climax came at the Montreal River, where Mr. McCormick had the train stopped so that we could feel the very heart-beat of the wilderness. An impetuous spruce-coloured stream, flowing from a pass, dropped into smoky depths. Walls sculptured by frost and wind harbored firs in their crevices, and on both sides rose mountains, each square mile of which afforded a fund of exploration. What an endless world, and how endlessly beautiful!

How did this "endlessly beautiful" scenery form? About 1.2 billion years ago, the earth's crust erupted in volcanoes and earthquakes. Incredible pressures caused the wide fault that became Agawa canyon. During the ice ages, ice sheets more than a mile thick covered the area, scraping and widening the canyon and depositing sediments on its floor—a fertile bed for future forests. Today, two different forest zones meet at the canyon: the Great Lakes-St. Lawrence forest, and the more northerly Boreal forest.

Train tours through the scenic Agawa Canyon leave from Sault Ste. Marie. At the canyon, the tracks descend 150m (500 ft.) over twelve miles to the canyon floor, then follow the Agawa River. The train stops in the canyon for two hours—long enough to climb to a lookout point, to take the Edgar H. Foote nature trail or just to enjoy a picnic amidst glorious scenery before having to reboard the train for the 3 1/2-hour return journey to the Sault. The Edgar Foote trail, a half-hour walk through mixed forest, introduces hikers to fault lines, drainage patterns, various native trees and wildlife. From mid-September to mid-October the dramatic Fall Foliage tour finds the canyon glowing with autumn colours while a winter wonderland greets the Snow Train between late December and early March.

The Group of Seven

> Well James, Me Boy, down on you knees and give great gobs of thanks to Allah... we have a car waiting us on the Algoma Central Railway!!!! A car to live in, eat in and work out of.
> —Lawren Harris to J.E.H. MacDonald, 1918

Painter Lawren Harris could not contain his exhilaration in this note to his friend and fellow artist, J.E.H. MacDonald. A boxcar for use as a travelling studio! His joy was only matched by his enthusiasm for the compelling beauty and power of the Algoma region—the "wild richness and clarity of colour" of the woods and "skies over the great Lake Superior which, in their singing expansiveness and sublimity, existed nowhere else in Canada."

For about four years, various members of the Group of Seven took these boxcar trips up the ACR, pulling onto different sidings each time. Their red boxcar was fitted like a rolling cottage studio complete with stove, sink, lamps, bunks, shelves, cupboard, furniture and a canoe and velocipede (a three-wheel, hand-pumped rail vehicle) for exploring the "wild, rugged, tumultuous country." They ventured north to the Agawa Canyon area, returning with enough sketches to keep them busy all winter creating canvasses that captured the land and its aloof beauty in ways no one had before. Their first exhibition in 1920 displayed paintings from the 1918 and 1919 boxcar trips. Using a bold new style, they interpreted the essence of Canada's wilderness landscape.

CLOSING "THE GAP": AGAWA RIVER TO MARATHON

Dramatic gorges and impenetrable woods are incredible wilderness scenery to some. But for roadbuilders they are a nightmare. As late as June 1959, the last 264kms (165 miles) of the Ontario section of the Trans-Canada Highway between the Agawa River and Marathon (better known as "The Gap"), was still incomplete. The stretch directly north of Agawa River was the worst. So bad, in fact, that the original Trans-Canada route was to bypass it altogether by going through Chapleau and Hawk Junction rather than Sault Ste. Marie and the Superior's eastern shore up to Wawa.

Radioing reports of the trek's progress from MacGregor Cove (see p.99)

Nothing was easy. Surveyors had to build rafts to cross lakes, swamps, and rivers. After a year and a half, 3 million pounds of explosives had cleared the way, 10 billion pounds of rock had been removed, 25 bridges and innumerable causeways over swampland had been built, and untold millions of black-fly and mosquito bites had been endured. Finally the road was widened and paved. The official opening was held on Sept 17, 1960 with a motorcade from the Sault to Wawa (see Wawa p.99). In the end, "The Gap" accounted for one-fifth of the entire cost of the highway in Ontario.

AGAWA ROCK PICTOGRAPHS: INSCRIPTION ROCK

Whether approaching by land or by water, the visitor senses the power of this place. A short forest trail passes through a wondrous narrow chasm left by an eroded rock dike. Cool, damp, sheer rock walls rise close on either side, and an enormous boulder balances precariously between the two faces. From the water, one can feel the strength of the 30-m (100-ft.) Agawa rock face plunging into Superior's waters. Low, early evening light suffuses the palette of warm pink and grey granite, orange lichen and ochre stains. Slowly the eye picks out the first red ochre pictograph.

According to Thor and Julie Conway's *Spirits on Stone: The Agawa Pictographs*, which includes interviews with Fred Pine, great grandson of the Lake Superior chief and shaman, Shingwauk, Ojibwe traditionally believe that the earth's energies are exposed at high rock cliffs. Along waterways, large birds often nested on these cliffs, reminding the Ojibwe of their protectors, the *Animikeek* or Thunderbirds, who flew between them and the spirit world. The rock faces were a point of contact between these two worlds, and they carried spiritual messages from past ages. These messages have endured in the form of pictographs painted in a penetrating red ochre and varnished by dripping minerals emanating from the rock itself.

There have been 117 recorded images at Agawa Rock most likely painted by shamans within the last 500 years. Today only 35 figures are visible. They provide insight into both the Lake Superior Ojibwe's earthly and spiritual worlds. Some denote success in warfare; others represent vision quests. Most are difficult to find. Each one resonates, warning yet beckoning.

Pictograph of the feared underwater manitou Mishepeshu, at Agawa Rock

Most arresting is the image of Mishepeshu, the Great Lynx, ready to strike, with head turned towards the viewer, horns to denote power and spines down his body and tail. Mysterious and dangerous, he is believed to live in and control the deep waters. Gifts of tobacco help appease his anger, and help ensure safe passage over the water. Only the very powerful, like spiritual leader Shingwauk (The White Pine) dared call on him for support. In the mid-1800s, Shingwauk was said to have gone to Agawa on a vision quest to gather fresh power. According to Thor and Julie Conway,

> He called forth Michipeshu, the guardian spirit of the underworld and minerals, especially copper. Shingwauk completed his fast, finished rituals which included rock art, and then led his warriors in a revolt against the copper miners [at Pointe aux Mines]. (For the story of this raid, see Pte. aux Mines p.40)

In another panel, a group of canoes is being led by totem animals of Ojibwe clans. It is thought to commemorate the successful crossing of Superior by Myeengun, The Wolf, and his men. Myeengun, a seventeenth-century chief and medicine man, had come from the Georgian Bay area to fight the Iroquois. In a four-day crossing, he canoed from

Superior's southern shore to Agawa, where combined Ojibwe forces successfully routed the enemy. (See Agawa p.56.) Once again, it was the Ojibwe protector Mishepeshu who was given credit for the victory. Shingwauk and Fred Pine both have said it was Myeengun himself who painted this scene.

The panel of a horse and rider is also thought to be Shingwauk's work. It may relate to a mid-nineteenth century conflict over spiritual leadership of the Lake Superior Ojibwe. Shingwauk was a powerful shaman in the Midéwiwin healing society in which the highest level that could be reached was the fourth degree. That may explain the panel's depiction of the Midé cross and four spheres. The small louse in front of the horse likely refers to Shingwauk's ability to transform himself in order to fly long distances on the back of a raven, even into the spirit world.

A delightful but not easily discovered panel shows a turtle (messenger to the spirits) leaving a long trail behind. Legend tells that the turtle created the Path of Souls (the Milky Way) by slinging mud into the sky... each piece becoming a star.

Fred Pine had this to say about Inscription Rock: "When I see one of those marks, I know what it is right away. But there's more meaning to it. It's like shorthand. You have to dream about it. It's an effort on your soul by the spirits." The site is sacred. Be sure to treat it as such. It is also dangerous. To view the pictographs requires going onto a sloping rock ledge well within Superior and Mishepeshu's easy grasp. In wavy conditions, the ledge is inaccessible. Watch your step in every way.

As we headed away from the pictographs, a thick fog rolled in, concealing them completely in less than a minute.

Sinclair Cove

This cove was known as *Saint Clair's* cove to brigades of voyageurs who used it as an overnight stop on their 720-km (450-mile) paddle between the Sault and Grand Portage. They would pull their birch bark canoes up on shore and patch them by torchlight, then dive into their standard meal of corn gruel mixed with bits of lard. It was this meal that earned them the nickname *mangeurs de lard*, or "pork-eaters." It would have been a great relief for these young men from rural Quebec to have survived the crossing of the open, unpredictable Agawa Bay. They feared the occasions when *la vieille*, the Old Woman wind, would suddenly whip Superior into a deadly sea for many of them could not swim. But even if they did, no one could survive Superior's frigid waters for long. The voyageurs often refused to travel in rough weather and if the offerings they sprinkled overboard did not appease *la vielle*, they lost precious days waiting for her to subside.

In *Caesars of the Wilderness*, Peter C. Newman vividly describes this inland navy of canoeists. At peak season, about ten freight canoes measuring 11-12m (36-40 ft). long, each capable of carrying 12 men and seventy 90-pound cargo packs, would leave from Laval every two days. The ideal voyageur was short—5'5"—and solid. He worked 18 hour days paddling 45 strokes per minute and was fiercely proud of his courage and endurance. On portages, men often carried two of the 90-pound packs, so it is not therefore surprising that the most common causes of death were heart attack and strangulated hernia.

This route saw hundreds of canoe brigades pass by, especially from 1783 when the North West Company was formed, until 1821 the year it merged with the rival Hudson's Bay Company. After 1821, the bulk of the trade no longer went to Montreal. Instead, pelts were sent up to HBC posts on Hudson Bay. Evidence of the voyageur encampments have been found at Sinclair Cove, along with pottery shards from earlier Indian settlements dating as far back as 500 B.C.

An active fishing station a century ago, Sinclair Cove was known as Whitefish Harbour. More recently, a small mink ranch was operated here for a few years around 1940. A government dock once stretched out into the lake but, damaged by successive storms, it was removed in 1991. Sinclair Cove can be accessed by car from the road to the Agawa Rock pictographs.

Lizard Islands

Rowe Is.
remains of cabin
Navigation light
Neptune wk.
Robinson fishery
site of Reliance wk
South Lizard Is.

Fishing at the Lizard Islands

It's a warm, summer day on South Lizard Island and Kevin Robinson is doing what many pay hundreds of dollars to do—he is fishing on Lake Superior. After a morning of pulling up nets, he arrives back at his camp where young children come down to the beach to assist with the catch. Soon, Kevin can retreat to a sauna on the small bay.

It sounds like paradise. It is. And it isn't. It's hard, dangerous work, work he doesn't want his children to pursue as adults (see Sandy Islands, p.28), even though his family has been fishing for generations. Kevin's grandfather, Peter, fished for whitefish, lake trout and herring in these same open waters—on a sailboat in the early years, later from a tug. Even then there were no assurances of safety. One stormy night he lost power as he was bringing the 12-m (40-ft.) *Neptune IV* into the camp. He dropped two anchors but they dragged and the tug was swept onto a reef, and then pushed on its side by the waves. A dock was built from which to winch the boat off the reef, but the boat broke in two. The remains still lie off the northern tip of South Lizard Island, the engine above water and the old steam boiler visible in the shallow waters.

South Lizard Island (once known as Fishery Island) has had a fishing station since at least 1871 when permanent buildings were erected by Messrs. Sharman and Roussain. At the turn of the century, the Dominion Fish Co. (a subsidiary of Booth Fish Co.) added still other buildings. Still visible are dock cribs and the remains of docks that were at least 15m (50 ft.) long.

Even if the work is difficult, the setting is glorious. South Lizard, a low island, is surrounded by shoals and beaches. Everything seems to move slowly and on a warm summer day when dragonflies dart among the reeds, it is easy to imagine that one is in a Louisiana bayou, instead of midway up Superior's exposed eastern shore. (Not so in December, see *Reliance*, below.)

The northernmost of the Lizard Island group is shown on charts as Rowe Island, but it is better known to local residents as Preachers Island, named for a group of ministers who spent summers there. The spot they chose for their large cabin was spectacular, on the island's north-east point near the wave-washed cobble beach and with a panoramic view of the blue, hazy, Algoma hills on the mainland.

During a harrowing storm in December 1922, crew from the tug Reliance *died trying to get off to South Lizard Island.*

THE HARROWING WRECK OF THE TUG *RELIANCE*

Superior wasn't co-operating. Thirty-five crew and passengers, mostly from isolated lumber camps and fishing stations, desperately wanted to get home to the Sault before shipping came to an official end on December 15. But because of stormy weather, the tug *Reliance* could make little headway. After two nights at Gargantua Harbour, it finally set out at daybreak, December 13, 1922.

Wheelsman, Jack Cadotte, an Ojibwe with extensive knowledge of the lake, soon regretted edging the Reliance into the open. They were hit by wind and a blinding blizzard. As waves broke over the bow, passengers urged Captain Williams to turn back, but he knew this was foolhardy. One massive wave striking broadside would capsize their vessel. Jack Cadotte knew it too, but approaching the Lizard Islands, he developed another concern. "It's getting high and choppy," Cadotte said, pointing to the waves cresting ahead. "It's got to be shallow in there." Captain Williams said nothing, so Cadotte repeated, "Hear that? That's surf. It's shallow." Again the captain did not respond, so the lower-ranking Cadotte continued to steer in silence.

When the *Reliance* struck the shoals, Captain Williams ordered the engines reversed. This forced the vessel down so heavily on the rocks that it bent the propeller and tore a gaping hole in the hull. The *Reliance* slid on her side like a wounded whale while passengers scrambled to keep their footing.

Captain Williams ordered one lifeboat to be lowered, placing Second Engineer Charles Currie in charge. With only three in a boat for ten, Currie drew a knife and hastily began cutting it loose. Jack Cadotte seized an oar and swung it like a baseball bat. "Let everyone else on!" he threatened above the screaming wind. Five more quickly scrambled in, including Cadotte and Mrs. Harten, the cook's wife, the only woman aboard.

Miraculously, they negotiated the 5 kms (3 miles) to the mainland. Half frozen, they staggered ashore into more than two feet of snow. Someone had accidently smashed the compass, leaving them with only a broken axe. Cadotte took his bearings. "We can make it to the Bussineau house near Agawa Bay," he said confidently. Assessing the spirit of the group, he added, "It's about eight miles away." He was lying, the nearest settlement was about double that distance through rugged country.

Pelted with sleet and snow and without food, the nine travellers scaled hills hundreds of feet high, crossing streams waist-deep in water. When Mrs. Harten collapsed from exhaustion, Cadotte carried her. When she could go no further, her husband stayed with her while the group continued the trek. After two arduous days and nights, some of the men finally stumbled into the Bussineau cottage. Currie arrived hours later; another man had collapsed in the bush. Two Bussineaus set out to search for the stragglers. After only two hours of sleep, Cadotte refuelled himself with a cup of hot tea and followed. All were returned safely.

Those back at the *Reliance* were experiencing their own nightmare. Attempts to reach the shore of South Lizard Island failed when waves swept away the second lifeboat before anyone could board. Because of this, two men decided to ride down with the last yawl. When an ice-covered rope became stuck in the pulley, the boat flipped and tossed them into the freezing lake. A third man slipped on the icy deck, hit his head, and plummeted into the water. All three died.

Constructing rafts out of gas drums, the remaining twenty-three made it to the safety of the island. There they huddled for six days until they were rescued by the tugs *Gray* and *Favorite*. There was one other notable survivor. The following spring, the *Reliance* was pulled off the shoal and towed to the Sault for repairs. The sturdy tug managed to serve at least five more seasons, chugging up and down past the Lizard Islands.

BEATTY COVE AND THE *TELEGRAM*

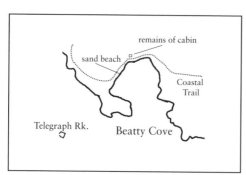

In the early 1890s, a traveller venturing up the eastern shore from the Soo would board the steamer *Telegram* which visited fishing stations between Sault Ste. Marie and Otter Head twice weekly. During the 1901 shipping season, the lightkeeper at Gargantua sighted the *Telegram* many times, but not after November of that year. The vessel is said to have foundered on a rock just west of Beatty Cove, a rock identified on a 1931 lake chart as Telegram Rock, but now named Telegraph Rock.

Protected by two headlands, on a late summer's day Beatty Cove is a slice of paradise. Its soft, warm, white sand beach invites laziness. Scattered driftwood stumps are silvery and iridescent. Just inland from the beach lie the ruins of a trapper's cabin. Only the wood stove remains, a reminder of frigid January nights when the wind and lake howled outside.

GARGANTUA HARBOUR

Fog and Gargantua were synonymous. The giant manitou, Nanaboozho, liked to play tricks on mortals, rolling fog off his palms just before fishermen headed out in the morning to set their nets, or just as they were about to reach the harbour in late afternoon. To Nanaboozho, fog was a toy.

Enjoying one of his usual pranks, Nanaboozho enveloped the steamer *Caribou* in thick soup for much of the trip up the eastern shore. The *Caribou's* captain stared out into the grey mist and occasionally pulled the whistle. As related by Gordon Macauley in "Ferries out of Owen Sound" in *Inland Seas*, steamer captains developed a sixth sense for navigating through fog. Cocking his ear to hear the faintest echo, the captain began to alter course:

... Another change of course and now—did the echo take just an instant longer to return? The skipper thought it did. Ringing for "slow ahead," commands were snapped at the wheelsman and the ship swung a bit one way then back again, following the echoes of her whistle. Suddenly to starboard loomed a huge towering mass and at almost the same instant to port loomed a smaller shadow. The ship, throwing off the clinging mist, scampered through a narrow chink in Superior's granite shoreline to enter a sun-drenched bay. Making a sharp turn to port she headed for a little cluster of weathered buildings nestled on the shore half a mile away. This was Gargantua Harbor.

When asked by one incredulous passenger how he had managed this feat, the Captain modestly replied, "I say, I guess it's done by ear, by nose and by God."

In 1903 and 1904 respectively, the steamers *Manitou* and *Caribou* began regular service from Georgian Bay's Owen Sound to Michipicoten, picking up fish at isolated stations along the shore. Many have fond memories of these trips, including on-board dances when the piano skittered across the floor in heavy swells. For people along the route, the steamers were their lifeline to the outside world.

One of these stations was Gargantua Harbour, a small, lively hub along a relatively uninhabited shore. It was established around 1871. Later, tourist cabins were built and the harbour occasionally became a haven for cruising yachts, its long dock serving as an impromptu dance floor. In the 1930s, fishing from stations like Gargantua was a great way to ride out the Depression, but things declined quite rapidly after that. In 1939 the *Manitou* was taken out of service and in 1942 the *Caribou* was given another route. The small community died out in the 1950s, their livelihood destroyed by overfishing and the invasion of the sea lamprey.

Much remains to explore. The harbour has two beaches—a long sandy one, and a wonderful cobbled beach made up of heavy, melon-sized, multi-coloured stones rounded by the waves of countless storms. On the west side of the harbour there are dilapidated cabins among lilac trees gone wild and a sea of raspberry bushes. One is tucked back from shore; and another, a fishing hut, opens to the water. Steps lead down to what was once the long steamer dock. For the snorkeller, massive dock cribs, as well as pots and pans, door knobs, cables and other hard-

Gargantua Fishing Station and Lightkeeper's house

ware are easily visible. Remnants of a barge lie in the sand, as well as the wreck of the *Columbus* (see p. 75).

From the northwest corner of the harbour, climb the green, mossy trail to a lookout point and bask in a panorama of beauty. Gargantua Harbour lies directly below offering a refuge from the blustery winds of the open lake. Devil's Warehouse Island dazzles against the infinite blue beyond. And northwest up the shore lies Warp Bay protected by Cape Gargantua.

LOUIS MIRON AND GARGANTUA ISLAND LIGHTHOUSE

The story of this light is the story of the Miron family. They tended the Gargantua Island lighthouse for three generations, from the year the tower was erected in 1889 to 1948, when it was automated. Louis, the first keeper, left his mark on peoples' memories, if not on the hard granite of the land. Born in the Sault in 1841, he first served as a winter mail carrier. Three times a month he drove a dog team and snowshoed 320-kms (200 miles) between Killarney and Sault Ste. Marie. Each one-way trip wore out a pair of snowshoes. In 1866, he was a volunteer guard protecting the Sault area against possible Fenian raids from the United States. He later guided canoe expeditions as far north as Moosonee. Married with children, he settled down, and in November 1889, he took the post of Gargantua lighthouse keeper, earning $450 for the eight month season.

To supplement his income, Louis fished, scavenged pulp that had washed ashore from passing log booms, and occasionally fed and boarded tourists. To complement their diet, the family raised pigs, grew potatoes and picked berries, and in autumn, they snared rabbits and partridge, sometimes hunting for larger game. As with all lightkeeping families, the Mirons were quite self-sufficient, even concocting their own remedies such as Duffy pure malt whiskey for coughs, one egg mixed with equal parts of vinegar and turpentine for sore muscles. For "thick" throat, a small towel was dipped in a vat of boiled young oak bark, then wrapped around the neck. Unfortunately there was no remedy for the stroke which took away Louis' speech when he was about eighty years old. He died five years later in 1927.

On his father's retirement in 1912, Charlie Miron assumed lighthouse duties for thirty years until Louis' grandson Tom (who had kept the light at Quebec Harbour for several years) took over. Near the end of Charlie's tenure, the original lighthouse on the exposed rock suffered a dramatic end. During a severe November storm in 1940, assistant William

Gargantua Harbour's first lightkeeper, Louis Miron, on right.

Lewis, stayed on the island to tend the light instead of returning to the mainland. The waves pummelled the lighthouse relentlessly and finally carried it away. Lewis and his 12-year-old daughter took refuge in a shack 50m (170 ft.) from the water's edge. The waves reached that far and froze so solidly that the next morning, the pair could not leave the shack until people arrived from the mainland to chop the ice away. The next year, a new light was erected only to be replaced by an automatic beacon in 1948.

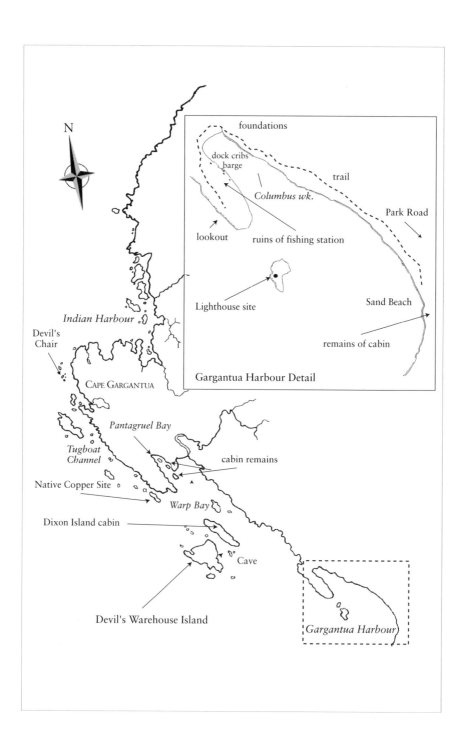

N

foundations

dock cribs
barge

Columbus wk.

trail

Park Road

lookout   ruins of fishing station

Lighthouse site

Sand Beach

remains of cabin

Indian Harbour

Devil's
Chair

CAPE GARGANTUA

Gargantua Harbour Detail

Pantagruel Bay

*Tugboat
Channel*

cabin remains

Native Copper Site

Warp Bay

Dixon Island cabin

Cave

Devil's Warehouse Island

Gargantua Harbour

THE WRECK *COLUMBUS*

The night watchman took a final drag from his cigarette, leaning against the rail of the 41m (139-ft) wooden tug *Columbus*. The September night was awash with stars, showering dim sparkles on the calm waters of Gargantua Harbour. Butting out his cigarette, he noticed sparks flickering near the smokestack. Seized with panic, he began beating them with his coat. But it was already too late. In those few moments, the situation had escalated beyond control. "Fire!" he yelled.

The crew spilled out of their bunks as flames spread across the vessel. "We're gonna' lose the dock!" someone shouted. "Cut the lines!" The crew scrambled ashore and by the time residents of the fishing station realized what was going on, the tug was already floating into the harbour, consumed in a ball of fire. Like a wounded animal dropping to its knees, she slid part way beneath the water and then, in one final motion, sank to the bottom. Here the *Columbus* has rested in about 9m (30 ft.) of water since that September night in 1910. Her boiler, propeller, machinery and the ribs from the hull make an interesting dive.

GARGANTUA AREA: IN THE SPIRIT OF THE GODS

One need only hear the names of locales in the Gargantua area —Devil's Warehouse, Devil's Chair—to sense that mystery and magic abound. Dramatically beautiful, Gargantua was the chosen site of the gods. In particular, it was home to the Ojibwe manitou, Nanaboozho.

The giant, Nanaboozho, could move from Devil's Warehouse Island to Devil's Chair in one step. Born of a human mother and a manitou father, Nanaboozho's blunders and follies made him one of the Ojibwe's most adored manitous. He could be impetuous and a buffoon. Though moody, fearful, lustful, envious, slothful, silly and prideful, he was also generous and big-hearted, and usually meant well.

Aeons of geologic time created this appropriately mystical environment for the gods. The narrow, deep Tugboat Channel passes through volcanic rocks that are twisted and wrenched in impossible shapes. Ojibwe entered the area with reverence and caution especially near the sizzling waters around Devil's Frying Pan, a flat, submerged rock ledge that surrounds and protects Devil's Chair, where tobacco offerings were dropped in the water.

With the coming of the missionaries, a collision between Christianity

Midéwiwin lodge belonged to the spiritual healing society

and Ojibwe cosmology was inevitable. The names Devil's Chair and Devil's Warehouse were given by early French missionaries to cast the Ojibwe hero, Nanaboozho, in a sinister role. However, it was easier for priests to dismiss him as a pagan idol than it was for voyageurs. They too must have felt an undeniable sense as their canoes slipped beneath the overpowering cliff at Devil's Warehouse. While the Christian God was known for bouts of wrath, locust plagues were not as immediately threatening as were storm, wind, waves and fog. Risking their lives on the open, unpredictable lake, in 10m (35-ft.) birch bark canoes, heavily-loaded with cargo, it was surely prudent to seek the manitou's goodwill with an offering. In this chaotic world, quite possibly, the Christian God might fall short of protecting them.

In Gargantua, they say, you are never alone. Some believe that because Gargantua is so pristine, mysterious powers can reverberate undiminished. Sceptical? Truth is in the sound. Paddle to Devil's Warehouse at sunset and listen... to the voices whispering in the breezes that ruffle the pine, and in the waves curling against the shore. Let Gargantua have the final word. (To learn about the name Gargantua, see Warp Bay and Pantagruel Bay. For more on Nanaboozho, see Sleeping Giant p.225)

Devil's Warehouse Island

Like the Ojibwe's Agawa Rock, the enormous sheer cliff face at Devil's Warehouse is a place where the earth is cut open, its energies exposed. Its towering presence inspires awe. Here and on the surrounding small islands was found the red-ochre rock which was ground and mixed with grease to form the Ojibwe's sacred paint used for rock pictographs.

It was also here that the Ojibwe kept some of their most sacred records, birch bark scrolls bearing pictographs of historical and religious significance. They recorded information from the Midéwiwin, a spiritual healing society which followed a deep spiritual path in order to communicate directly with the manitous. After a prescribed number of years, the scrolls were recopied and the old decaying scrolls were used in important ceremonies and potent medicines. It was reported that a number of these scrolls were discovered on the island in the 1970s and have been since lost.

Devil's Warehouse is still alive with spirits. Their eyes follow as you pass beneath the massive wall stained by orange lichen and delicate mineral washes of orange, red and green. They reside deep within the island's crumbling caves and grottos, perhaps those where the Midé laid their scrolls. One of these caves is particularly compelling. Interior stone breaks away in thick flakes like subtle purple, red and green-hued fish scales. Shapes and shadows beckon or repel the unprepared visitor, depending on the time of day, the time of year and the mood of the lake. Cobbled beaches dot the shoreline, their grey-white tones contrasting with the red ochre. Thick mosses drip with dew and ferns shiver in the slightest breeze. Everything is touched by a quiet magic. This spiritual ground does not demand reverence. It gently draws it out of you.

Tugboat Channel and Devil's Chair

Nanaboozho's Domain

Long before steamers and fishing tugs plied this shore, the Tugboat Channel belonged to the canoes of voyageurs, missionaries and natives. And long before people were on the earth, it was the world of the gods.

The weary shoulders of a long-crumbled mountain range rise like the broken back of a prehistoric beast. The hills and shoreline are volcanic in origin. Some are the colour of dried blood, stained by the pigment used by shamans for pictographs. Unbridled forces gave birth to this land and millions of years have carved it away.

Set apart from the craggy shoreline, Devil's Chair rises out of the blue water—massive pyramidal rock, imperious among dangerous rocky shoals. According to legend, the giant Nanaboozho rested here after bounding across the lake. (He is said to have left a giant footstep on Devil's Warehouse.) As the son of the wind, Nanaboozho not only controlled fog but all weather. Thus the Ojibwe, not wanting to tempt fate, left offerings of tobacco at the base of this magnificent throne to ensure safe passage on the water. Voyageurs followed their lead.

Should you venture out to Devil's Chair, do so with caution. Beware of the Frying Pan, and watch the weather. Water and sky can change in an instant from clear blue to steel grey. (A trail continues from Warp Bay to the shore across from Devil's Chair with a couple of back country campsites nearby.)

WARP BAY AND PANTAGRUEL BAY

Voyageurs likely named the region and bay after Gargantua and Pantagruel, well-loved characters created by the sixteenth-century French satirist, François Rabelais. King Gargantua was noted for his mammoth size, his "gargantuan" feasts and festive parties. Pantagruel was his son, a young, jovial drunkard who entertained with a brash, bawdy sense of humour. It is easy to see the connection the voyageurs made between these characters and the manitou, Nanaboozho, who entertained Ojibwe with his many follies and foibles.

These two bays are sanctuaries in which Gargantua's stunning beauty can be enjoyed in relative calm. Pantagruel Bay offers a breathtaking view out to Devil's Warehouse and the inland hills. The marsh at the end of the bay attracts a variety of wildlife. It is even possible to explore between the bays and around small islands by wading in shallow, sandy channels of warm water, a rare occurrence on Lake Superior. Some remnants of cabins—a few doorknobs, a rusted frying pan, a bed frame, fireplace and water pipes—can be found.

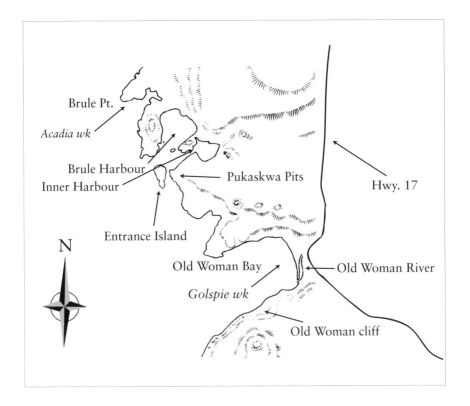

Old Woman Bay

The Controversial wreck of the Golspie

As the shadows shift along the sheer rock headland of Old Woman Bay, an ancient face emerges. Trees cling to the windswept cliff far above the normal water level, a reminder of the height waves can strike during late autumn gales, gales urged on by what the voyageurs called *la vieille*, the "old woman wind."

Not only Superior's wind and waves have claimed untold victims, her sheer remoteness and hostile environment have taken their share. Consider the fate of the steamer *Golspie* in the raging December storm of 1906....

Having been promoted from engineer, Captain Harry Boults was new to command when he lost steering on his way to Gargantua Harbour. The *Golspie* reeled and flailed and began taking on water.

Boults and his crew of eighteen—mixed Canadian and British sailors (and an Irishman)—could only hang on and pray that their 55m (182-foot) vessel would not be dashed against the rocks.

Swept into the shelter of Old Woman Bay, their relief was palpable. The safety of land was within reach. Soon, all hands and the few remaining provisions—twelve pounds of flour, a few chunks of beef, some buns, tapioca and canned goods—were aboard the vessel's sturdy lifeboat.

Safely ashore, Captain Boults ordered his First Mate, a man named McLeod, to sail the yawl with twelve of the crew, blankets and provisions, north around Brûlé Point to Michipicoten. At the mission, they were to send word of the shipwreck to the vessel's owners and direct a rescue party back to Old Woman Bay.

Once away from the protection of Old Woman Bay, they were soon numbed by a strong freezing head wind. Only three were able to manage the oars. Forced to land, McLeod had to devise a new plan. The seven foreign sailors, whom he considered ill-prepared for an overland journey, were to stay with the yawl while he set out with the Canadians.

A number of the men who had been left behind felt McLeod had discriminated against them. What if McLeod's group did not reach the mission? If they waited too long they might be too weak to head out on their own. And besides, how far could the mission be? They must be able to reach it by nightfall! Leaving their blankets behind, the naïve group headed into the rough country of the north shore. In the end, only seven men made it to Michipicoten: all of McLeod's men but only two from the other group. Days later, the rest were found crawling on their hands and knees. One delirious man had thrown away his shoes and was stumbling through the snow in stocking feet. All of them had to have their feet amputated, and one lost his frozen hands as well. (Presumably those left with the wreck were also rescued.)

An inquiry into the disaster noted that those men who recognized the risks and obeyed instructions were all Canadians. The Englishmen, Scots and Irishman who naïvely believed they could challenge the land, paid dearly. The owners of the *Golspie* were also blamed for neglecting to send out a search vessel when the ship was overdue. The tragedy led to a lively parliamentary debate on worker's compensation for anyone injured on the job.

There are periodical reports of pieces of the wreck being seen in Old Woman Bay, but shifting sands soon cover any traces.

BRÛLÉ HARBOUR

The harbour is named after Etienne Brûlé, the first European believed to have set eyes on Superior (even though it is doubtful he actually made his way this far up the shore). The entrance is difficult to spot, but once inside, the harbour is a hidden treasure (especially to those who have raced threatening clouds and steel-grey waves up the unforgiving, cliff-lined shore from Grindstone Point). Completely sheltered, the harbour's eastern arm is ringed by brilliant green hills. Treed down to the waterline, hardly a ripple disturbs the placid green water. Beavers go about their business; ducks and loons play in the marshes.

On the mainland, south of the harbour entrance is an ancient, raised cobble beach. Cobbles along the waterline are bleached and polished, but above an entangled line of driftwood, they look very different. Undisturbed by waves, these rocks are covered in green, black and grey lichen. Many are split apart, giving the beach the appearance of a patch of cracked, liver-spotted old skin. There is a primeval stillness about the scene. It is not surprising then to discover evidence of early peoples who roamed these shores. Several strange, rounded pits dot the cobbled beach. Known as Pukaskwa Pits, (see p.136) their purpose is a mystery.

At the spot where beach and forest meet, a marvelous thing happens. The "forest" turns out to be more like a thin stage curtain. Stepping through it unveils a remarkable scene: shelves of beaches stretching up the hill... and back into time. For each layer marks the waterline of a slowly retreating post-glacial lake. As the volume of meltwater diminished, the lake level (which was as much as 45m (150 ft.) higher than at present) dropped, stranding a succession of beaches. This phenomenon has also been affected by another force. Once the weight of glacial ice lifted off the land, the earth's crust began to slowly rebound. And it's all recorded here, in the shelves of round cobbles, high above the water's edge.

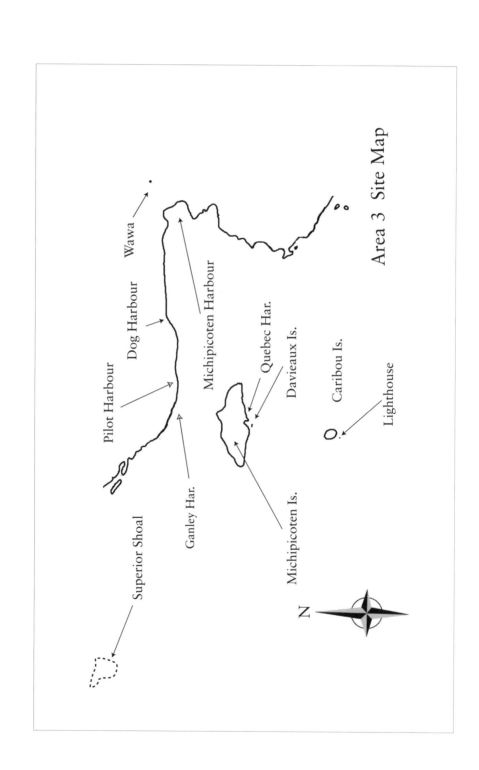

Area 3 Site Map

Wawa

Dog Harbour

Pilot Harbour

Michipicoten Harbour

Quebec Har.

Davieaux Is.

Caribou Is.

Lighthouse

Ganley Har.

Michipicoten Is.

Superior Shoal

N

3

AREA THREE: MICHIPICOTEN AND THE ISLANDS

THE UPS AND DOWNS OF THE MICHIPICOTEN TRADING POSTS

When the French lost their trading territory on Hudson Bay to the English in the 1713 Treaty of Utrecht, they looked to the continent's interior and to the west for their furs. They also looked at ways to block Indians from trading with the Hudson's Bay Company. They decided to erect a string of three posts, *les postes du nord* in order to intercept Ojibwe taking pelts to the forts on Hudson Bay, and to protect the interior from HBC incursion. They built Fort Kaministiquia to guard the western route; Nipigon Post to guard the northern route; and an outpost at Michipicoten to deter Lake Superior Ojibwe from taking the Michipicoten-Missinaibi-Moose River route to the HBC post at Moose Factory on James Bay. After the 1763 Treaty of Paris, Canada became property of Britain. The French left the post to independent traders like Alexander Henry. The situation changed after the formation of the North West Company in 1783. Michipicoten became a NWC post. By 1795 the NWC posts had become so effective at blocking furs, that Hudson's Bay Company directors in England finally decided to be more proactive, and to establish rival posts inland from Hudson Bay. At Michipicoten, instructions were to construct:

> ...a House of 30 feet long 24 feet width 18 feet height... [with] a Trap-Hatch through the Roof to look out in Times of Danger, and one Row of Strong Stockades round the Whole.... Cause the woods to be fell round about you, so that the Indians may not annoy, Surprise, or set you on Fire.

Michipicoten Post, 1908

Perhaps intimidated by these instructions, the first trader begged off the following spring. The job went next to Henry John Moze, who arrived in June 1797. Told he could build anywhere except on Mr. Henry's "Potatoe Ground," Moze chose a location on the north bank, across the river from the North West post.

Despite Moze's efforts, the Hudson's Bay was unable to compete with the North West Company. They abandoned the operation after six years only to reopen in 1816. By that time, both posts were competing for a dwindling fur supply. The company's Chief Factor noted,

> ...the trifling Trade procured at this place is scarce worth mentioning, and I am sorry to observe the future prospects are not flattering.... Only three packs of furrs were procured there last Year by our Opponents & 4 others from an Outpost situated between Meshippicoton & the Sault St. Maries....

After the two rivals were amalgamated in 1821, the Michipicoten post was kept open, although most of the trade was shipped to Europe via Hudson Bay. Until 1887, the Michipicoten post managed all the Company's Lake Superior District. Keel boats were constructed to transport pelts to Moose Factory and bateaux were built to deliver supplies to outposts such as the one at Pic River. For a time, Michipicoten was even involved in com-

Donald MacMillan Family and friends at Michipicoten Post, c. 1908

mercial fishing. After the Robinson-Superior Treaty of 1850, it also became a distribution centre for treaty payments, which helped ensure that Indian trappers would continue to use the post. By the late 1870s, the fortifications enclosed a spacious 8-room, 2-storey house with veranda, a storey-and-a-half trading store, provision store, carpenter's and blacksmith's shops, a dairy and stable and more, all at the preferred south shore site.

The arrival of the railway in the 1880s diminished the importance of the Michipicoten post. The CPR tracks were constructed near the height of land making it easier for native trappers to deal with traders along the train line than to haul their pelts out to the Superior shore. Operations were transferred to Chapleau and the Michipicoten post closed in 1895. The discovery of gold near Wawa brought a brief reprieve but by 1904, the post's fate was sealed.

For fifty more winters, the main building remained standing but few cared about preserving this historical site or its records, which had been left scattered on the floor. Local resident Lyman Buck was shocked to see Jack Kennedy, a man who lived at the post, use some of abandoned records to light the fire one morning. Did Kennedy not recognize their future value? To which he replied, "Oh, to hell with it!" After Kennedy, the Great Lakes Power Company bought the property in case there was a problem with one of their dams and the area flooded. Unable to maintain the buildings, they tore them down in 1952. A local newspaper lamented, "The crowning blow of humiliation, struck by hammer and crowbar this summer brought the sturdy old dwelling to its knees as though in wanton desecration of its brave significance." Many buildings in Wawa were built from the salvaged lumber and beams. In the 1960s, only the crumbling stable, the powder

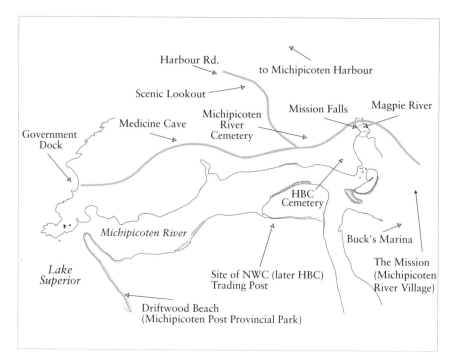

magazine, stone fireplaces, and a few headstones testified to the existence of this once-vital fur-trading post.

Over the years, silt carried down from the Michipicoten and Magpie Rivers amassed into an island. Now, instead of a grand approach, one can only take a very small craft up the narrow channel separating the island from the former post site. Behind high grasses lies a fairly open field, dotted with raspberry and red currant bushes and a few roses, probably planted by Francis Hector Clergue's sister Helen during their years at the post. On the foundations of the two-storey building, visitors have placed pieces of metal discovered at the site as a gesture of remembrance.

One passionate admirer of the past did more than make a small gesture. In the 1960s, Al Turcott constructed Fort Friendship, a replica of an eighteenth-century fur trading post. Unfortunately, this has also been abandoned. Mr. Turcott died in 1974 and was buried beside his dream. There is access to Fort Friendship from the road leading to Michipicoten Post Provincial Park. A local business rents canoes and can give directions to the original fort site. Ask at the Information Centre in Wawa.

THE MICHIPICOTEN MISSION AND MORMON TOTEROADS

When the Hudson's Bay post expanded in the 1860s, the Ojibwe people living adjacent to the post were forced to relocate. They moved across the Michipicoten River to a site that became known as the Mission because of the Jesuit Sainte Margaret-Mary Church, the focal point of the community. (It burned in 1980.)

At the height of the CPR construction in the early 1880s, the Mission grew into a thriving freight and supply depot. Steel rails were shipped to docks at the Michipicoten River and Michipicoten Harbour. From there, teamsters (thought to have been Mormons from Pennsylvania) hauled the rails across the Magpie River or by mule team along a corduroy and gravel road to their camp at the west end of Wawa Lake (now the town of Wawa). They constructed two steamboats to ferry the rails to the east shore of Wawa Lake, where they were reloaded onto mule-drawn sleighs for the trip to construction sites at Grasset and Missinaibi.

As work along the line was completed, the teamsters turned their mule teams loose, abandoned their cabins, and moved on. Some of the cabins were recycled. One became part of a gold-rush hotel, another a jail. (The last cabin was demolished in 1958 to make room for a parking lot.) Many

The Michipicoten Mission July 1st Celebrations

local roads and highways follow the route of these old corduroy roads. Corduroy logs can still be seen—and felt—poking up through the gravel on the road running down to Government Dock.

From the water, the former Mission (now Michipicoten River Village) is just up the road from Buck's Marina. If approaching from Highway 17 south of Wawa, take the sign marked Michipicoten River Village heading west. (Most of the Ojibwe moved from the Mission to the nearby Gros Cap First Nation reserve in the late 1930s and early 1940s.)

MAGPIE RIVER

Past Michipicoten River Village, continue along Harbour Road to the Magpie River Bridge, where for years, logs thundered over the three sets of falls on the swollen spring waters. With any luck your visit will be more pleasurable than the 1848 scientific expedition led by Louis Agassiz, who enjoyed the "very pretty falls on the Magpie River," but would go no further:

> Neither the love of the picturesque however, nor the interests of science, could tempt us into the woods, so terrible were the black flies.... One whom scientific ardor tempted a little way up the river in a canoe, after water-plants, came back a frightful spectacle, with blood-red rings round his eyes, his face bloody, and covered with punctures. The next morning his head and neck were swollen.... Mr. S. said he had never seen the flies so thick.... He consoled us, however, by the information, that it was nothing to what they have further north.

CEMETERIES, GOVERNMENT DOCK, MEDICINE CAVE

Across the Magpie River bridge, and at the next bend, a trail heads left ending at what remains of an old *Hudson's Bay Company* cemetery.

Continuing on the Harbour Road past the *Michipicoten River Cemetery* (this one is visible from the road), the left fork heads to the former *Government Dock* where the steamers *Caribou* and *Manitou* once docked. Along this road, there is also a small, unmarked trail leading off to the right, and ending after a five-minute walk at the *Medicine Cave* which was at one time a sea cave. It has been suggested the cave was possibly used for medicine and healing by local Ojibwe, and fragments of nineteenth-century glass, iron, china, pottery and a small hearth have been found.

At the top of the hill on the Harbour Road, a wonderful panoramic view looks over Michipicoten Harbour, where in good weather, Michipicoten Island can be seen about 40 kms (25 miles) away. At dusk, the jet black land silhouetted against glistening silver waters epitomizes the cold power of the North Shore.

MICHIPICOTEN'S WILD YEARS: MONTANA CHARLIE

In the early 1880s, the Canadian Pacific Railway brought with it all the colour, excitement, temporary affluence and hair-raising shenanigans of frontier days. For workers, carving a right-of-way through the inhospitable northern Ontario bush was a test of dreary endurance. To make things worse, CPR officials banned the sale of alcohol within ten miles of the rail line. This prohibition, of course, only ensured a flood of both alcohol and its accompanying "service industries." Ed Butts reports in "The Outlaws of Ontario," that "one search of a railway car turned up 14 kegs of hooch hidden in potato barrels, a jar of rye and two barrels of ale in a container of peas, and a small quantity of gin."

Shootings, fights and brawls were commonplace among the bootleggers, prostitutes, gamblers and thieves. Even Michipicoten's head constable, Charles Wallace, ran a bootlegging business. "Montana Charlie," as he was known, and his gang of thugs, the Wallace Gang, took over Michipicoten. After masked gunmen riddled the constable barracks with hundreds of bullets, mob rule prevailed. The gang raided the jail and posted death threats against anyone who opposed them.

Constables from Toronto arrived and rounded up several of the men, but the ringleaders escaped. Again the barracks were attacked. This time a policeman and a cook were injured. The Toronto contingent left once things appeared to be under control. The very next day, Wallace and his gang boldly paraded through town, Wallace carrying a Winchester repeating rifle, with four heavy revolvers and a large Bowie knife tucked into his belt. The men boarded the steamer *Steinhoff*, and in a farewell gesture, blasted one hundred rounds into the railway offices. Wallace miraculously escaped two more manhunts before being caught in the woods while chopping wood. Even then, he was released from a Toronto prison after only a few weeks before he disappeared for good... or so the story goes.

WAWA AND THE BRIEF AFFLUENCE OF WILLIAM TEDDY

There were other things Indian trapper William Teddy would rather be doing than drawing water from Wawa Lake on a warm summer's day in 1897. Maybe pull a few trout out of the lake for dinner? Just then his wife, Louise Towab, returned and showed him some shining pebbles in the bottom of her pail. Light bounced from their surface in yellow rays. No, the golden glow wasn't sunlight, it was.... "Where'd you get these?" he asked, turning them over and over in the light.

Louise took him to a spot on the water's edge and pointed. A few feet from shore veins of gold shimmered beneath the water. "This will make us rich!" he shouted, sweeping his hand over the find. But even a hundred years ago, $500 didn't make you rich. Rumour has it that's how much Teddy was paid for revealing the site.

Whispers grew to mutterings, which grew to shouts, which ended in the headline: *GOLD*! Prospectors, shysters, merchants and dreamers flooded the once-quiet Mormon settlement coming from as far away as the Maritimes, New York, Boston and the Dakotas. The Hudson's Bay Company resurrected its Michipicoten post and the Ontario Government dispatched an inspector from the Bureau of Mines to add the necessary element of bureaucracy. The first mining office in Ontario was opened at the post.

In 1898, two Irish partners built Wawa's first hotel, naming it the Balmoral after Queen Victoria's new summer residence. The Balmoral featured a 40-foot mahogany bar, cleverly made a foot higher than normal to prevent enthusiastic rough-necked patrons from leaping over it to help themselves to whiskey. In an area at the back, known as the Snake Room, inebriated customers could sleep off the effects of the Balmoral's bounty. (One commentator called the Balmoral the most productive gold mine in the area.)

Enthusiasm for the town turned into visions of grandeur. The main thoroughfare was named Broadway while other street names reflected an American influence: McKinley, Cleveland, Madison and Chicago. Schools, a hospital, churches and a jail were constructed and in 1899, application was made to have the townsite registered as Wawa City. (The

William Teddy and his wife, Louise Towab, the discoverers of gold at Wawa

word Wawa apparently was derived from the Ojibwe word for Wawa Lake, *Wawagonk* or *Wawungonk*, meaning "place of clear water," rather than a widely-held meaning, "wild goose".)

For a few prosperous years, gold money flowed into town, along with earnings from logging, fishing and shipping. But in 1906, production dropped abruptly. The Great Wawa Gold Rush was over and the 1,100 big spenders and colourful characters moved on. Even though iron mining continued, the ore was sent by rail directly to Michipicoten

Broadway Avenue, Wawa, after the 1920 forest fire. Only the Balmoral Hotel and a few other buildings escaped the flames.

Harbour, bypassing Wawa. With only a few families remaining, Wawa became a ghost town.

And William Teddy? For a while, with his hat band sprouting ten-dollar bills, he was the envy of the boys at the billiard hall. Then, as a devout Catholic, he decided to make a pilgrimage to the shrine at Ste. Anne de Beaupré in Quebec. Unfortunately, on his way through Montreal, he succumbed to some of the city's attractions. By the time an Indian agent brought him home, Teddy's share of the Great Wawa Gold Rush had evaporated. And Louise Towab, who was, after all, responsible for the discovery? She was left with a new $15 stove and a barrel of molasses she managed to buy before her husband headed east.

THE HELEN MINE

In the late 1890s, people were constantly approaching Francis Hector Clergue with new ideas, hoping that some of his financial magic would rub off on them. One day in 1898, a watchman at Clergue's pulp mill in Sault Ste. Marie approached the magnate saying a prospector had sent some "solid gold ore" from near Wawa. Clergue took only a quick glance at it. Then he took a closer look. "That's not gold," Clergue said. As the disappointed watchman started to walk away, Clergue grabbed the rock. He had recognized that the ore was iron pyrite—"fool's gold." This rock was especially rich in iron ore and if there was enough of it.... "Where did you get this?" Clergue demanded. "They said there's a whole mountain of it north of Wawa Lake," the watchman replied.

Clergue wasted no time boating up to Michipicoten Harbour. From there, his party clambered inland twelve miles to the shore of a small lake at the foot of a veritable mountain of iron. Within a few weeks, Clergue had purchased the mineral rights and launched an iron mine named in honour of his sister Helen. The economic spill-offs were set immediately in motion. For starters, the mine would need excavating equipment and offices plus cooking facilities and bunkhouses for the men. To carry the ore, a twelve-mile railway had to be constructed from the newly-christened Helen Mountain to Michipicoten Harbour. And, of course, the Harbour had to be dredged in order to handle the steamships that would be needed to transport the ore to Sault Ste. Marie where an entire steel mill complete with blast furnace and rolling mills would have to be built. But most importantly, Clergue needed more employees. When there were not enough skilled

Helen Mine, 1908

men to operate the mine Clergue arranged for the immigration of workers from Italy and other European countries.

Within two years of having recognized the iron pyrite samples, Clergue had accomplished an astonishing feat. The Helen mine had the largest production of any iron mine in Canada. An underground tunnel extended 78m (260 ft.) into the heart of the ore bed. Horse-driven tramcars and later an electrical cable system transferred the ore to a crusher. From there railway cars carried it to Michipicoten Harbour where it crossed a 225m (750-ft.) trestle before landing on an 82m (275-ft.) dock ready for lading onto one of four steel freighters. Also stretching into the harbour was a warehouse on a massive pier. A sawmill, offices, hotel, stores and housing for employees dotted the shore. About 440 men worked at the mine which was almost like a self-contained town. Single men lived in two-and three-storey bunkhouses and ate in a common cook house, while families had small detached homes. Cougar Lodge provided a meeting place for card games, concerts and festivities.

While the Helen Mine flourished, F.H. Clergue's fortunes did not. By 1903, his ambitions had exceeded his credit and his empire collapsed. Workers went unpaid, sparking a riotous strike (see p10). After a reorganization, mining resumed both at the Helen mine and at a newly discovered site near the Magpie River.

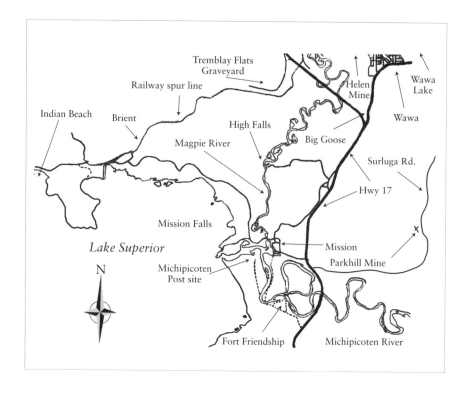

By the end of World War I, the Helen mine's richest ore had been removed and the operation closed. The Magpie Mine closed two years later. The Helen Mine site was devastated by a forest fire in 1921. It reopened in 1939 thanks to a new process for utilizing the remaining ore, a war-time demand for iron, and the financial leadership of Sir James Dunn. The "new" Helen Mine continued to operate for many years.

Several other gold and iron mines came and went. For a short period between 1942 and 1946, there was a thriving iron mine on Parks Lake called the Josephine Mine. A townsite was developed but in 1946, the lake broke through into the underground mine. The Parkhill gold mine, which was productive in the late 1920s, was gone by World War II. Today, bush has largely taken over, but some cement foundations and tailings can be found. The Surluga Road provides very limited access. And what of Ben Boyers and Jim Sayers, the prospectors whose discovery started the great iron rush? In their honour, the lake at the foot of Helen Mountain is now called Boyer Lake and a nearby body of water is known as Sayers Lake.

In a violent 1941 storm, waves washed through Clergue's Wigwam depositing furniture in the lake

SOREN LASSEN'S RAILWAY DIARY, 1899-1900

It sounds so easy. Simply because one industrial magnate needs to get iron ore to the Sault, a 12-mile railway link to Michipicoten Harbour was born. Soren Lassen's diary, dedicated to his wife and children from "their grieving husband and father," tells another story. Lassen, an academic and a lawyer who had been financially ruined in Denmark, left his family and arrived penniless on this side of the ocean. He signed on as a railway construction worker for $1.75 a day. After a steamer trip to Michipicoten Harbour, he was taken to a cabin which slept 72 men on bunks covered with hay and fir twigs. English, French, German, Swedish and Norwegian were all spoken. Arriving at the end of November 1899, after paying for rail and ship fare, Lassen found it difficult to save for winter boots with his wages. As for the camp itself? "What a pigsty we live in; lice and fleas are rampant. The boys are just as filthy as are the Indians, and it is not uncommon to see a boy half naked creep up to wherever there is light and ransack his underwear for lice." "[I] rubbed my skin with petroleum jelly in order to prevent the lice from eating me, I changed my woolen underwear into underwear which was not clean but which had hung outside in the cold for twenty-four hours to kill the lice with which it was infested."

The men worked from dawn to dusk using only picks and shovels. Despite being in poor health, Lassen advanced rapidly. One of his first jobs was to set and ignite the dynamite, a dangerous task causing the routine loss of life or limb. He then progressed through assistant warehouse keeper, bookkeeper, inspector of meats and slaughterhouse, assistant surgeon, interpreter, barber, medical instrument maker and carpenter.

His diary includes a description of a Christmas Eve when he was invited to dine at the Clergue residence on an island called the Wigwam in Michipicoten Harbour. He needed a clean shirt which meant he had to use caustic soda to whiten it and in so doing took the skin off his hands. He could not dry his clothes by the stove or they would become covered with soot, so he wore his clothing wet. The group rowed out to the island and enjoyed a rare, wonderful feast. At its close, the mail bag was dumped and the men scrambled to receive their gifts and letters. Lassen received nothing. Lassen concludes his diary by recording his grief over news that his wife had left him, and a plea to his children to accept his good intentions and to learn from his mistakes.

(Navvies who died during the railway's construction are buried at the Tremblay Flats Cemetery.)

MICHIPICOTEN HARBOUR

With one sweep of his long entrepreneurial arm in 1899 the legendary Francis H. Clergue transformed the quiet, picturesque harbour of Michipicoten into a major industrial port. Clergue was the Maine-born businessman behind the Lake Superior Power Corporation, a pulp mill in the Sault, nickel mines, and the emergence of Sault Ste. Marie from a quiet northern town into a key industrial centre.

Clergue needed iron ore and the discovery of substantial quantities near Wawa filled the bill. Sault Ste. Marie was the logical location for his new Algoma Steel plant, and Michipicoten Harbour, 19 kms (12 miles) from the mine, was the logical port from which to ship the ore to the Sault. Soon, steel rails were running from the mine site to the harbour (see Soren Lassen above) and a dock for freighters was built.

It is perhaps not too surprising that this hard-driving man's idea of a vacation cabin was right in the harbour, with the hiss and clang of heavy industy all around. On a small island on the east side of the harbour he built "The Wigwam." It was a cottage with distinctly quirky character-

Minnie M. *at Michipicoten Harbour, 1908.*

istics—like its owner. Connected to the mainland by a spindly suspension bridge, its access was guarded by two trained bears chained to stakes. Obviously few unexpected visitors arrived to disturb this spot, which for Clergue must have been a welcome escape from the pressures of business.

Perhaps Clergue should have spent more time in the office, because his empire collapsed in 1903. His power companies were split between U.S. and Canadian interests; the paper mill was sold to Abitibi; the Algoma Eastern Railway was absorbed by the CPR; Algoma Central spun off as a separate corporation and Algoma Steel was reorganized under Sir James Dunn. Clergue moved on to other projects in other places, but the changes he initiated along Superior's eastern shore are felt to this day.

Between 1940 and 1960 there were about 500 people living at the Harbour. Iron ore and pulpwood were still being shipped out, while coal, coke, fuel and limestone were coming in. Although coal and lime are still being brought in for sintering, there are only a few remaining residents remain in this semi-ghost town. The dock remains, as do remnants of the pier. The Michipicoten Harbour lighthouse at Perkwakwia Point still marks the harbour entrance.

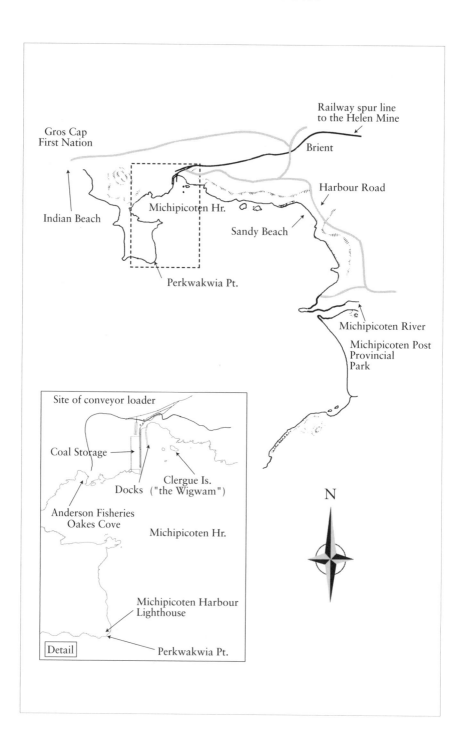

Brient

The town owed its existence to the Algoma Central Railway. In 1912, a maintenance centre to service the massive hissing steam engines and a dozen workers' homes grew up along the old gravel road east of Michipicoten Harbour. When the railroad switched to low-maintenance diesel power in the 1940s, Brient faded away like a distant train whistle. Now only a few foundations remain as the meadow slowly reclaims the land.

Wawa vs. Jamestown

In 1947, there was a proposal to rename Wawa, Jamestown after Sir James Dunn, owner of Algoma Steel, the company which employed 770 of the town's almost 3,000 citizens. Some locals promoted the idea, while others were horrified. For twelve years the controversy raged. Some families stopped speaking. Stores lost customers. There were even two separate chambers of commerce! The post office and ACR station caved in to the pressure and raised large JAMESTOWN signs. Justice came swiftly. Mysteriously, the post office sign lost its J and A, leaving the word MESTOWN. Finally in 1960, the conflict ended. Wawa had won the day.

The Trans-Canada: The Long-Promised Road

"Wawa Demands Promised Link to Agawa: Outlet in any other direction also welcomed." This road, long promised, had never appeared. In 1951 to stir up publicity, a group of four men walked from Wawa down to the Montreal River along the proposed route. One of members, Ed Nyman told Rick Vosper, "it wasn't very far... fifty to sixty miles through there to Montreal River.

Demonstration for completion of Highway 17

It's a good walk but we took seventeen days—for the purpose of stirring up publicity. They reported us lost in the bush."

Many residents couldn't wait for the road's completion and so it was a common sight to see cars spinning their wheels on sand-covered hills and crawling across the rough log bridge at Old Woman River. Because these impatient drivers were a real hindrance to the work crews, guards and barricades were placed at the exits from town. As reported in the Sept. 14, 1960 *Sault Star*, just days before the opening, anticipation was running high: "Imprisoned most of their lives within the massive granite hills of the Michipicoten country, the Wawans are wild to burst their bonds and soar out into the great wide world on the new Trans-Canada Highway." It went on to say that residents already owned 700 cars even though there were only 45 miles of road around the town. The official opening was September 17, 1960. Despite the teeming rain, thousands of townspeople and visitors turned out for the official end to their isolation.

The highway represented the final link in the Ontario portion of the Trans-Canada Highway, and the last section of the Circle Route around Superior. Soon after the opening, 4,000 cars created an hour-long traffic jam. Restaurateurs ran out of food, "no vacancy" signs appeared, and trailer parks and tent sites sprouted.

To commemorate the event, Wawa residents commissioned a giant plaster Wawa Goose, (the town symbol) with wings raised ready for flight. Today a steel goose, made of ore from the Helen Mine, has replaced the original.

THE COASTLINE WEST OF MICHIPICOTEN

Dog Harbour and False Dog Harbour

The coast west from Michipicoten provides few places of refuge for mariners. Around Point Isacor, several miles of cliffs plunge into the cold depths of Superior, making the two Dog Harbours all the more important. In *False Dog Harbour*, one first notices the sheer rock wall bearing graffiti from past "guests," dating back to the 1930s. Any frequent traveller of this region has a story about waiting out bad weather here. Brad Buck, of Buck's Marina in Michipicoten, jokes about carving his name and the date in the wall of the old cabin on the beach. It was 1971, and as a teenager, he and two friends were stuck here for eight days during a blow.

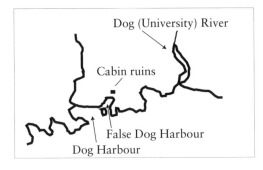

Dog (University) River

Cabin ruins

False Dog Harbour

Dog Harbour

In *Dog Harbour*, there are only scant reminders of the small Booth Co. fishing station. The buildings are gone but the dock cribs are visible in the southwest corner of the harbour. On our visit, fog flowed down the ancient hills like rivers. In the harbour, the air was calm and still. A porcupine trundled out of the bush, offering us only a disinterested glance. A fish tug appeared for a split second, then disappeared in the thick fog. Straight out through the thick atmosphere are two of the most remote islands on the Great Lakes: Michipicoten, and beyond it, Caribou Island around which considerable mythology has sprung up.

Michipicoten Island: Magic and Copper

The Ojibwe avoided Michipicoten Island. Long ago, a group of Ojibwe were snowshoeing over the frozen lake when, without explanation, the ice began breaking up. Terrified, they ran towards the island but the closer they came, the further it drifted away. And so the belief was born that Michipicoten was a mystical floating isle.

This is also the domain of the powerful underworld manitou, Mishepeshu, a giant serpent who controlled copper. Anyone foolish enough to challenge him would suffer tragic results. Once a group of Ojibwe arrived to gather precious pure copper nuggets. Believing the manitou would not disturb them, they stayed the night before heading home laden with treasure. Not far from the island, they heard a powerful voice thunder, "Who are these robbers carrying off from me my children's cradles and play things?" Shortly after returning to the mainland, the trespassers died in agony.

Knowledge of the island's potential wealth spread. In 1610, explorer Samuel de Champlain was given a foot-long piece of copper, said to have originated at Michipicoten. (Some believe this is confirmed by his 1632 map on which he marked an island that appears to be Michipicoten, "where there is a mine of copper.") Centuries passed, but inevitably attention returned to the 24-km (15-mile) long island laced with the precious metal. It is rumoured that when the first surveyors waded ashore, their Indian guides refused to land with them. Obviously Ojibwe fears had not diminished.

In the late 1800s, miners, fishermen, mill workers, a farmer, a shop-keeper and a lightkeeper with his large family were drawn to this large, mysterious island floating 45 kms (28 miles) offshore.

THE JONES LOCATION: MICHIPICOTEN'S MINING LEGACY

On the west side of Michipicoten is the Jones location, where the Upper Canada Mining Company purchased the island's first mining grant in 1846. In 1854 natives drove the miners off the island, but they kept coming back. Other companies followed but could not make a substantial profit. In 1882, the Lake Superior Mining Company sank four shafts totalling 319m (1,065 ft.) but with little reward. Its successor, the Quebec Mining Company, fell into bankruptcy. Perhaps it was true, that Michipicoten's copper belonged to the manitou, and those attempting to extract it would be cursed.

As companies struggled to survive, their miners faced a pitiful existence. An 1850 newspaper article describes,

> descending a shaky ladder into a scene close to Hell. Ankle-deep in black, glue-like mud, with claustrophobic black walls, illuminated by feeble yellowish flicking candles, and separated from instant death by a few rotten props, men breathed humid, bad air, while tearing fiercely at dripping, ragged rocks.

The 1880s site operated by the Michipicoten Native Copper Company included the operations buildings, a smelter, boilers, crushing house, hoisting shaft, etc. and crude boarding houses, each sleeping about a dozen men. A farm and portable lumber mill on Schafer Bay supplied meat, milk, oats and construction wood. The ore was placed in a railway car and pulled by horse along a track skirting the shoreline to a shipment dock near the current Quebec Harbour range lights.

One of the few impressions of the mine comes from the diary of C.S. Gardiner, a camp cook and carpenter in the late 1800s. He described the miners as a motley crowd of Cornishmen, Yorkshiremen and Irishmen with a smattering of Canadians and Norwegians. "...They hoist the blasted rock

One of the many mines that operated on the west end of Michipicoten Island

and ore out of the shaft by means of a huge bucket... lowered and lifted by steam power." The miners descended the shaft in the swinging bucket, carefully hugging the drills to their sides. If the drill snagged the shaft, the bucket might overturn, as in the case of one Cornish miner who tumbled to his death. He was buried on the island. The following year, his body was exhumed and sent to Bruce Mines on the North Channel where there was a large Cornish community.

It was difficult to keep personnel. Companies paid a miner's transportation to the island, but subtracted the cost from his wages. One carpenter from Montreal worked only one day before slipping off to a higher paying job building a house for the island's shopkeeper. The shopkeeper, Mr. Grierson, carried a grudge against the mining engineer and captain. He sent a boat at night so that the carpenter could steal tools from the mine. Unfortunately, the mining manager and engineer doubled as the island's Justices of the Peace. Diarist Gardiner was sent to deliver the arrest warrant, accompanied by lightkeeper Hyacinthe Davieaux who had been sworn in as constable.

When confronted, Grierson flew into a rage. Brandishing a butcher knife, he jumped up on to the shop's counter. The ceiling was so low that he looked more silly than threatening, bent over like a hunchback and flailing his weapon. A member of Grierson's family arrived with a gun. Wasting no more time, the lightkeeper-constable tackled Grierson. Appearing in front of the J.P.s the following day, Grierson was instructed to return the tools and pay the carpenter's passage to Montreal.

Locals say boilers and old machinery still mark the site. Former islander Mort Purvis recalls his father Ivan visiting the mine in the 1930s, "blankets and bedding were hanging on ropes to keep them away from the mice—it looked like [the miners would] be back the next day, but they never returned." Going to the Jones Location is not recommended: the property is privately owned and brush conceals a number of dangerous, uncovered ventilator shafts. The blacksmith shop, a fine remnant of the old mine, was dismantled and rebuilt at the Quebec Harbour fishing station site.

WRECK OF THE *CHICAGO:* DRIVEN OFF COURSE

Superior was in a welcoming mood the day we set out to find the remains of the *Chicago* and *Strathmore.* The water was tropical green, smooth as glass, with a clear view twenty feet down where rocks loomed up like the knobby backs of monsters. The serene day juxtaposed with treacherous waters gave the area a sinister feeling. It was easy to imagine the fate of the *Chicago,* pitching and rolling out of control, trapped by churning seas as the rocks below shredded its hull.

Blizzard and magnetic disturbances brought the Chicago *onto Michipicoten's west shore in 1929.*

In October 1929, the 3,200-ton *Chicago* had left Duluth and was crossing open water when she was caught in an early blizzard. Northeast winds howled at 80 kph (50 mph), heavy snow shrouded the vessel in a blinding white-out and waves towered at 9m (30 ft.). In those conditions, even an experienced captain like P.C. Farrell could do little more than hang on. He estimated they were near Ile Parisienne, almost 160 kms (100 miles) to the southeast but he was not sure because the compass was thrown off by the area's magnetic rock. Suddenly the boat slammed into a shoal... off the western tip of Michipicoten Island.

The crew was ordered to stay aboard until morning. Then, as the doomed *Chicago* began to slide off the rocks, its 32 men launched the lifeboats and managed to land safely on Michipicoten Island with bedding and food. Eight of them set out through dense forest for Quebec Harbour and eventually all were brought to the mainland, leaving the shattered wreck behind.

Loaded with cedar shingles, paint and flour, the *Chicago* lost its cargo to the waves. Word spread like wildfire as locals plundered the bounty, flipping pancakes for quite some time, painting their cabins with bright coats of paint, and shingling their roofs. Today, remnants of the *Chicago* can be found spread downward from about 1.8m (6 ft.) to about 20m (67 ft.). Lying on its side, the wreck includes an anchor, windlass and chain.

WRECK OF THE *STRATHMORE*

A November 1906 gale overtook the *Strathmore*, a 61-m (205-ft.) wooden steamer laden with prairie grain on its way from Fort William. Driven onto rocks just north of Schafer Bay, Captain Sullivan ordered the crew to man the pumps, but they were no match for the seas that drowned her boiler fires. The thirteen-man crew launched the yawl and negotiated the wild water to the Quebec Harbour lighthouse where they were picked up two days later. The *Strathmore*'s anchors were salvaged, at rest today at the Sault on the grounds of the Canadian canal.

Remains of the *Strathmore*—a twisted mass of metal shrapnel and a large propeller—are scattered 1.5-1.8m (5-6 ft.) below the water's surface.

AT MICHIPICOTEN ISLAND.

Busy Quebec Harbour, 1882. Agate Island Lighthouse at right, Quebec Harbour light at left. Davieaux Island is in the background.

AGATE ISLAND

By the late 1870s, the island's abundant supply of agates had been largely picked over by eager tourists and by lightkeeper Hyacinthe Davieaux, who supplemented his government income by selling them to visitors for a $1 a pint.

On the sharp tooth-like volcanic rock of tiny Agate Island, we found a great number of small gems still flecking the surface. Agates are fine-grained quartz banded with brightly-coloured concentric rings. These minerals, formed over a billion years ago in gas bubbles left in cooling volcanic lava are revealed through slow erosion of the surrounding basalt. Combing the area, our eyes wandered from the showier crystalline white and purple of the agates, to captivating muted shades of cobalt blue, purple, green, orange and terracotta red in other scattered stones.

There is another treasure on Agate Island. Where a tired pine leans away from the wind at the tip of the island, Michipicoten's first lighthouse once stood. Erected in 1872, it was moved by scow in 1917 to serve as the front lighthouse at the Quebec Harbour range lights. Operated until 1938, it was replaced by a house with a light perched on its dormer, the only range light of its kind in Canada. The original Agate Light was moved behind the house, relegated to a storage facility. Today, only rusting iron posts mark the foundations on Agate Island.

Davieaux Lighthouse: The Third Lighthouse

Both the beauty and solitude of lightkeeping can still be experienced here, sitting on a bench atop the windswept point near the light tower. On a clear day, Caribou Island appears as a hazy form on the southern horizon. Lurking beneath the expanse of open water in between are the shoals that may have gouged the hull of the *Edmund Fitzgerald*, on that stormy November day in 1975.

Davieaux Light is named for the first lighthouse family to serve Michipicton Island. Hyacinthe Davieaux and his wife looked after both the light on Agate Island and one on the eastern side of the mouth of Quebec Harbour. When Hyacinthe died at the Agate Island lighthouse in 1910, his son Charles, took over.

In 1917, the Lighthouse Board of Canada decided that Michipicoten's lighthouses were inadequate. The Agate Island light was moved to become one of two range lights directing boaters into the harbour, and the tower on the eastern shore was moved to Davieaux to serve as an interim tower while a new, reinforced-concrete lighthouse was built there. The assistant keeper lived in a "shelter shed" on Davieaux, while Charles Davieaux and his family lived at the range lights, crammed into the old musty Agate lighthouse. Here he and his wife raised six children.

Each evening, Charles would row across to the island to spend the night, rising at midnight to wind the clockwork mechanism that turned the light. Morning often brought weather too rough for the return trip and so he was sometimes forced to remain on the island for days on end. In his absence, his family attended the range lights which had to be kept burning steadily through the night. The government did not build a proper house at the ranges until 1938, five years after Charles had died at the age of eighty-four.

Davieaux Lighthouse is named after the Davieaux family that kept the various Quebec Harbour lights for generations.

QUEBEC HARBOUR: A FISHING LEGACY

In an effort to prevent the drain of native trappers to the rival American Fur Company, the Hudson's Bay Company started a commercial fishery in 1839 in Quebec Harbour. The American Fur Company had begun to employ Indians year-round, as trappers in winter, fishermen in summer. In 1860, American fishing tycoon, Alfred Booth chose Quebec Harbour to set up an operation which prospered for many years. During the Great Depression of the 1930s, the location was taken over by James and Ivan Purvis who wanted to expand their fishing operation westward from Manitoulin Island. James was no greenhorn—the family had been in the fishing business since 1879. Running Quebec Harbour with his son Ivan, he saw the fishing station grow into a community of seventy people.

Each spring, the Purvis tug would arrive at villages such as Thessalon and Batchawana to hire men for the new season. For each tug Purvis needed three men to handle the nets, one for the fish, two firemen, an engineer and a captain. He also needed shore crew, packing men and cooks. Purvis would choose a few from the many hopefuls congregated at the docks. He dispensed ten-dollar bills—a respectable sum for the lean 1930s—for anyone needing a bit of cash to get started.

The fishermen chose a seven-day work week in order to earn as much money as possible. Besides, there was little to do with time off. It was strenuous work. Each day, three tugs set 315 kms (197 miles) of nets. Still, many fishermen chose to "share-fish" in the evenings as well, by setting nets in the harbour from small boats. For every pound of fish they caught, Purvis would split the profit.

When the boats came in, each fisherman was responsible for putting two

Posing with a big one, Quebec Harbour fishing station

cotton nets on the drying racks. A 9-kg (20-lb.) fish could leave a gaping hole in a net, so the nets were constantly being mended. The fish were wheeled into the packing house, packed in ice, and graded by fats and leans. (The ice was manufactured in a large brine tank cooled by a Lister diesel engine and the frozen blocks were hauled out with a winch and crushed.) Fishermen prided themselves on their knowledge of fish, but none could match the expertise of the packing crew. Their ability to pinpoint where a fish came from by its appearance was not only uncanny but of great benefit, especially the day the Purvis tug rescued a broken-down American fishing vessel. While packing the Americans' catch, the crew realized it was comprised of fish found only in Canadian waters. The authorities were notified and the tug was towed to the Sault, where the Americans paid a hefty fine to get it back.

Poaching was frowned upon, but somewhat ignored. Fishermen of both nationalities tried to stay on friendly terms with each other in case they found themselves in a pinch. However, the poaching around Caribou Island became so flagrant that the Department of Marine and Fisheries had to intervene. To catch culprits red-handed, officials hid one of their vessels behind the lighthouse, but they failed to make an arrest. They were shocked to learn later that the lightkeeper had been signalling their presence to American tugs by blocking out a portion of the lanternroom! Mort Purvis recalls, "when it was found out the lightkeeper was more friends with Americans than the Canadians... I don't know how he got his groceries and spools of thread after that. Silly ass!"

Mort Purvis grew up at Quebec Harbour and recalls that life there was not all work. Everyone's favourite gathering place was the cookhouse and store (the only building surviving from Booth Fisheries). The men would crowd in and roll dice or flip coins to see who was going to buy the next round of coffee or chocolate bars. In the large room above the packing house, Purvis recalls, "You could get a hell of a barn dancing going... fiddles, guitars, that sort of thing. I think a lot of them were natives from Manitoulin and Batchawana... some pretty musical fellas." When they weren't fishing, men filled their evenings with poker games, dice and billiards. Electricity was provided by the two-cylinder Lister diesel that also operated the icemaker and pump. Mort remembers it was shut off promptly at 10 p.m.: "They'd just slow it down, and everyone would see the lights dim and, quick! Get your oil lamps going."

The bi-weekly tug run to the Sault to deliver fish and buy fresh groceries was a big event. Before leaving Ronnie Gordon would take orders.

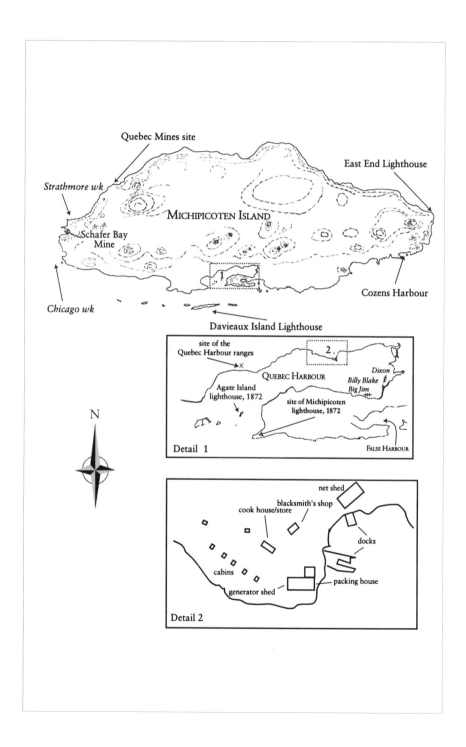

Quebec Harbour dock, lined with net-drying racks

In the Sault, a man named Nichol McAuley would try to fill them. He would call around town and have the items delivered to the dock.

> Once Ronnie told Dad [Ivan Purvis] 'we've got to apologise to Nichol, I got a letter back on my list:' 'Ronnie I filled your order. All but the boots. Did you want high boots, low boots, leather boots, rubber boots, laced boots, and does the size matter?' Ronnie had put down: one pair of boots. Nothing else.

In the 1940s, the parasitic sea lamprey had clenched its jaws into the fishing industry and by the 1950s the fishery could no longer compete. In 1959, Ivan Purvis sold the operation to Ferroclad Fisheries. Family members continue to maintain a summer cabin on the south shore of the harbour.

Much of the once-vibrant fishing station is still standing. Neat shelves still line the walls inside the cookery and store. The old square log blacksmith shop is still there. A few metal drying reels are rusting in the overgrown grass and the tin-roofed net shed, cabins and packing house can be seen along the waterfront. Above its door is the name plate from the *Captain Jim*, one of the company's wrecked fishing tugs in the harbour.

QUEBEC HARBOUR WRECKS

There are three wrecks in Quebec Harbour. Local beavers favouring the *Captain Jim* have built a sprawling lodge around the hull and exposed boiler. The old tug developed a chronic leak that eventually overcame the pumps. One day, while rounding the island, a young fisherman, Joe Thibault, thought the tug was going to roll over because of the slogging weight of the water. He was about to jump overboard when the captain hauled him back and put him in the wheelhouse. If they were going down, it was best to hang on to the boat. They managed to limp into dock and the following day, the old *Captain Jim* was put out of its misery by being run across the bay and scuttled.

Nearby, lie the ribbed remains of the *Hiram R. Dixon*. The 44-m (149-ft.) *Dixon*, built in 1883, formerly belonged to the Booth operation. It met its fate on a shoal and was stripped, scuttled and burned in August 1903.

Rising out of the water is the rusted ribbed skeleton of the *Billy Blake*, a steam tug with a special function. Mort Purvis reminisces,

> it was real handy when steam'n a pig to get the bristles off. You run the steam into a big 45-gallon tank of water to heat it up really hot, dunk the pig in—not enough to cook it but enough to loosen the hair. That's what they called steaming a pig—'fire up the Billy Blake!'

Perhaps it tried to steam one too many plump snake-fed island pigs, because the last time, the tug caught fire and sank.

EAST END LIGHTHOUSE AND THE ORDEAL OF THE SHERLOCKS

As the crow flies, it is a mere 45 kms (28 miles) from Michipicoten Island to Gargantua. But in December 1916, it took the East End lightkeeper William Sherlock and his son James, over a week to make the crossing. "We left our lighthouse on the 14th because our docks had been swept away," William recounted to a reporter. "If we waited any longer, we wouldn't [have been] able to get out." Provisions were low and it would be suicidal to spend a winter on Michipicoten Island without preparation. With twenty-five gallons of oil, an emergency sail and some provisions, father and son and their small dog pushed off at 2 p.m. in an open 5.4m (18-ft.) boat.

Halfway across the open water, a dreaded nor'easter rose and the temperature plummeted, setting in motion a series of torturous events. "Our pump froze and we had to take to the oars," William explained later. "Our boat began to take in water and we gradually had to throw everything we had overboard, just to keep afloat." First went the oil, then the emergency sail and finally most of the provisions. Water splashing over the gunwales froze into a thick coating of ice. The men were scarcely able to bend their arms or knees. At one point, an oar slipped from James' hands and, reaching to retrieve it, he fell overboard. Only his father's quick response prevented certain death.

Hearing the roar of the surf on a rocky beach, the two men managed to land on Leach Island. They made a fire from driftwood and tried to repair the boat. It had now been four days since they had left Michipicoten Island. Once again they tried to reach the mainland.

"We struck out for the North Shore, which was three miles distant," William recalled, "my son at the oars and me bailing all the way." It took

East End lighthouse. Keeper William Sherlock and his son nearly died trying to cross to the mainland after the shipping season

five painful hours in high winds and bitter cold. Gargantua was still 2 1/2 miles (4kms) away. Severely weakened from exposure and hunger, it took them another three miserable days, crawling most of the way, to reach the safety of Gargantua Harbour, where they were transfered to hospital in the Sault. Even though their hands and feet were badly frozen, the Sherlocks made a full recovery. And what of their small dog? "We killed him when we reached the North Shore," William explained solemnly, "and this kept us alive until we struck Gargantua."

The previous year, 1915, the government had stopped picking up light-keepers at the end of the shipping season. The Sherlocks' ordeal did nothing to change this dangerous policy. Sadly, two years after this incident, fate caught up with William Sherlock. At the end of December 1918, George Johnston, lightkeeper of Caribou Island, telegraphed the Department of Marine in Ottawa reporting that Sherlock had not arrived on the mainland. A disinterested bureaucrat replied:

> ...it is just possible that Lightkeeper Sherlock after leaving Michipicoten Island was forced to take shelter under the lee of the island and finally made his way back to the station or to Quebec Harbour; or that he was driven out of his course and made some habitation on the north shore.... I understand that there is a missionary, Rev. Father Richard, leaving Sault Ste. Marie about the present time, and that he travels by dog team over all that extent of country where Lightkeeper Sherlock may have landed.... Ask him to make enquiries at the various places he visits.

Neither William Sherlock nor his boat were ever recovered. (For more about the lightkeepers' plight see Caribou lighthouse p.117 and the *Lambton* p.118.) William's wife took over as East End keeper, retaining the position until 1925. The lighthouse was automated in 1983. East End light is an impressive sight. Erected in 1911, it is one of nine flying-buttress towers built in Canada between 1906 and 1912. Its six buttresses support some of the load of the lanternroom and prevent the 21-m (70-ft.) tower from swaying in high winds. The East End and Davieaux Lights were constructed during a campaign to improve safety conditions for the growing freighter traffic. Frequent fog coupled with magnetic disturbances in the area are a hazard to navigation.

CARIBOU LIGHTHOUSE: THE MOST ISOLATED ON THE GREAT LAKES

In 1886, an 18-m (60-ft.) lighthouse tower was built on Caribou's tiny sister island to keep ships away from the treacherous Caribou Shoals. This was the most remote lighthouse on the Great Lakes at 104 kms (65 miles) from the nearest port, Michipicoten Harbour and it was subject to the full

Caribou Island Lighthouses, George Johnston, inset. Caribou Island tower was replaced by a taller, stronger tower with flying buttresses in 1911.

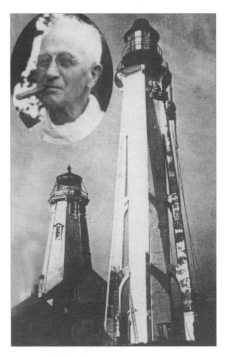

onslaught of Superior's fury. No wonder that in 1911, the government commissioned a second, more secure concrete tower, 27m (90 ft.) high, strengthened by six flying buttresses.

Because of the extreme isolation, Caribou's keepers and assistants were chosen carefully for their hardy and resourceful natures—traits perfectly describing George Johnston, the keeper of Caribou lighthouse from 1912-21.

In his first season, Johnston realized he had packed a good supply of cartridges but no gun. Unfazed, he carved a wooden stock from a piece of sturdy driftwood, adapted a metal vapour tube from the light as a barrel, and fashioned a breech and firing pin. The makeshift weapon had poor aim but could still bring down rabbits to supplement the family's diet of mostly fish. When Johnston broke his shin, he gritted his teeth against the pain, set the bone and attached a splint. After constructing crude crutches, he devised a type of peg-leg and soon he was once again managing the steep lighthouse ladder.

The lighthouse could not save all shipping from disaster. On one memorable occasion, Johnston was startled by the ominous call of a ship in distress. With the island cloaked in fog, he followed the shoreline in his boat and was suddenly met by the beached 160m (536-ft) freighter *Westmount*. She was not badly damaged, but her enormous grain load held her fast. George took the Captain the 48kms (30 miles) to the Quebec Harbour fishing village on Michipicoten Island where he could send for help. Before long, a tug towing a barge arrived and removed enough cargo to allow the *Westmount* to float free.

Johnston's son Pat, now in his late eighties, has fond memories of island summers shared with brothers Roger and San. They picnicked on Caribou Island and spent hours beachcombing the golden sand for corks from the fish nets, bottles, crates and other treasures tossed from passing boats. More exciting was being chased by ill-tempered caribou while family members were rabbit hunting or berry picking. After one such incident, George

Caribou Island, the most isolated lighthouse on the Great Lakes. New tower is to the left, the original tower is at right.

George Johnston remodelled his "death trap" left, to get back to the mainland after the shipping season of 1919.

discovered his wife up a 7.5 m (25 ft.) tree, only her rubber boots showing below the foliage.

The annual visit from the government supply boat was a favorite event. Dressed in their best clothes, the boys would watch the men unload parts for the light and fog plant, and roll barrels of kerosene and lubricating oil up to the storeroom. As the ship departed, they would help their father salute it with the low moan of the fog horn. The fog horn also provided a treat. As its engines were thermo-cooled, the water would heat up during extended periods of fog, to be replaced with cooler fresh water. The runoff allowed the boys to have a warm bath.

Lightkeeper Survives Nightmarish Journey

George Johnston survived many close calls on Caribou, but he never expected to be placed in the gravest danger by his own employer. It began with a terse letter from the department in 1915. As a cost-cutting measure, the Canadian government would no longer provide a ship to take light-keepers off and on the lights. Johnston imagined the Ottawa bureaucrat sniffing, "Shouldn't be a problem. After all, we provide each keeper with a boat." One hundred and four kilometres (65 miles) across to the mainland in an open 9-m (30-ft.) sailboat in December? As far as Johnston was con-cerned, they had issued Lake Superior keepers a death sentence. But Johnston was not a man to sit still. With $400 extra dollars supplied by the government, he set out to make his boat more secure. He bought a Detroit engine that ran on kerosene, added a small weather-tight cabin built from scrap lumber and canvas, and installed a coal-fired Quebec Heater. Other keepers were not as fortunate. In 1916, the Michipicoten East End keeper, William Sherlock and his son, nearly died after days of being trapped on the open water. Tragedy also struck Otter Island's lightkeeper Robert McMenemy. Suffering from pneumonia, he landed his boat to warm himself by a fire... and was discovered later that winter, frozen, leaning against a tree. In 1918, fate also caught up to William Sherlock. Neither his body nor his boat were ever found (see p.112). These losses did nothing to change Ottawa's mind. It was only a matter of time before Johnston would be put to the test as well.

Shipping season had officially ended on December 15, 1919, but George and his assistant were trapped at Caribou Island by unrelenting storms. For days, they waited for a break in the weather. The reprieve came on Christmas Day. That afternoon they made it to Quebec Harbour on Michipicoten Island, 48 kms (30 miles) away, but plans for an overnight stop were frustrated by the mass of ice choking the Harbour. Drifting just outside, a storm rose pushing them toward the ice. Forced to head for open water, Johnston threw the sea anchor, praying it would hold them in a slow drift. Waves and spray slapped against the boat, coating it in ice. Come dawn, George had to ram his shoulder against the frozen door to force it open. Thick, falling snow obscured Michipicoten Island. The nightmare had begun.

For several days the two men huddled in the cabin. The storm was too much for the engine and so they drifted, listening to the grating sounds as ice floes struck the wooden hull. With each blow, Johnston held his breath, half expecting the hull planking to burst. When the wind and rolling finally subsided, they pulled in the sea anchor and set compass for the mainland. They arrived New Year's Day, after eight days on the open lake.

THE MYSTERY OF THE CGS *LAMBTON*

After nine years of service, Johnston was leaving Caribou light to take the position of fog alarm inspector. The new keeper, George Penefold was enraged to learn the government expected him to reach the mainland at the end of season with only a small boat. He began a fierce writing campaign that eventually convinced the government to rescind its dangerous policy.

The Lambton vanished with all hands. There are reports of it being sighted as a ghost ship.

In 1921, the CGS *Lambton* was entrusted with responsibility for dropping off and picking up lightkeepers. That autumn, Johnston was shocked to witness the crew chopping ice from the steering cable. Originally built as a tug, she rode low in the water, exposing the steering quadrant to freezing spray. In addition, the lifeboats were on the uppermost deck. Johnston feared in a storm that the crew would not be able to reach them. He wrote a stern letter to the government asserting that the *Lambton* was dangerously ill-suited for the Great Lakes. When his warning was ignored, his wife, Louise, picked up her pen. It was unconscionable, she wrote, that the government would place anyone in such danger. Her husband had a large family and could not afford life insurance on his wages. The following spring, Johnston did not board the *Lambton*. The ship and all aboard were never seen again.

Evidently while helping to free another ship from the ice in Whitefish Bay, the *Lambton* damaged its steering gear. The captain proceeded with a makeshift steering arrangement, travelling in the company of two other vessels. About 48 kms (30 miles) past Whitefish Point, the storm forced the accompanying ships to turn back. The *Lambton* pressed on.

Around noon, a passing steamer reported sighting the *Lambton's* crew fighting to control the ship by using cables attached to her steering quadrant. This was a virtually impossible system in such conditions. The following day, wreckage from the *Lambton* was seen about 40 kms (25 miles)

southeast of Michipicoten Island and 24 kms (15 miles) east of Caribou
Island. Johnston was part of the search party that first discovered one of the
lifeboats. Johnston deduced from its crushed air tanks, that the boat had
sunk with the ship. The pressure of the descent had collapsed the tanks
before it could break loose and resurface. Just as he had warned, with
waves sweeping the upper deck, the crew had likely been unable to reach
the lifeboats. All 22 men perished, including the new Caribou lightkeeper,
George Penefold.

But that was not the end of the *Lambton*. Some believe she is part of the
fleet of ghost ships, their phantom shapes seen briefly between dusk and
dawn. One such *Lambton* sighting, confirmed by several witnesses, took
place near Gargantua in the fall of 1922.

SUPERIOR SHOAL:

The Underwater Mountain and Vanished Ships

June 1929. A tense silence pervaded the pilothouse as Captain Greene's
gaze fixed on the echo sounder of the U.S. Coast Guard survey vessel
Margaret. "The thing must be registering erratically," he muttered.
Moments before, the sounder had monitored depths in the hundreds of
metres; now suddenly it registered only 15m (50 ft.)—far too shallow for
this open part of Superior. They were virtually at the Lake's east-west mid-
point! Captain Greene ordered the vessel to retrace its course. Again the
equipment registered extreme depths, and then a mere 13m (43ft).

The *Margaret* had stumbled upon a hidden danger: a mountain of rock
thrusting up in places to within metres of the surface. A chill ran though the
men. Sitting directly in the shipping lane between the Lakehead and the
Sault, these rocks might offer an explanation for some of Lake Superior's
mysterious ship disappearances... such as the *Inkerman* and *Cerisoles*.

The French minesweepers *Inkerman*, *Cerisoles* and *Sebastopol*, were
built at Fort William. On November 13, 1918, they set out from Thunder
Bay on their maiden voyage to France, manned by experienced sailors.
Sebastopol arrived safely while the other two ships were never seen again.
Although both carried wireless equipment, no radio message was ever
recorded. The year after they vanished, a body washed up on Michipicoten
Island. Many years later, skeletal remains were uncovered east of Port
Coldwell. They were believed to be crew from the French boats, but were
hastily buried before official confirmation. Adding to the mystery, none of

the usual flotsam was ever found.

An intriguing conspiracy theory developed. Two weeks after the minesweepers left Fort William, an executive of the builder, Canadian Car, allegedly claimed the ships had sailed through the Sault locks and made Port Colborne on Lake Ontario. When asked why no record of their passage could be found, he replied that the captains must have neglected to report it. An unlikely explanation. The French Navy also reacted peculiarly. Asked if France had given up hope of ever seeing the ships again, one official merely shrugged. This raised the suspicion that the vessels were not lost, but had steamed across to an American port as part of some secret agreement between the French and the Americans. A number of speculations floated around: the boats were shoddily constructed; they were sabotaged (after all it was war-time). And now Superior Shoal joined the list.

A year later, in 1930, when the Canadian Hydrographic vessel *Bayfield* arrived to survey the 4-km (2-mile) long shoal, the crew had the unsettling feeling of sailing over a veritable graveyard. A course variation of only 5 kms (3 miles) could mean the difference between a safe depth of 300m (1,000 ft.) and a potentially deadly one of only 6m (21 ft.).

On the *Bayfield's* first attempt to discover what wrecks might be clinging to the rocky incline, her grappling hook took hold of rigging from a sunken ship, but failed to raise it. The crew did manage to salvage an unidentifiable fire-axe and some tangled fishing net. Perhaps some fishermen, motivated by greed, had kept the shoal's existence a secret for decades.

It turned out that many fishermen did know about Superior Shoal. There were tales of phenomenal catches, such as an amazing single-run haul of three tons which turned out to be unsaleable because dealers complained the fish had a peculiar flavour. Rumours spread about fish caught on the shoal having revolting mutations and protruding teeth. Before reaching market, they had to be decapitated. While conducting its survey, the *Bayfield's* crew had noted a tug from Michigan quickly pulling in its nets and scuttling back to port. Evidently, U.S. fishermen had been poaching the site for years. Canadians avoided blowing the whistle, and even spread negative reports about their catches in an effort to steer others from the valuable fishing ground. Tragically, no one reported the menace to the shipping industry.

Efforts to blast the shoal were ineffective, but at least it was accurately charted on navigation charts during WWII. Every captain sailing Lake Superior gives wide berth to the mysterious graveyard of Superior Shoal.

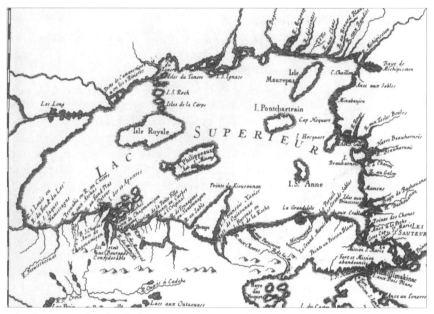

The fictitious islands of Philippeaux and Pontchartrain

THE IMAGINARY ISLANDS OF PHILIPPEAUX AND PONTCHARTRAIN

Copper mining opportunities in Lake Superior caught the attention of a shrewd negotiator best known for his experiments with electricity. Following the American Revolutionary War, Benjamin Franklin was appointed to negotiate boundaries between the U.S. and the British territory to the north. Someone alerted him to the likelihood of copper deposits on Isle Royale, and taking advantage of Britain's unfamiliarity with—some would say careless neglect of—its remaining colonies, Franklin persuaded Britain to set the boundary north of the "Royal Island" which forms the "eye" of Superior's wolf-head shape.

Even a brief glance at a map of Superior reveals the illogic of Franklin's boundary. By virtually every measure—geological, climatic and historical—Isle Royale belongs more to Superior's North Shore than to the state of Michigan, which administers it today.

There is some consolation for Canadians, however. Along with Isle Royale, the U.S. was awarded the island of "Philippeaux," which lay midway between Isle Royale and the Keweenaw Peninsula. Like Isle Royale, Philippeaux was believed to be rich in copper ore, which would be a major asset to the fledgling new country.

One problem with this generous grant is that the island of Philippeaux doesn't exist. It has never existed, except in the imagination of Sieur de La Ronde, whose appointment as commander of the fur-trading post on Madeline Island had been opposed by the French minister, Jean-Frederic Phélypeaux, Compte de Maurepas. While La Ronde searched for rumoured copper deposits on Superior's south shore, Maurepas was sceptical. Yet by the early 1730s, La Ronde was sailing his 40-ton barque built at Point aux Pins, the first decked craft on the lake. To finance his venture, he borrowed 30,000 livres from a Montreal financier.

While La Ronde succeeded in locating some copper deposits near the Ontonagan River, he never found the fabled islands of copper of which the natives told. But that did not prevent him from reporting their existence. What better way to placate a senior French official than to claim a major geographical landmark in his name? And if one island named for La Ronde's reluctant benefactor would work, why not two? Or even three? La Ronde's "optimism" produced a pair of fictitious islands in Lake Superior, which he named for the French official who doubted his abilities. In addition to Philippeaux, La Ronde claimed that an island named Pontchartrain—which was the title awarded to the father of the Comte de Maurepas—lay between Isle Maurepas (now Michipicoten Island) and Isle Ste. Anne (now Caribou Island).

His information was used by respected cartographers for the rest of the century, and when U.S. and British negotiators pored over John Mitchell's 1755 map while drafting the Treaty of Paris in 1783, Franklin had a line drawn across Superior encompassing both the actual Isle Royale and the imaginary Isle Philippeaux. (For more on the border, see Pigeon River, p. 258.)

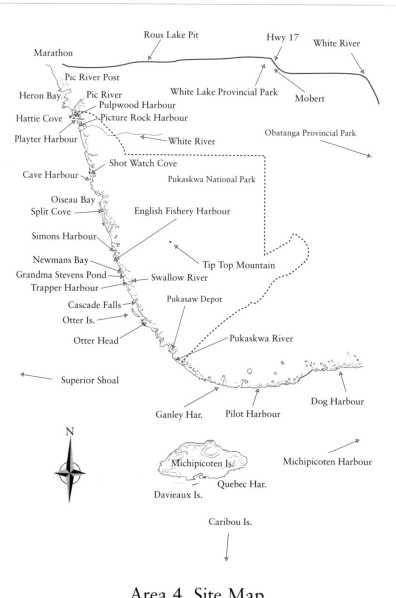

Rous Lake Pit

Hwy 17

White River

Marathon

Pic River Post

White River

Heron Bay

Pic River

White Lake Provincial Park

Mobert

Pulpwood Harbour

Hattie Cove

Picture Rock Harbour

Playter Harbour

Obatanga Provincial Park

White River

Shot Watch Cove

Cave Harbour

Pukaskwa National Park

Oiseau Bay

Split Cove

English Fishery Harbour

Simons Harbour

Newmans Bay

Tip Top Mountain

Grandma Stevens Pond

Swallow River

Trapper Harbour

Cascade Falls

Pukasaw Depot

Otter Is.

Otter Head

Pukaskwa River

Superior Shoal

Ganley Har.

Pilot Harbour

Dog Harbour

N

Michipicoten Harbour

Michipicoten Is.

Quebec Har.

Davieaux Is.

Caribou Is.

Area 4 Site Map

4

Highway 17 West from Wawa

OBATANGA PROVINCIAL PARK

10,000 years ago, barely a blink of an eye in geological terms, the last of the glaciers shrunk north leaving 100 square kms (38 square miles) of what is now Obatanga Provincial Park under deep glacial meltwaters. Over time the waters drained away, leaving a region randomly littered with massive boulders, and gravel and sandy beaches. Today, moose, black bear, mink, beaver and otter reside along the shores and among the stands of Jack Pine, Black Spruce, White Birch and Trembling Aspen (whose heart-shaped leaves rustling in the breeze inspired natives to call it "noisy leaf").

This area is part of the immense Boreal (northern) Forest which drapes thirty-five percent of Canada's land area, from Newfoundland west to the Rockies and north to Alaska. The trees are hardier than their southern neighbours—the Sugar Maples, Yellow Birch and Eastern Hemlock—of the Great Lakes-St. Lawrence Forest Region.

Nature has endowed boreal trees with the ability to flourish in a short growing season and in an eco-system prone to fire. Forest fires can be devastating, but they actually assist the Jack Pine to open its seed cones. The fire's heat melts the thick resin that keeps the cones dried shut, thus releasing the seeds to germinate in the ashes. (Much of the Jack Pine in the Park is the same height, because it all grew after a forest fire in 1910.) In contrast, the Black Spruce holds its cones close to the top of its trunk where flames are less likely to reach. In damp areas, the spruce dips its lower branches to the ground where the tips take root under moss and leaf litter and send out roots to start new trees. As a forest matures it is these two coniferous species that tend to take over.

To explore the different forest environments, Obatanga Park offers hikers two looped trails: one 2.8 kms (1.7 miles) and the other 4.5 kms (2.8) miles). Canoe routes cover both the parks 32 interconnecting lakes and parts of the historic Dog (University) River. It is a rigorous 50-km (31-mile) paddle from Heart Lake down river to Lake Superior.

WHITE RIVER, WINNIE, AND AN ICE-BOX REPUTATION

Snug in his Montreal mansion, William Van Horne, the strong-willed Vice-President of the CPR, could soften the impact of a Canadian winter with a roaring fire and a snifter of good brandy. But he didn't want to be *reminded* that his employees north of Superior might be experiencing even bitter winters still. And so, when he saw that a major CPR divisional centre had been named Snowbank, he insisted it be changed to White River. But no mere name change could moderate one of the most severe winter climates in all of North America. After 1935, the railway community cannily

Captain Harry Colebourne feeding Winnie, the bear he bought at the White River Station, that became the much-loved, Winnie the Pooh

turned this negative into a positive. White River began billing itself as the coldest community in all of North America, based on a recorded temperature of -72 degrees Fahrenheit (-58 degrees Celsius) and reinforced its claim by erecting an oversized thermometer along the Trans-Canada Highway. It is not known whether this distinction drew tourists to White River, or repelled them.

Much more attractive is the legend of the small bear cub from White River. This was not just any cub. Purchased in 1914 on the White River CPR platform by Harry Colebourn, a young military officer from Winnipeg, the cub became the regiment's mascot. When Colebourn was called to serve in France, he left the bear at the London Zoo.

There was something special about this White River bear. She had a gentle nature, a clever personality and a special rapport with visitors to the zoo. She was named *Winnipeg*, after Colebourn's home town. By the time author A. A. Milne visited the zoo in 1925, his son Christopher Robin in tow, Winnipeg had become *Winnie*, her antics inspiring one of the best-loved series of children's books ever written. Since then, millions of people around the world have grown to adulthood with fond memories of Winnie the Pooh, a native of White River, Ontario.

THE MOVING CRATER

It is one thing to hear water running beneath the ground. It is quite another to imagine it could cause two sections of road and a forested area to disappear into a huge crater 30-45m (100-150 ft.) deep, one-third of a mile long and a quarter-mile wide. It began as a gravel pit, but the underground water mixed with fine sand, silt and clay to form a viscous fluid that flowed with some momentum into the Black River, leaving behind the gaping, ever growing crater.

To view it, take the first small dirt road which heads north from Highway 17 west of Rous Lake about 24 kms (15 miles) east of Marathon).

WHITE LAKE PROVINCIAL PARK

White Lake is part of the enormous White River system that was used extensively for logging. The White River canoe trip can begin either from the town of White River or, for the full 192-km (120-mile) route, from its source at Lake Negwazu, north of Obatanga Provincial Park. For park information, call (807) 822-2447 (For the river trip's end, see White River p.159)

WHITE RIVER: POW LUMBER CAMPS

During WWII, some of the thousands of German Prisoners of War who were brought to Canada were imprisoned in camps along Lake Superior's north shore. Many were put to work as loggers. Charlie Quinn, a former worker at the four White River POW camps, estimated that over one thousand prisoners worked for the Abitibi Power and Paper Company. Cutting trees was dangerous work requiring stamina and training and the spring river drive was particularly perilous. The Germans were treated carefully, as authorities feared that harming a German soldier might cause retaliation against Canadian POWs abroad. According to Quinn, no German was killed on the job at White River—quite a record for the early logging industry.

According to Quinn, there were different types of POWs:

> Some were Devils—a Nazi was in a class by himself, he was surly. One camp had 125 Air Force men—they were harder to handle. They thought they were better. We had one camp, a Navy gang—also tough to handle. But the regular soldier, he was all right.

Despite being imprisoned in a place with record cold temperatures, some prisoners maintained their sense of humour. On one occasion, two Germans managed to acquire civilian clothing and tricked the head foreman into believing they were unemployed Canadian lumbermen. Quinn relates: "[The foreman] Dan goes, 'No this is a German prisoner of war camp, no civilians can work here.' They put up quite an argument that they could get on with the Germans. 'No,' Dan says, 'you have to get the hell out of here as quick as possible.'"

The impostors continued to goad the foreman, claiming they had walked a long distance and were hungry. Dan offered them lunch but they continued to plead until he threatened to chase them off the camp. "Then the German said, 'Well if we show you our credentials can we stay?' The imposter threw off his jacket, and there was the big red patch." (A large red dot was painted on the prisoners' uniforms as a target at which guards would aim if a prisoner attempted to escape.) The embarrassed foreman let

Many German WWII POWs worked at logging camps on the north shore. Note the target on the back of their uniforms in case they attempted escape.

out a string of curses as the prisoners grinned.

There were some more serious confrontations. At one point, convinced the war was over, the prisoners went on strike. The commander retaliated with orders to place the men on a diet of bread and water. When the prisoner in charge of ration pick-up was informed, he stormed out of the room. Quinn ran for backup, only to discover that all the guards had fled into the woods. Within ten minutes, the German returned, along with a hundred prisoners lined up behind him.

> He says very firmly to us, 'What's the verdict?' Dan answers, 'No coffee, sugar, butter or tea that's the verdict.' So there was Dan Steel (the clerk), Gordon Ball (the logging boss), and me–just the three of us. The German comes in, he didn't put a hand on anybody, he just elbowed past. All the prisoners are crowding into the room too. There was a case standing where the axes were. So he took an axe out and pinched the locks open. He took out the rations—not an ounce more than the rations.

Quinn was sent to the Magpie River camp for help. Before long, a platoon of about 100 men arrived.

> We called the prisoners into the cookery, and kept the meeting going until we heard the tractors come in. Major Draper said, 'Now when you fellows walk out of here there is a live machine gun on every corner of every building. The orders are shoot to kill. One mis-move, that will be the end of it.' When the Germans walked out, sure enough, there was a machine gun on every building.

The Germans were punished. They took their blankets. They took their lamps and mattresses. Put them on bread and water twice a day. They paraded them for thirty minutes, twice a day, up the road and back. And if you think bread and water don't bring you down to size you think again–I've never seen such a sorry looking bunch of men. They all went back to work. It was quite an experience. The guards who ran away were all captured and put under house arrest and charged with cowardice.

When the end of the war was announced, the reaction of prisoners, many of whom had come to enjoy life in Canada, was somewhat surprising. Quinn recalled:

Some of them cried, some of them laughed... some of them said 'I knew it would happen but it didn't happen quick enough.' The Nazis were really upset about the loss... they didn't speak. The others had to be quiet so there would be no retaliation against them by the Nazis. The fellows I knew–they were pleasant. They said, 'so long as I can run away before they can find me I will stay, and if I do get back I'll look you up.' But none ever looked me up.

HBC's Mobert (Montizambert) Post

MOBERT (MONTIZAMBERT)

Once the CP Railway came through in the early 1880s, many of the Ojibwe trappers who had previously travelled down to the Pic Post to trade (see p.152), set up at Mobert. They were closer to their hunting grounds, and closer to better trading opportunities. The Hudson's Bay Company followed, closing the original Pic Post in 1888.

PUKASKWA NATIONAL PARK

The wild shore of an inland sea, Pukaskwa National Park is one of Canada's best-kept secrets, the largest national wilderness park in Ontario, and a place of undeniable grandeur.

The Park's mandate is to protect an outstanding example of the Canadian Shield and of the Lake Superior shore. Its territory, the bulging peninsula between the Pic River in the north and the Pukaskwa River in the south, is covered by thick Boreal forest. A pale green lichen, Old Man's Beard, drips from spindly branches, giving the forest an ancient, eerie feel. Tangled lower branches effectively deter human passage. Although tracks of moose, white-tailed deer, black bear, lynx, red fox, fisher and wolves are common, a visitor rarely encounters them.

In addition to the impenetrable forest, the terrain is completely broken up. Swiftly-flowing rivers left behind by retreating glaciers, cut steeply-carved valleys and gullies through the Precambrian bedrock of the interior uplands all the way to Superior's rugged coast. The shoreline of coves, inlets, shoals and jutting headlands is like a jigsaw puzzle. Between the Pic River in the north and the Pukaskwa River in the south, the Park is about 73 kms (46 miles) as the crow flies, but about 128 kms (80 miles) along the shoreline.

Under brooding grey clouds, the massive rocky headlands gleam in a silvery light. Under clear blue skies they stand out stark and powerful. The waters can change quickly from steel grey to brilliant blue, turquoise and emerald green. Long beaches and dunes of gravel, cobbles or fine white sand dot the shore and mark Superior's fluctuating waterlines. In areas windswept by the prevailing westerly wind, only a few stunted trees successfully cling to cracks in the rock. But in protected coves they grow gracefully down to the water.

On the raised cobble beaches, mysterious depressions called Pukaskwa pits were left by early inhabitants, most between 1,000 B.C. and A.D.1500 (see p.136) Others who left their mark were later Ojibwe, voyageurs, fur traders, prospectors, fishermen and loggers.

The deeply-faulted terrain explains why surveyors avoided this area when laying out the Trans-Canada Highway. The long stretch between Wawa and Marathon circles well north of the bulging Pukaskwa peninsula, isolating the shoreline and interior. Only the north-westerly slash of a power line mars the almost 1,900 square kilometres of wilderness. Since there are no inland trails, most visitors arrive at the park's northern entrance at Hattie Cove, and either stay in the area, or take the magnificent coastal hiking or canoe trails south. (For Park information, see Hattie Cove, p.151)

PUKASKWA RIVER

The exact origin of the name Pukaskwa (pronounced Pukasaw) is unknown. In one version of the story, Joe Pukaskwa killed his wife Sarah, and threw her burnt bones and ashes into the river. ("*Pukasu*" is said to refer to bones being burned on a fire to cook the marrow.)

The Pukaskwa River offers one of two remote whitewater river canoe routes in the Park. It is an exhilarating 10-14 day trip, with 57 negotiable rapids on the 283-m (850-ft.) drop between the headwaters and the river mouth at Lake Superior. At Two Pants Portage, the river surges over Lake Superior's ancient shoreline and through a kilometre-long walled gorge. Along the route, old dams left over from the pulpwood runs (see Pukasaw Depot) are still visible. *Note: The river can be paddled only in May and early June, since by mid-June, water levels are normally too low. Portage trails are not maintained.*

From Lake Superior, the river mouth is well concealed by a gravel spit. Heading upstream, the surprisingly tepid river meanders lazily through verdant green for the first short stretch. Then at the base of a massive chasm, huge boulders are strewn as if tossed there by the gods from the towering cliffs. In the words of Superintendent of Indian Affairs, Thomas G. Anderson in 1869, the falls "hasten down with the wildest speed conceivable, as if to escape the threats of the over hanging precipice on either side...."

Pukasaw Depot

PUKASAW DEPOT: LIFE IN ISOLATION

Remote Pukasaw Depot grew out of the small logging camp Grant Perry established in 1904-05. Perry's operation lasted until 1910... the year the log boom holding his entire year's supply of wood, broke, and dumped in the lake. Between 1917 and 1930, the Depot was a logging base for the Lake Superior Paper Company's pulp operations up the Pukaskwa River. On either side of the quiet-flowing Imogene Creek were an enormous bunkhouse, a doctor's house, blacksmith shop, harness maker, cookery, warehouse, offices, cabins, stables, hay sheds, and root cellars.

The men worked in camps located along the branches of the Pukaskwa. Cutting of spruce and balsam began in October and ended in February, when the logs were hauled to the rivers and left on the ice behind dams. At first, the logs were cut in 16-ft. lengths and driven down the river after spring break-up. But the longer the logs, the more wood was wasted, and the greater the likelihood of a jam developing. So in later years, wood was cut into 4-ft. lengths. The logs were stored in a large boom at the mouth of Imogene Creek until they were picked up by tug and towed to the pulp mill at Sault Ste. Marie (see the big tow, p.32).

Group at Pukasaw Depot, 1920s

Lee Fletcher grew up at the Depot in the 1920s, and remembers the provision boats arriving in the fall from the Sault:

> They had a little track and rail car from Perry's wharf—you can still see
> the old cribs for the wharf along the shore. They would load the supplies in the rail car and horses would haul it up the hill, then 5 or 6
> teams of horses would haul it to the warehouse or the root house. I
> remember in 1925 or 1926 they brought in 7 tons of lard and lots of
> beef on the last boat in December. The beef was frozen and they kept it
> in the bunkhouse and cookery. We used to worry whenever we got a
> thaw.

Crews were hired from the Sault area, Quebec and as far as Scandinavia.
Most were farmers from Buckingham, Quebec who turned to pulpwood
logging for their "winter cash crop." Many of the Scandinavians were from
Finland and they brought their culture with them. Fletcher elaborates:

> The Finns were very rabid about cleanliness. The first thing they'd build
> at a camp was a steam bath. The steam bath was usually finished before
> the other cabins were. On Wednesday and Saturday nights they'd have
> a steam bath, which was good for fly bites. You'd get a good feeding
> and have a steam bath, which took out the poison.

The Finnish camps must have been a delight compared to those without bathing facilities. ("The only time anyone had a bath was once in a while when we went through the ice—everybody smelled the same!")

In the winter and early spring, the only way out was the 112-km (70-mile) White River trail. Depending on conditions, a round trip took 7-14 days, and so most men stayed put, although the odd Scandinavian made his own skis and took off. Because of the isolation, news from the outside was treasured. Radio batteries and newspapers were too heavy to bring in by sled and so any paper that did arrive ended up in tatters, having been passed from hand to hand. To fill the lonely hours, the men turned to chess, jigsaw puzzles, practical jokes, winter sports and the occasional batch of moonshine.

For some, however, games were not enough. Despair drove to suicide a former editor of a Ukrainian newspaper in Toronto. Apparently, he began a writing marathon. When questioned, he said he was writing to warn his people never to come to a logging camp. One morning in February 1923, he ate a hearty breakfast, turned to the cook and said, "I'm going to finish myself off this time." He walked to the lake, pulled his cap over his face and crawled through a hole in the ice.

As in all logging camps, work was hard and dangerous. As related in *The Lumberjacks*, disaster struck Joe Lefebvre when he and his brother rigged a block and cable to take sleigh loads of wood down a steep hill. The log being used as a brake suddenly swung and hit Joe on the side of the head, breaking his jaw and throwing him in front of the horses. Despite blood coming from his eyes and ears, he grabbed the reins. But the horses could not hold back the load and the sleigh hit him in the chest.

> I tied my jaw shut with string and my brother helped me walk the three-and-a-half miles to camp. I was 18 days in that camp before they took me out. The superintendent had a special sled made for me, and Eric Skead, one of the jobbers, a very good dog sled man, drove me out 70 miles to White River in 30 hours. The usual trip took a week. My wife had to stay in camp because she had three children, the youngest born six days before the accident.

After a long winter, the arrival of the first boat was met with great anticipation. All the women and children from the camps would come down to the Depot and stay in the "harem," to wait. Lee Fletcher recalls,

> We didn't know when the boats were coming in until the damned things
> arrived, and then there'd be a great stampede. You couldn't see the dock
> from the Depot. One of the captains was kind of a joker. He'd sneak in
> very quietly and tie up and sit there for an hour or so before someone
> would notice the tip of the mast sticking up over the hill, and all hell
> broke loose then.

Until Pukasaw Depot was silenced by the economic doldrums of the
Great Depression, it sent 30,000 cords of pulp wood a year to the paper
mill in Sault Ste. Marie. The loggers came out in the spring of 1930 and
never returned. Only a few families like the Fletchers and Mills remained,
riding out the Depression by trapping. Since then, the community at the
mouth of Imogene Creek has slowly crumbled. Out of more than 20 buildings that once made up the Depot, the only easily identifiable structure is
the Fletcher/Mills cabin, or what remains of it. Balsam fir and birch thrive
in the log foundations of other long-vanished cabins. As though grown
weary, the elaborate iron cross made for two Lafleur children who died in
a cabin fire, leans further every year. On the outcropping east of Imogene
Creek the large rings that once bolted the log booms to the shore can still
be seen.

RICHARDSON ISLAND AND RICHARDSON HARBOUR

Pukaskwa Pits - Mysteries of Time

It is appropriate that the shores of such a mystic lake hold a mystery
beyond our understanding....

Colin MacMillan was hunting partridge near Richardson Harbour one
beautiful late-September day in 1949 when he came upon an extraordinary sight. Across the raised, rocky beach set well above the level of Lake
Superior, he saw what he first thought was a low stone wall. But it wasn't
exactly a wall. It was more like a pit with walled sides. Neither the weather nor an animal could have made such a structure. What could it be?

MacMillan had happened upon one of Superior's great archaeological
mysteries: Pukaskwa Pits. They are found on raised cobble beaches, sometimes 30m (100 ft.) above current beach levels. The earth's crust in this
region has been rebounding from the weight of the glaciers (imagine what
2,400m (8,000 ft.) of ice covering the region for thousands of years could
do) since the last retreat 10,000 years ago. This "isostatic rebound" has
been occurring at an average rate of 15m (50 ft.) per thousand years (the

rate is now only 0.3m (1 ft.) per century).

Although pits are known elsewhere, some of the most outstanding examples, over 250 of them, have been found along this stretch of the Park's shore. They are of different designs from simple depressions to pits surrounded by walls of rock. Many are circular or oblong, averaging 1.8m (6 ft.) across. Larger pits are sometimes referred to as "lodges"; smaller pits are called "hearths." Sometimes there is only one pit on a beach. At other locations several are joined together.

Little is known about these pits which originally would have been constructed on lake frontage. Archaeologists have found little to go on. Excavations have unearthed only fragments of pottery, flints, caribou teeth and charred bones. More revealing clues may be lost having sifted down through the cobbles.

While the age of the pits is difficult to determine, most were probably made by Algonkian people about 1000 B.C. to A.D.1500. The larger pits, or "lodges," might have been temporary dwellings that were covered over or domed. Maybe they were duck blinds or food caches. The smaller "hearths" could have been fireplaces or places to smoke fish.

Could others have been used for sweat lodges? Or, might they have been used in ceremonies? Perhaps there is a connection with the Midéwiwin, the elaborate religious healing society of the Ojibwe. Some believe they were used by adolescents for "vision quests." In Ojibwe tradition, adolescents (usually boys) would withdraw to remote locations where they would fast for days, seeking a vision of the guardian spirit who would accompany them through life. This guide often took the form of a bird or animal and could be summoned through dreams, fasting, concentration or offerings.

Further up the shore there is a site which may have had an important spiritual significance. After climbing fourteen beach layers through the spruce forest, one comes upon a peaceful, meditative place. Spread over the cobble expanse is an extensive complex of connected rock walls built around large depressions, the whole encircled by a masssive oblong wall two-feet thick. Stone cobbles are covered with dark grey and green lichens. The sound of birds and distant waves are calming. Blueberry bushes and birch trees, their leaves making dancing patterns in the sunlight, grow out of some of the enclosures.

The Pukaskwa pits are fragile and could easily be damaged by curious visitors. Be aware of them when walking across cobble beaches and keep your distance.

OTTER HEAD AND THE GREAT TIN SWINDLE

Peter McKellar was known for his many traits: excellence as a surveyor and geologist; honesty; a streak of Scottish stubborness; inventiveness (he designed not only a rock crusher and pulverizer but a rotary engine to power it); not to mention a black beard that sprouted from his chin like a well-cultivated shrub. When the Silver Islet Mine (near Thunder Bay) heard that a major tin deposit had been discovered near Otter Head, the mine operators sent McKellar to investigate.

In the spring of 1873, McKellar and his party rounded the spectacular Otter Head. Paddling up the Pukaskwa River they encountered a group of prospectors. When asked about the vein's location, only one of them actually knew but he refused to take anyone—not even his own partners—to the site. McKellar smelled a rat. He walked around the region, but nothing suggested the presence of tin. Just before McKellar departed, the prospector agreed to show some samples from the claim. McKellar noticed they did not look freshly broken, and they were covered with sediment as if they had been kept under running water. The samples were fakes. He would stake his reputation on it.

Peter McKellar

Meanwhile the eyes of greedy investors were already clouded with dollar signs, especially after a New York newspaper reported the Otter Head tin deposits could be "traced with the naked eye from cliff to cliff across the rugged highland." McKellar scoffed at the idea. No one listened. Even his own employers questioned his judgement.

In November, travelling on board a steamer from the Sault to Thunder Bay, McKellar watched open-mouthed as the steamer made an unscheduled stop at Otter Head. Sounding its whistle in an apparent code, it unloaded several barrels. Earlier McKellar had been tipped off about the barrels and had quietly inspected them. They contained cement "salted" with tin ore.

In spite of McKellar's warnings, money began pouring into the bank accounts of the Otter Head mine promoters. The frenzy grew and

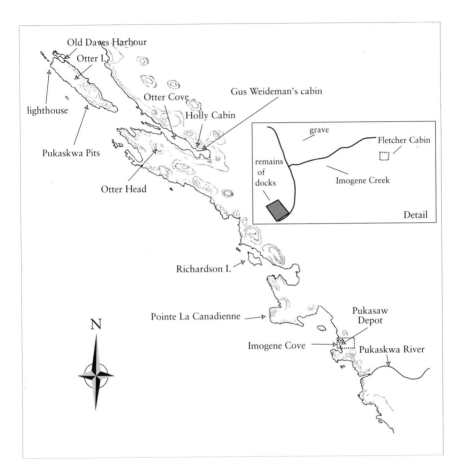

McKellar's Silver Islet employers had grown impatient with their sceptical geologist by the following spring. After all, some of the industry's most highly-respected mining experts were jumping on the bandwagon.

A group from Silver Islet set out by snowshoe and toboggan on the 300-mile journey to Otter Head. McKellar insisted on accompanying them. He examined drilling samples that showed tin ore in a substance that looked suspiciously like cement. He also noted several discarded barrels on the way to the claim—the very same barrels he had seen on a steamer the previous November. Finally, McKellar was given an opportunity to examine the site for himself and he quickly exposed details of the fraud. The prospector and his confederates had chosen the location carefully, removing a vein and replacing it with the mixture of grey cement and tin ore. It was in precisely the kind of rock matrix that a geologist might expect to

Otter Head first appeared on a Jesuit map in 1672. For voyageurs, it marked the halfway point between the Sault and Fort William.

yield a vein of tin ore.

Following McKellar's revelations, the great Otter Head "tin bubble" burst. The prospector was convicted of fraud and imprisoned. Everyone congratulated Peter McKellar for his perspicacity. He merely nodded and returned to work.

Tête de la Loutre, or Otter Head first appeared on a Jesuit map of 1672. In the mid-nineteenth century, John Bigsby of the British Boundary Commission described it as "an upright slab, from thirty to thirty-five feet high, placed on some scantily-clad rocks, 120 feet above the lake." This distinctive rock was apparently named by the Ojibwe who compared it to an otter's head sticking out of water. For voyageurs it had a different meaning. It was the spot that marked the halfway point on their gruelling journey between the Sault and Fort William.

OTTER COVE

The Legends of Gus Weideman

Of all the trappers who have ranged this shore, one of the most legendary was "Big Gus," a rugged individual who marched to the beat of a different drummer. Soon after Gus Weideman arrived at Pukaskwa Depot in the mid-1920s, rumours began to fly, each more scandalous than the last. Weideman was a sailor from Lithuania; he was a criminal on the run from

Trapper Gus Weidman, "Big Gus", had a shotgun-sized hole in his cabin door to ward off unwelcome visitors

the law; he had killed a man in Europe... or maybe in Montreal.

Some of the legends were based on fact. Gus, powerfully built and dedicated to physical fitness, was precisely the type of individual who would seek a solitary existence in a remote and challenging corner of the world. Lee Fletcher recalls:

> Gus arrived about 1924.... He was a very powerful man who trapped at Otter Cove and did a bit of poaching, especially beaver. The game wardens were scared of him, really scared. They always approached his camp with their guns drawn. One year he got three months in jail, January, February and March, and said it was the best winter he had ever spent—he didn't have to shovel snow and got three hot meals a day!

Fletcher has seen "Big Gus" single-handedly heft a 400-pound barrel of coal oil onto the back of a wagon. Yet he was not just a strong man of the land. Others have whispered in awe about his extensive knowledge of European languages, history and philosophy. Evidently he kept up with current events by reading magazines he collected from yachts. His favourites were *Time, Reader's Digest, Atlantic Monthly* and *The Saturday Evening Post.*

For several years, Gus trapped, fished and poached from the tiny cabin he supposedly shared with a tame otter and a snake he encouraged to come up through the floor to deter mice. He also supplemented his income through tourism, betting boaters $100 a pop that he could canoe up to a moose and jump on its back. The lucrative sideline ended one day with a swift antler prod and Gus's leg broken in four places. Aside from his perilous antics, life along the North Shore was hard, and Weideman was as prone to the risks as anyone. Somehow a rusty spike was driven into the side of his head. He is reputed to have rowed to Otter Island lighthouse before being taken to the Sault for treatment. Another version of the story has him removing the spike with a pair of pliers, then, when the wound became infected, to having lanced it with a hunting knife.

To deter intruders, Big Gus added a special feature to his cabin door. He carved an opening just large enough for the muzzle of his shotgun, to welcome unexpected visitors, like game wardens. The cabin remains standing today in thick undergrowth, a fitting reminder of the legendary stranger who lived in it many years ago. (In an ironic twist, the nearby cabin, kept by Leland Holly and his family as a summer retreat from 1957-77, is now a warden's station.)

OTTER ISLAND LIGHTHOUSE: TWO WEEKS OF TERROR

At first, Gilbert MacLachlan was annoyed. Then he grew concerned. The horror came later. The night of November 30, 1930 had been about as bad as a lighthouse keeper on Superior's North Shore could expect. A storm had brought heavy snow, strong winds and temperatures of 25 degrees Fahrenheit. MacLachlan had remained all night at his post in the octagonal wooden light tower.

"I'm starving," MacLachlan said to his assistant, John Moore. "What's left to eat?" "Not much 'cept biscuits," Moore replied. The season was almost over and they were down to the last of their provisions. "Biscuits'll do," grunted MacLachan. Moore nodded and shrugged into his coat. It was a fair journey to the house, a third of a mile. MacLachlan turned his attention back to the light. When he finished replenishing the oil he would tend to polishing the lens. He would have to check the fog plant later, start preparing things for the journey to the mainland in a couple of weeks.... As time passed, the hungry MacLachan became concerned. Suspecting Moore had fallen asleep in the house, he headed down the steep lighthouse stairs... and caught his breath. At the foot lay a small pool of blood.

Rushing outside, the lightkeeper followed the trail of blood all the way to the house, where he found Moore's stiffly frozen body. Controlling his panic, he carried the body inside. Evidently after being injured Moore tried to crawl to the safety of the house. While the lightkeeper had been polishing the lens and grumbling over his assistant's tardiness, Moore had been bleeding to death in the frigid December air.

For a moment, MacLachlan considered lighting a fire. Then he realized the heat would thaw Moore's body. It could be days before anyone arrived to help. In shock, MacLachlan stumbled to the fog alarm building and began sending out a distress call. For three days and nights, the mournful blast of the Otter Island fog horn echoed like a dirge up and down the Pukaskwa peninsula.

Otter Island Lighthouse, note the beaver weathervane

Finally Jack Mills arrived by boat from his residence 19 kms (12 miles) down the shore. He promised to telegraph for a lighthouse tender to be dispatched, but bad weather delayed the alert. For another nine days, MacLachlan, subsisting only on soda crackers and water, shared the lonely outpost with his assistant's frozen corpse.

On December 12, almost two weeks after Moore's accident, a tender arrived to carry the keepers, one dead, and the other near emotional exhaustion, to the Sault. The following spring, Gilbert MacLachlan returned to the Otter Island light for another shipping season. (Otter Island light was erected in 1903 and is still in use. For the assistant keeper's house, see Old Daves Harbour, below.)

OLD DAVES HARBOUR

On a warm summer's day, this refuge at the north end of Otter Island is calm and serene. Through the clear, green water, objects at great depths seem just below the surface. The harbour was named after "Big" Dave, a fisherman who operated here in the early 1900s. After WWII, the Talarico Company employed twenty people, including crew and families, at their station. The buildings sag but their greying boards and green roofs add to the picturesque harbour, which is still frequented by the fish tug, the *Last Time*.

Inside the charming lightkeeper's residence, a log book invites visitors to sign. Many of the comments are from thankful kayakers and canoeists who took refuge here after being caught in a sudden storm. A trail from the house leads to the lighthouse.

Big Dave's home, 1909.

SWALLOW RIVER/TRAPPER HARBOUR

In several sheltered bays and river mouths, there are remnants of log cabins occupied by trappers who set up trap-lines in the Park region in the 1920s and 30s. Most were Ojibwe, French Canadians or former lumbermen who would trap in winter and fish in summer. All were rugged individualists.

On the north shore of the Swallow River, just inside the river mouth stands a cabin that was likely used by French Canadians Art Laroque and Henry Brisbois, in the 1930s. John Marsh's study, *The Human History of the Pukaskwa National Park Area 1650-1975* quotes Gordon Primeau speaking about Laroque. He was:

> a quiet person, never divulged anything to anybody... we used to bring him books... he was a fanatic, book fanatic. And we'd come there to his camp in the summer and he'd be sitting on the rocking chair there reading, and there'd be five of us standing there. When he finished that chapter, then he'd say, 'Hello.'

Olav Bjornaa recalls the two trappers Laroque and Brisbois had tame groundhogs which would come when called and sit with them at the table in their spotlessly clean cabins.

GRANDMA STEVENS POND

In the early 1900s, the Stevens yacht, *Cambria*, was one of the first cruising yachts in the area. The matriarch of the family would not let her wheelchair slow her down. She would have herself lowered over the *Cambria*'s sides, rowed to shore and carried to her favourite trout fishing hole, an inland pond.

NEWMANS BAY

The bay is named after trapper and cedar-strip boat-builder, Billy Newman. Fisherman Olav Bjornaa recounts an old tale about the bay in which a sailing schooner from Duluth met its doom on Superior Shoal. One man survived by tying himself (and a corpse) to a spar which drifted into Newmans Bay. (See Superior Shoal, p. 120.)

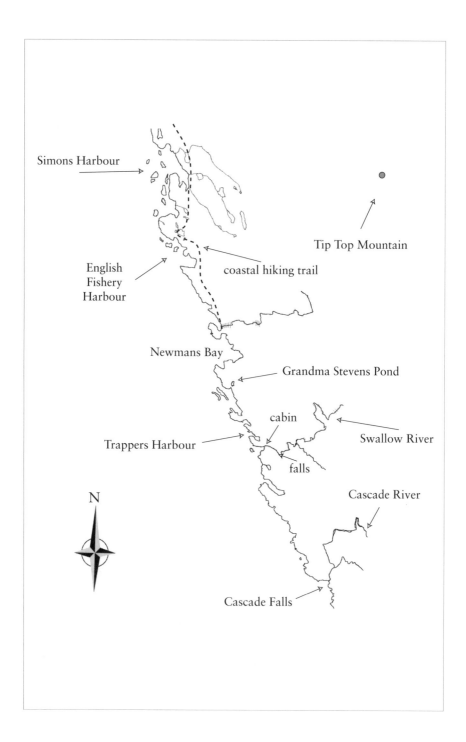

Simons Harbour

English
Fishery
Harbour

Tip Top Mountain

coastal hiking trail

Newmans Bay

Grandma Stevens Pond

cabin

Trappers Harbour

Swallow River

falls

Cascade River

N

Cascade Falls

English Fishery Harbour

If you look hard enough at the north end of English Fishery Harbour, you can find a hidden accessway for canoes to reach Hideaway Lake. A few kilometres north along the coastal hiking trail brings you to the top of the hill behind the lake where there is a spectacular 360-degree view.

Simons Harbour

Simons Harbour was once the site of a small fishing camp operated by Booth Fisheries. It is still a haven for anyone caught in a Superior storm. One such reluctant visitor was Bruce McCuaig, who runs a charter service delivering hikers and canoeists down the Pukaskwa shore in his big tug, the *Century*, "the best boat on the Great Lakes." Bruce claims he never worries about the weather "because its going to do what it's going to do whether I worry about it or not." With a smoke in one hand, a can of Pepsi in the other and an impish grin on his face, McCuaig recalls the night he and a friend were stuck in Simons Harbour during a blow. They decided this was a good time to stop smoking—after they finished their open packs of course. At that point they would quit, cold turkey. By Wednesday, with the last smoke long gone, their resolve was now so weak that they decided to radio for a helicopter if the weather did not let up by the following day. (It did.) Recognizing that the cigarette crisis did not, perhaps, warrant helicopter relief, McCuaig adds, "besides, I needed my Pepsi!"

Tip Top Mountain

At 630m (2,099 ft.) above sea level, Tip Top Mountain is one of highest peaks in Ontario. Ambitious climbers (including Gus Weideman) (see page 140) have reached the summit. But with no trails through the thick tangled bush, bogs and steep-sided valleys, this is no country stroll.

SPLIT COVE

So-named in Bonnie Dahl's *The Superior Way*, the cove's shape resembles a molar tooth complete with roots. Actually it is two coves separated by a peninsula. Many of the coves along the Pukaskwa shore have several names: Ojibwe names, names used by the Park, local names, and names given by tug operators and others who have passed through. Whatever one chooses to call this cove, with its deserted, fine white sand beaches rimming "warm" turquoise waters, dramatic headlands, and spots where the boreal forest drips right down into emerald green waters, it all adds up to a taste of paradise.

OISEAU BAY

For a few years in the mid-1940s, logging operations to build the new town of Marathon were centred around Oiseau Bay. A camp was located a

bit inland on the north shore of Oiseau Creek, but a flash flood in 1986 wiped out all traces. Nor are there many reminders of the sawmill that once stood at the south end of the bay. Just in from the long, white sandy beach stretching along the wide curve of the bay, trapper Dan Goodchild had a cabin. Dan's son Protheus recalls, "he travelled a lot of the bush. That was his life, he wanted to be in the bush all the time. When you're out there, you've got freedom." It is possible to follow several of Dan's old trapping trails inland by watching for the blazes carved on the tree trunks.

Trapper Dan Goodchild kept a cabin at Oiseau Bay

Cave Harbour and *Misamik*'s Head

At the northwest point of Cave Harbour, there is a cave facing west shaped like a beaver's head. According to a local legend, the giant [Nanaboozho] was hunting *Misamik*, an equally huge beaver. Spotting him, the giant was too impatient to set a trap. Instead, he decided to pull the beaver's dam apart. Once the water ran out of the lake, the beaver would come out. Finally, the beaver appeared and the hunter started chasing him around the beaver pond [Lake Superior]. Misamik tried everything to get away. As the beaver approached Cave Harbour, he desperately tried to hide under a rock. It was not a good plan. He hit his head so hard that it made an impression in the stone. (The cave can be reached by water or by walking along the shore from the coastal hiking trail.)

Shot Watch Cove

After a local trapper's death, little was found around the small "line shack" he kept near the beach, except for an old pocket watch with a bullet hole. Was the watch a shooting target? No one knows for certain.

White River

In contrast to blustery Lake Superior, on a late summer's day, the White River is remarkably tranquil. The current flows warm and languid under cedars that bow gracefully out over the water. The upriver journey ends at a pool below a set of rapids, where a portage trail leads up to the spectacular Chigamiwinigum Falls. You hear them before you see them and they take your breath away. Edging out onto a swaying suspension bridge, you can see a cauldron of whitewater boiling through the rock canyon far below.

Until the 1960s, the river was the scene of exciting log drives from White Lake. Each spring, the powerful water drove the pulpwood through this gorge at 45 mph on their 96 km (60 mile) journey to Lake Superior, where they were marshalled into booms at the White River mouth or in nearby Playter Harbour.

For whitewater enthusiasts, the navigable rapids of the White River are an adventure. Depending on one's starting point and pace, the trip takes 4-8 days. The full trip from Lake Negwazu, the river's source, to Superior is 184 kms (115 miles). (For more information, consult the Park's guide to canoe routes.)

PICTURE ROCK HARBOUR

It is said that the "drawings" on the rocks at Picture Rock Harbour were created by scraping off lichen from the rock face (See Les Petits Ecrits p.185). The drawings are gone but the harbour still has its unusual red rocks. Not the natural, dull brick-red one would expect, but a brilliant almost fake-looking red that glows in the magic hour of sunset. This harbour marks the division between the granite that runs south and the greenstone belt of Playter and Pulpwood Harbours to the north.

Along the beach are massive boom logs with rusting chains still attached, stacks of sun-bleached driftwood, and remains of a cabin kept by the McCuaigs, who beachcombed the coast for stray pulp logs. The family had a licence to pick pulp from the Pukaskwa River in the south as far up as Terrace Bay, including the Slate Islands. They started in the 1940s and stopped in 1983, the year Marathon Corporation's drives on the Pic River ended. The McCuaigs would pick over the shore every three years, working about ten days in one location, storing the logs in that bay, then moving down the shore. (A Marathon tug would pick them up.)

PLAYTER HARBOUR

Around Playter Harbour lie some of the oldest rocks in the Park. Mostly pale grey to greenish-grey "greenstones," they are early Precambrian metavolcanics. Some are shaped like long, narrow pillows and are thought to have formed as lava under water.

PULPWOOD HARBOUR

The McCuaig family stored pulp logs they had beachcombed here during the spring and early summer. Once the river current on the Pic had subsided, they would move the logs into the river for storage. Bruce McCuaig still keeps his tug, the *Century*, tied to old boom logs attached to shore (see Picture Rock Harbour, Simons Harbour p.147).

We have an explanation for the place name. Guarding the entrance to the harbour are sharp, jagged tooth-like rocks that could gnaw any hull into pulpwood.

HATTIE COVE

Pukaskwa National Park Entrance

When in his later years, the infamous Gus Weidman built a cabin on the north shore of this cove, the location was known as Mud Bay. When, in 1978, this location was picked to be the visitor's entrance to Pukaskwa National Park, "Mud Bay" did not make the grade. The name was changed to a more welcoming, locally-used name, Hattie Cove. Preservation of the environment is the park's priority and so when planners designed the park, they sought to maintain the integrity of its natural wilderness in subtle ways. For example, the roads curve instead of being straight with the standard ditch or clearing on each side. Planners wanted people immediately to feel the presence of nature enclosing them. And one does. Clumps of pale green "Old Man's Beard" lichen sway in the breeze, draped over spindly Black Spruce. The damp forest floor, into which little light penetrates, is carpeted with brilliant green sphagnum moss. White-throated sparrows call out their haunting tune.

Hattie Cove has campground facilities and a visitor centre with interpretative displays and regular informational programs. The short trails around the cove offer surprising contrast, from rocky headlands jutting out into Superior, to fragile dunes and the lichens and other rare vegetation they support.

This strong wild land will slowly reveal itself to those who take the time to explore. Hattie Cove is the start of both the **Coastal Hiking Trail** and the **Coastal Canoe Trip**. The rugged, at times treacherous, trail leads 60 kms (47 miles) south to the North Swallow River along dramatically beautiful shoreline. It is clear as far south as Oiseau Bay, but below, it becomes hillier and more difficult.

The 256-km (160-mile) canoe trip begins at Hattie Cove and follows the coast south and east to Michipicoten. On this demanding trip, prepare to encounter fog, wind, waves, cold temperatures, frigid water... and breathtaking scenery. Thomas McKenny, who travelled through in 1826, said it well, "The elements appear to have nothing else to do but amuse themselves." There is inland, flat-water canoeing on Lurch, Birch and Louie Lakes, although with no road, access is difficult. Both of the river canoe routes, the White and the Pukaskwa, are fast-running and filled with rapids. For more information, write to: The Friends of Pukaskwa, General Delivery, Heron Bay, Ont. P0T 1R0. The park office can be reached at (807) 229-0801.

PIC RIVER AND THE TRADING POSTS

It took the voyageurs about a fortnight to travel from the Sault to Grand Portage, paddling against the west wind through Superior's frigid waters. Therefore when Daniel Harmon and his brigade spied Pic River fort on their first journey west in 1800, they were ecstatic. At sight of the North West Company's buildings set behind a nine-foot-high stockade, many of the 350 men raised their paddles and cheered.

Fort Pic was a welcome stop on the trip west. It also marked the entrance to an important canoe route up the Pic and Black Rivers to James Bay. An earlier post consisting of a warehouse and two-room log house had been established near the mouth of the Pic between 1775-91 by independent fur trader, Gabriel Coté. When the North West Company took over, they built a shed, a 5-room house with glass windows and a stable. A third post, operated by the competing XY Company—"the new firm"—included a substantial warehouse and residence, plus a forge and powder magazine.

The river mouth had been a gathering place for centuries. The sluggish mud-coloured River "Pic," or "Peek," is possibly an abbreviated form of the Ojibwe word *pekatek*, meaning "mud." (It also may refer to being able to see the "long stretch of river," *Bigitigong*, from Lake Superior.) The Pic provided an important route north into Cree territory. Sturgeon, char, whitefish, pike and pickerel were bountiful, and a remarkable stretch of sand dunes led to a large, open, grassy area suitable for Ojibwe encampments.

Twenty-one years after Harmon's first visit, the North West and Hudson's Bay Companies joined forces, and the Pic Fort became an HBC post. By the native summer grounds and a good river route to James Bay, the location suited the fur traders well. However, their prosperity didn't last. The downturn also hurt the local Indians who were already suffering heavily from disease. In John Marsh's study, "The Human History of the Pukaskwa National Park Area, 1650-1975," he quotes Chief Factor Thomas McMurray reporting in 1832,

HBC Pic Post, c. 1900. Over time, the post has been covered over by sand. But on occasion, sands have shifted to reveal the tops of pickets.

> I passed an agreeable winter at this Place, and am as happy & content, as a poor Old N'Wester, can be.... Small furs have failed, and Indians, for want of the Means of Subsistence owing to the disappearance of Hares... suffered much from starvation, of course, their exertions were damped, and they made no hunts.

Trapping continued in a small way. Marsh reports that in 1877, primed furs from Fort Pic numbered: 27 bears, 97 beavers, 68 fishers, 238 lynx, 3 silver foxes, 10 cross foxes, 7 red foxes, 228 martens, 333 minks, 1179 musquash, and 55 otters. There was also some commercial fishing.

In November 1882, Chief Factor Gilbert Spence saw a large, unfamiliar canoe rounding the bend in the river. Fearing attack, Spence hid his wife and children at the rear of the post while he and two servants took up positions with their rifles. The canoeists turned out to be surveyors for the Canadian Pacific Railway. The idea of a railway was news to the isolated family. During its construction years the railway proved to be a boon for the HBC. But on completion of the railway in the mid-1880s, the Pic post declined. Indians began trading with independent traders along the tracks. In an 1884 letter from Spence to P.W. Bell at Michipicoten, Spence wrote: "Our collection of furs are very small as none of our Indians has been down scarcely. No doubt some of the beggars are trading along the

Railway line with the C.P.R. people." In an effort to remain the centre of economic exchange, the HBC followed the Ojibwe who had moved upriver to Heron Bay and to Mobert, nearer the railway, and by 1888 the Pic Post was closed.

In the late 1930s, the area once again gained attention. The Marathon Corporation recognized that the site of the old Hudson's Bay post would be ideal for a logging camp. Land contours were smoothed for easier vehicle travel, disturbing the buried remains of the fort. Parts of the stockade that were uncovered in the 1940s are once again buried under the constantly-shifting sand.

PIC RIVER MOUTH SAND DUNES

It is an atmospheric place. In the chilly early morning air, mist rises from the relatively warm waters of the Pic River. From Superior, the path of the river is traced in a serpentine trail in the sky. The site has been inhabited since the middle Woodland period (c.500B.C.-500A.D.). One can almost hear the laughter of children playing in the dunes and the quiet words of the elders coming from the camp.

Englishman Dr. John J. Bigsby described the Pic River: "...it pours out an ash-coloured, and, when swollen, a reddish-yellow water, tinging the lake for a mile or two round its mouth, and derived from beds of yellow and white clay some distance up the river." A marvellous dune complex on the north side of the Pic River mouth is the largest on Superior's north shore. Slowly the sand dunes advance in a north-easterly direction, eating into the spruce forest where rare grasses and plants, such as Franklin's Lady-Slipper and Northern Twayblade—two species of orchids—are found.

Periodically the wind shifts the dunes to reveal shards of pottery, chard pipe-bowls and arrowheads, and occasionally something more....

THE HIDDEN GRAVE

The following story is reported by Wayland Drew in The Haunted Shore. It was the morning after a great storm. Two men out for a stroll along the beach idly scanned the sand. One of them noticed what looked like a line of logs sticking up. It was the palisade of the former post. Further digging exposed a carefully-stitched roll of birch bark. Obviously something valuable was inside.

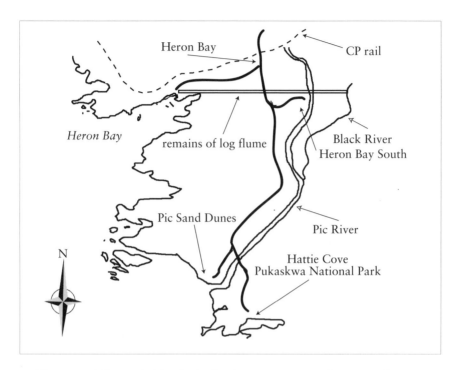

They carefully peeled back the bark covering, revealing a wicker wrapper... and a wrapper of doe skin... and then, the skeleton of a little girl, with a string of beads in her hands. The two men crouched, lost in thought. They gently rewrapped the little corpse and reburied it in the sand. Following another shift in weather, the palisade was once again covered, along with the unnamed little girl buried by grieving parents so many storms ago.

LOUIS AGASSIZ'S "BREACH OF PROPRIETY"

It was a superb fish, the most impressive sturgeon Louis Agassiz had ever seen. Agassiz, a noted Swiss-American biologist from Harvard University, was leading a scientific expedition along the North Shore in 1850 to study the lake's natural species.

When an Ojibwe fisherman dragged his catch on shore, Agassiz approached. "Ask if we may study and sketch the fish," Agassiz instructed his interpreter. The Ojibwe agreed and settled back to watch as one of Agassiz's party took out easels, pencils, and other equipment from his pack.

The scientist and his friends began measuring the great fish, commenting on its features. The sketch proceeded slowly. It was criticized, erased and started over again. The work was leisurely and methodical.

The Ojibwe man and his family watched patiently. After several hours, noting the Ojibwe hadn't moved, one of Agassiz's party asked why. "They are waiting for you to finish," the interpreter replied. Agassiz's man was confused, "Do they find our work that interesting?"

The guide shook his head, then pointing to the sturgeon said, "That is their dinner. They haven't eaten all day." The Agassiz narrative reads, "We were shocked at having committed such a breach of propriety, but the sketch not being finished, we proposed to them to lunch meanwhile on some of our port and biscuit, to which they readily agreed." When he finally left Pic River, the Harvard professor not only took with him fresh knowledge of Lake Superior sturgeon but also a lesson in good manners.

HERON BAY

Heron Bay was established as a railway village after the arrival of the CPR in 1885. Coal brought by steamship was unloaded at a small island known as CPR Island and carried by rail to chutes alongside the main line, where steam locomotives waited to be refuelled.

THE GHOST TOWN OF HERON BAY SOUTH:

The Roar of the Flume

Flume in foreground, and village of Heron Bay South in background.

Lumber operations suddenly mushroomed in the mid-1930s when two rival paper companies—the Ontario Paper Company owned by the Chicago Tribune, and Marathon Pulp Mills of Canada headquartered in Wisconsin—leased timber land on the Black and Pic Rivers respectively. There was only one problem: the rivers join about two miles from the mouth of the Pic.

Logs from the Black River crossed the Pic River on this elevated flume.

Both companies wanted to float their pulp logs down to Superior. How could they keep them separate?

The solution was dramatic enough to be reported in *Ripley's Believe It Or Not*. Both firms contributed to the cost of constructing an elevated flume, to carry the Ontario Paper Company's logs 5.6 kms (3-1/2 miles) from the Black River to Lake Superior. This meant crossing over the Pic River and so a 90m (300-ft.) bridge was constructed 24m (80 ft.) above the water. But that wasn't all that was needed. A 90m (300-ft.) wharf, a barking plant and a pumping station to supply the flume with water were also erected. Beside the flume bridge over the Pic River, a new village named Heron Bay South arose.

The imaginative project proved successful. In 1939, its first full year of operation, 25,000 cords of pulpwood were shipped to the Ontario Paper Company's newsprint mill in Thorold. Heron Bay South expanded. However, by 1964, the company was cutting trees so far inland that it made more sense to ship the logs by rail making the flume obsolete. One by one, the structures at Heron Bay South began to disappear and eventually the flume itself, although its massive supports still stand. At the Heron Bay South community site, the road and some foundations remain.

MARATHON: ONE BOOM AFTER ANOTHER

While some communities experience a boom once in their history, Marathon is among those that boast three. Marathon's roots trace back to the mid-1880s and the construction of the CPR. Then known as Peninsula Harbour, it was a community of clapboard hovels that earned the label, "the wickedest town in Canada."

Peninsula Harbour was a base of operations—of all kinds. Bootleggers, gamblers and prostitutes all helped to separate the hard-working railway navvies from their earnings. When men weren't gambling or brawling, they wrestled steel rails, wooden ties, coal, food, horses and equipment off steamships and onto wagons for the trip inland to the rail line. Two particular steamers, *The Butcher Maid* and *The Butcher Boy*, meant stevedore work of a different kind. Cattle were driven up the hill to the line, then from camp to camp. Each camp slaughtered its own meat and wrapped the carcasses in cheesecloth before hanging them on tree limbs for storage.

At its peak, thousands of men worked in and around Peninsula Harbour. However, with the rail line completed, the crowds drifted away and Peninsula Harbour began to fade. For several years, a granite quarry was the area's principal industry. Then, during the Great Depression, it also closed but its stone can be seen in Toronto's former Eaton's College Street store (now College Park Mall), as well as in Detroit and Chicago. By 1935, Peninsula Harbour was little more than twenty-eight residents and a post office.

Nevertheless the village was far from finished. In the 1940s, the Marathon Paper Mills Company decided to build a large pulp mill and chemical plant nearby. Within three months of the announcement, more than five hundred men were hard at work. In gratitude, the town changed its name to Everest, the surname of Marathon's president. Mr. Everest may have been honoured, but postal authorities were unimpressed. Stating the new name would be confused with the community of Everett, they refused to recognize it. Everest became Marathon once again.

Marathon may have had a name, but there were no telephones, street lights or sidewalks, and its dirt roads were impassable after a rain. Marathon's first bank opened in 1944 after the bank manager jumped off the train with $2,000 stuffed in a packsack. Bankers' hours did not apply at his log-and-canvas Dominion branch. The teller was available even at midnight!

The construction phase was long. Dormitory life was tedious for the single men, and annoying for wives (many of whom were war brides) waiting for the completion of family homes. 1,300 men were employed to construct the mill and townsite. Chapples, Marathon's only grocery store, had difficulty keeping up with demand. The owner's apology, "We haven't any now but we are expecting them by the end of the week" was recalled in Jean Boultbee's *Pic, Pulp and People*. One exasperated shopper retorted, "Oh, Chapples is the mother of Marathon. They are always expecting!"

In 1960, the long-awaited completion of Highway 17 from the east lessened Marathon's isolation. The town boasted 2,000 residents... that is until boom number three.

In 1981, gold deposits at nearby Hemlo proved to be the largest discovered in Canada in seventy-five years. By the time the first gold bar was shipped from the mine four years later, the town had mushroomed into a community of over 5,000 people. Today Hemlo boasts three of Canada's largest gold mines, and Marathon continues to thrive.

Marathon's Dominion Bank branch opened in 1944. (Note the name Peninsula crossed out and replaced by Everest in 1941)

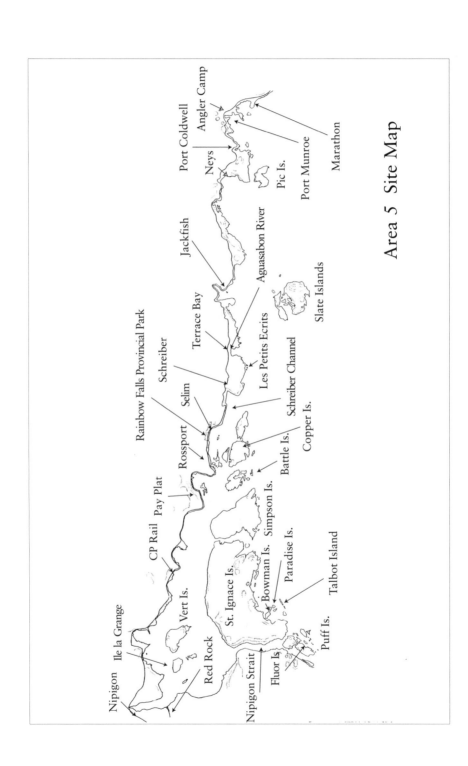

Nipigon

Ile la Grange

Red Rock

Vert Is.

CP Rail

Pay Plat

St. Ignace Is.

Nipigon Strait

Fluor Is

Bowman Is.

Simpson Is.

Paradise Is.

Puff Is.

Talbot Island

Rossport

Rainbow Falls Provincial Park

Selim

Schreiber

Terrace Bay

Jackfish

Les Petits Ecrits

Aguasabon River

Schreiber Channel

Copper Is.

Battle Is.

Slate Islands

Port Coldwell

Angler Camp

Neys

Pic Is.

Port Munroe

Marathon

Area 5 Site Map

5

AREA FIVE: SUPERIOR'S NORTH SHORE AND ISLANDS

ANGLER POW CAMP

The Escape that Shocked the Country

During World War II, Canada interned 35,046 Prisoners of War and Japanese-Canadians in 26 main compounds and dozens of smaller camps in Canada. Prisoners worked at lumbering, farming and manufacturing. Lake Superior's inhospitable and remote shore hosted three large POW compounds at Angler, Neys, and Red Rock. A number of smaller logging POW camps were located in the rough interior along the White and Magpie Rivers. Of all the attempted escapes from Canadian POW camps, the largest and the most cunning was masterminded at Angler just west of Peninsula Harbour.

It was mid-April, and tension was running high amongst the 559 German prisoners. After months of clandestine preparations, the date of a planned escape—April 20th, the Fuhrer's birthday—was drawing near. Compasses had been fashioned from magnetized razor blades and needles; prisoner uniforms had been redesigned as civilian clothes; maps had been drawn, copied and distributed. Tin cans filled with kitchen fat would serve as candles (complete with wicks made from underwear drawstring). They had even blackmailed a guard into handing over a radio, which they hid in a model of the prized German battleship, *Bismarck*. Camp authorities congratulated the prisoners on their workmanship, unaware that the ship's gun

Angler POW camp during WWII

turrets were knobs for operating the forbidden radio.

The tunnel stretched 45m (150 ft.) outside the camp wall. Side tunnels enabled men to move from barrack to barrack as they covered for tunnel excavators at roll call. Since Angler was situated on sand, digging had been relatively easy. The challenge was to prevent the tunnel from collapsing. Reinforcements were constructed from wood braces that were wrenched from beneath the barracks and painstakingly sawed to size using straightened phonograph springs stretched between two handles.

Every detail was checked and rechecked. Everything was in place... and then it began to rain and rain for three days straight. Tension grew while tunnels filled with water. On the morning of April 18, 1941, the horrified men discovered the excavation was beginning to collapse. By noon, 30 cms (12 inches) of water filled the tunnel. They would have to leave that night after roll call or not at all.

At dark, they lowered themselves into the freezing water of the black tunnel. Crouching in a line, they waited for the men at the front to open the tunnel outside the fence. Every noise made their hearts skip a beat: was that gunfire? They knew if they were caught escaping they would be shot.

Finally, the line began to move. One by one they emerged from the tunnel, scrambled across a gully and stole into the refuge of Superior's dark forests.Then one escapee stumbled over the digging tools left near the tunnel opening. Alerted by the sound, a guard decided to investigate. Moments later, he bounded to the phone. The unthinkable had occurred: an unknown

Corpses of Angler escapees shot by Canadian authorities were returned to the camp on dogsled, April 1941

number of German POWs had escaped.

Only 28 of over 80 hopefuls managed to escape. Five were shot (and two later died) as they emerged from a nearby railway shack. Four others managed to board a boxcar on an eastbound freight train. Unfortunately for them, one POW's cough alerted an RCMP officer. Most of the remaining escapees were quickly tracked down and returned to the camp.

Prisoners Horst Liebeck and Karl Heinz-Grund were more successful. Arriving at the CPR tracks just as a westbound freight train slowed for a curve, they managed to haul themselves aboard. Leaping from car to car, they searched for an entry point. Finally, one hatch began to yield. After what seemed like hours, it gave way, revealing an unwelcome cargo—a full load of block ice. Military guards stopped the train three times. Afraid they would freeze to death, the men left the car at Kenora, and headed into the woods. They built a fire, changed into civilian clothes, grabbed a much-needed nap and even shaved before boarding another westbound train to Winnipeg where they purchased a newspaper with headlines announcing their escape.

Liebeck and Grund continued west hoping to reach Vancouver and eventually Japan. But their luck ran out in Alberta. A suspicious railway guard in Medicine Hat alerted police, and the two men were captured while walking along the highway. To the Germans' utter amazement, local citizens treated them like celebrities. Well-fed, they were sent back to the camp, but only after signing autographs for well-wishers who gathered to see them off. Back at Angler Camp, even the Commandant shook their hands, "As a sportsman I congratulate you"—then sentenced them to 28 days in solitary confinement.

At the end of the war, the prisoners were repatriated to Germany. Horst Liebeck never forgot the beauty of the Ontario wilderness or the warmth of the Canadians he met during his brief fling with freedom. Like several hundred other POWs who waited out the war in Canada, he later returned to find employment, raise a family and entertain his grandchildren with harrowing tales of his great escape.

In 1942, Angler became an internment camp for over 700 Japanese-Canadians. 300 were subsequently released to work leaving 425 at the camp. The very rough road leads south to the site from Highway 17. Today, only foundations and scattered items can be found there.

PORT COLDWELL: OF FISH AND RAILS

Port Coldwell sprang to life thanks to its excellent harbour. Near good fish stocks, it was also a supply depot for the construction of the railway in the early 1880s. The village was named after Robert Coldwell, a well-liked Scottish foreman of a CPR blasting crew.

In addition to the fishermen's homes, Port Coldwell (also referred to as Port Caldwell) consisted of a few railway section houses, a small station and a general store. After the construction workers left, fishermen maintained the railway tradition of serving liquor at the store, where patrons requested their libation from a neat row of teapots. The arrival of a steamboat, or of a train to fill its water tanks or load crates of frozen fish were welcome connections to the outside world.

Not that there was time to be bored. The fisherman's routine began at daybreak as they reefed their sails and headed out 40 kms (25 miles) into unpredictable Superior. Arriving home, many of the men had to soak their cramped fingers in warm water in order to straighten them after an exhausting day of hauling nets and dressing fish.

Around 1915, the five Nicoll brothers arrived from Blind River, determined to break the monopoly held for so many years by the Booth Fish Co. The brothers were shrewd and introduced innovative ways to catch and pack fish. They opened new markets for their own product, and paying fair prices to others, they successfully set up a market for fresh fish using the railroad. Soon, lake trout and whitefish from the Nicoll operation were being served aboard CPR dining cars on the transcontinental route, and in many of the finest restaurants across Canada and the U.S.

The fishermen's sailboats were retired once the Nicolls bought three steam tugs in the 1920s. By now, the more than 100 residents had a school, a small chapel and a boarding house for visiting Mounties, miners, loggers and preachers. Each summer, a tent village was set up by natives during blueberry-picking season. As many as 15 tons of blueberries were loaded onto trains destined for Saskatchewan's Saskatoon Fruit Company.

In 1922, artist A.Y. Jackson and others of the celebrated Group of Seven discovered the picturesque cove. Each October, they would arrive, pitch their tents just west of Coldwell Bay and take expeditions to Pic Island, the Slates, Jackfish, and other compelling sites. Jackson describes "a feeling of space, dramatic lighting, the stark forms of rocky hills and dead trees and beyond, Lake Superior, shining like burnished silver."

In the 1950s, an unwelcome visitor arrived via the St. Lawrence Seaway: the sea lamprey. This creature survives by fixing its rasp-like mouth to the

Steamer coming into Port Coldwell

sides of fish—it favours lake trout—and sucking nourishment until the host fish dies. Lampreys have no natural enemies in the Great Lakes. Whitefish and trout have no natural defense against them. As the fish catches drastically declined, so did the population of Port Coldwell. The closing of the fishery in the 1960s and the destruction of the old CPR village store in 1963 marked the passing of an era.

Today the main road still winds from the railroad tracks down to the sheltered harbour. Remnants of a dock remain, but all of the buildings are gone. In the cemetery, a granite stone surrounded by wildflowers marks the grave of Robert Coldwell. Before his death in Scotland, he expressed a wish to be buried, not in his homeland but in the Canadian North Shore community that still haunted his memory.

NEYS PROVINCIAL PARK: A FORMER POW CAMP

Today, visitors follow trails along the shores of Neys Provincial Park, to enjoy the same views that hundreds of desperate men once risked their lives to escape. The inmates of Prisoner of War Camp 100 were mostly Germans, with a few displaced Japanese-Canadians who were imprisoned from 1941-46. Forced to work logging the Pic and Little Pic river valleys, the prisoners were soon cutting most of the pulpwood used by the Pigeon Timber Company. In 1943, Prisoners accounted for 90,000 of the total 98,000 cords of wood harvested by the company. It was cheap labour. While regular loggers were paid $6 per cord of wood cut and piled, prisoners earned only $4.50, of which $4.00 went to cover food and clothing. The balance was credited to their personal account.

German POWs were divided into two categories: the "greys," largely comprised of ordinary soldiers, and the "blacks," potentially violent die-hard Nazis, considered an escape risk. Neys was one of Canada's nine "black camps." As a result it was enclosed with three separate barbed-wire fences, 3m (10 ft.) high, with a guard tower at each corner. But this did not deter men from attempting to escape. Pauline Dean's *Sagas of Superior* highlights some of the more creative failures: two POWs who carved a kayak with the intention of crossing the lake; and the prisoner who whittled a set of wooden skates but learned, to his dismay, that Superior does not freeze across to the American shore.

One fatal escape involved Germany's 1936 Olympic high-jump

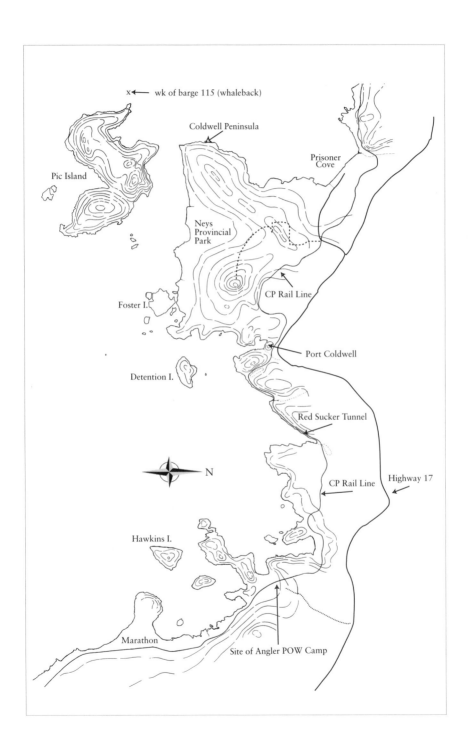

Neys German POW camp during WWII

champion, Martin Mueller. The policeman who apprehended him was seen afterwards in Jackfish at the Lakeview Hotel, shaking so badly he could barely hold his drink. He recounted running into Mueller in the dark in a rock cut near Jackfish. Although Mueller was armed only with a stick, he refused to surrender, forcing the officer to shoot him. Ironically, when the collapse of Nazi Germany was imminent, escape attempts were more often made to avoid returning to the homeland. Some POWs had grown fond of Superior and desperately wanted to start a new life in Canada.

At the end of the war, Neys became a processing camp for POWs detained in Northwestern Ontario. They were inoculated and given shoes, towels and three sets of civilian clothes. Until it was dismantled in the early 1950s, the camp was turned into a minimum-security work camp for prisoners from the Thunder Bay area. Apparently, more than a few of the barracks and other buildings were recycled into garages and sheds in Marathon. Although little marks this site where so many men longed for their freedom, strong winds off the lake periodically sweep away the sand, revealing cobblestone paths laid by the POWs.

Visitors now come to Neys to camp, boat, picnic and hike along scenic trails including the 2-km (3.2-mile) Lookout Trail, which offers a spectacular vista over the lake. Not surprisingly, they also come to enjoy Neys' beautiful 1.5-km (2.4-mile) long sand beach.

MAJESTIC PIC ISLAND

The Tragic End to Barge No. 115

Lawren Harris' powerful, stylized paintings of Pic Island evoke the very essence of this majestic island, its steep slopes rising out of the water to a peak of 240-m (800-ft.). Over 70 years after Harris painted the scene, we boated at dawn toward the formidable deep-purple silhouette looming over a silver sea. The same penetrating colours that Harris so dramatically conveyed on canvas. As we drew closer, Pic Island's impressive shape became more defined, deep vertical gashes creating the illusion of flying buttresses on a magnificent natural cathedral.

Pic Island is one of the few places in the region where herds of woodland caribou still roam, protected both by law and by the island's own passive hostility. Its defenses are effective. Boaters are warned to expect major compass deflections, especially off the east shore. Southerly winds often envelop the island in a cloak of fog. Except for Windy Bay, surrounding waters threaten visitors with jutting rocks and lurking shoals. On the west shore, the remains of a vessel are vivid testimony to one such victim.

Do not be fooled by the wreck's utilitarian name, *Barge No. 115*. This ship was part of a bizarre, innovative fleet designed by a man who withstood professional ridicule and changed shipping history. The inventor was Captain Alexander McDougall. His invention was a kind of vessel called a "whaleback." Designed with a rounded top and a flat bottom for maximum cargo hold, the shape was supposed to ensure strength and stability. Capt. McDougall tested miniatures in a large water tank in his home, demonstrating models to respected seamen. The response was always the same: "She'll roll over!" "You call that damned thing a boat? Why, it looks more like a pig!"

In 1888, McDougall himself financed the first whaleback, *No. 101*. Sailors called the freak vessel "McDougall's Nightmare." And in fact, shortly after it was launched, *No. 101* was accidentally towed onto rocks and smashed. Undaunted, the inventor went to Colgate Hoyt, an associate of John D. Rockerfeller, who needed to transport quantities of ore. Hoyt backed the dreamer and formed the American Steel Barge Company.

With Hoyt's capital, *Barges No. 102* and *103* were soon under construction, in spite of jeers from the shipping community. To everyone's astonishment, these ships performed well in all conditions. Whalebacks were soon sailing the ocean, and in 1893, the first whaleback passenger

Initially scorned by sailors as a "Pig Ship," the whaleback's unique design became popular in the early 1890s.

vessel, *Christopher Columbus*, was unveiled at the Chicago World's Fair. No one was laughing now. The inexpensive "pig-ship" became a growing threat to conventional ships.

The fleet did suffer a casuality or two. Laden with iron ore in mid-December 1899, the 76-m (256-ft.) *Barge No. 115* was under tow by the whaleback steamer, *Colgate Hoyt*. A sudden storm rocked the vessels so badly that the tow-line snapped. The *Colgate Hoyt*'s crew feared the worst. Before the barge vanished behind a wall of falling snow, blood-coloured water revealed a leak in the iron-filled cargo hold.

For five horrifying days, No.115 floundered in huge swells until Superior tossed it aground on Pic Island. With waves pounding the barge, the crew launched a raft, hoping to reach the mainland. After days adrift, they finally landed near Pic River. Soaked and frozen, the captain and his men tramped two days through dense bush before reaching a train station. The nine men were in grave condition after nine days of severe weather on only two days of rations. When the iron whaleback was discovered, it had been smashed beyond recovery.

In total, forty-three of these whaleback vessels were constructed. By 1896, nine years after the introduction of No. 101, the design had become obsolete, mainly because its small hatches hindered quick loading. The design was modified several times, creating ships known as "monitors," "turret ships," "turtlebacks" and "straightbacks," oddities that rocked convention.

ASHBURTON BAY AND THE DOOMED *JUDGE HART*

It was every captain's nightmare. Captain Burmister watched from the lifeboat as his 75-m (252-ft.) vessel began to disappear under Superior's angry grey waters.

Loaded with over 100,000 bushels of wheat at Port Arthur on November 24, 1942, Capt. Burmister's freighter, the *Judge Hart*, had headed out in typical November conditions: northwest winds peaking at 35 mph accompanied by rain, sleet and snow.

By 5 a.m. of the 26th, the *Judge Hart* was in serious trouble. Seas were crashing over the deck; blinding snow reduced visibility to zero; and perhaps most frightening of all, the ship was becoming encased in ice. To provide visibility, one of the wheelhouse windows had to be kept open. Inside, the temperature dropped so drastically that the wheelsman suffered frostbite.

The freighter pressed on, but by noon the next day, ice and wind had ripped away the vessel's radio antenna and the ship's depth-sounding machine was too coated in ice to function. Without communication, and unsure of their location, tensions grew. Somewhere off the Slate Islands, they were granted a short reprieve. The wind abated enough to slow the engines so that the men could chop ice off the bow and windlass. Capt. Burmister planned to use the anchor as a lead line to test the water's depth, but sooner than expected, he discovered their location with disturbing accuracy.

With a terrifying crunch, the *Judge Hart* ran aground. She was taking in water until a tarpaulin stretched over the hole did the trick. It seemed to be holding until the following day when the weather took a turn. Pounding waves began to ease the *Judge Hart* off the rock despite the engine's efforts to thrust her forward. Anticipating the worst, the Captain sent most of the crew to ships that were standing by. After the *Judge Hart* slipped off the rock and began to drift, Captain Burmister, himself, abandoned ship and watched it sink beneath the water.

According to Cris Kohl's *Dive Ontario Two!*, in 1990, divers discovered the *Judge Hart* in near-perfect condition in about 46.5m (155 ft.) of water near Simons Rock in Ashburton Bay, a set of radio headphones still sitting on the counter.

STEEL RIVER: MEETING THE DEVIL IN GOD'S COUNTRY

The North Shore has always known characters like Wild Bill Frazer—rough, gruff, rich in backwoods lore, somewhat lacking in social graces. Wild Bill owned the Lakeview Hotel in Jackfish, and also served as a canoe guide for the CPR in the 1920s and 1930s. One day, two British tourists, a bishop and a minister, arrived in Jackfish as guests of the Railway. Both were eager to take the CPR's three-day tour of the Steel River, Devil Lake and Big and Little Santoy Lakes. They clutched a promotional brochure promising "a most interesting one-hundred-and-seventy mile canoe cruise in virgin country" and "a sportsman to serve as an interesting and useful guide." *Interesting* is definitely what they got.

Wild Bill was an excellent guide with one odd quirk. He could not function without swearing. Every swarm of blackflies, every difficult portage and every uncooperative tent stake was addressed with a stream of profanity. The Anglican bishop and his ecclesiastical companion were increasingly scandalized by Wild Bill's foul tongue and made their displeasure known. Surely a grown man could face the challenges of God's country without invoking His name!

For three days, Wild Bill endured their scolding. He neither replied nor made any effort to curb his "expressive style." Finally, near the end of the trip, when they had reached the mouth of the Steel River, Wild Bill Frazer had had enough. *A History of Jackfish* relates that he overturned the canoe dumping the passengers and their possessions into the lake just beyond a sandbar, roaring, "All right, you Protestant bastards! I've put up with you for three long days. Well, you can just walk home from here!" With that he righted his canoe and paddled away, leaving the clergymen to flounder in the drink. (This was Wild Bill's last guiding expedition for the CPR.)

JACKFISH: FROM NORTH SHORE HUB TO GHOST TOWN

About 25 kms (16 miles) east of Terrace Bay along Highway 17, a gravel road at the top of Jackfish Lake hill heads south towards Superior, ending at the railway tracks. In order to reach the ghost town of Jackfish, walk west along the tracks. After traipsing through several rock cuts, one spies the crumbling cement coal chute and the water tower—once Jackfish's very reason for being. Without refilling the water tanks at stops such as

Jackfish, no CPR steam train could complete the long journey from Sudbury to Thunder Bay.

At the height of the summer shipping season, the scene was a busy one. Alongside the 180m (600-ft.) trestle dock, a coal freighter from Pittsburgh prepared to unload its cargo. Carrying two to three tons at one time, small gondola cars would transport the coal to a spur line to be loaded onto railway cars. Three hundred men worked from six in the morning to eleven at night. Without wearing hard hats, they worked on sagging planks high above the ground, and under the coal chutes. This was the Depression, and they were thankful to have a job. Despite the long hours, they still had enough energy to kick up their heels at dances held on the coal boats every other night. Fiddles, harmonicas, and accordians sang out into the wee hours.

As a fishing station, Jackfish had humble beginnings. The Norwegian fisherman Ben Almos started it all. Arriving in the 1880s he must have felt right at home here among the rock-bound inlets of Jackfish Bay. As the industry expanded, schoolboys could earn pocket money by pushing wheelbarrows piled high with boxes of frozen fish from the packing house up to the tracks. Women carrying buckets of water from the lake to their homes would nod to the fishermen as they were putting their nets onto drying reels.

Jackfish c.1940s

For a few years in the 1930s and 1940s, a pulpwood operation thrived. Cut in camps near Big Santoy Lake, the logs were floated down river to Jackfish. Some were loaded directly onto freighters for transport to mills in Green Bay, Wisconsin. Others were transported in giant booms to the Slate Islands where they were loaded onto U.S.-bound vessels.

The town prospered. The one-room schoolhouse was well-attended, as were the social clubs. Jackfish's hockey team was one of the best on the North Shore. Once a month, clergymen would arrive to hold services in the Catholic and Protestant churches and the priests would send a local child door to door reminding the residents to attend. No herding was necessary to swell the ranks at Jackfish's notorious watering hole, the Lakeview

Waiting for the train

Hotel. It was a magnet for residents, nearby loggers and anyone on the north shore who could hop a train to town.

The hotel had a reputation for rowdiness. Jack Yates, the bartender and bouncer, once found himself bounced through the window, over the porch and into the yard. Serious brawls were broken up by Johnny Lia. Yates would bang on the staircase, and the large intimidating Finn would appear. Another of the town characters was Rodin, a Norwegian hermit. Children used to raid his strawberry patch until he employed the ultimate deterrent—he spat his chewing tobacco all over the fruits and vegetables.

In the latter part of the Depression, a large L-shaped government dock was built. Jackfish seemed destined to become one of the most important towns between the Sault and Thunder Bay. But luck was not on its side. First the arrival of the sea lamprey sucked the life out of the fishery. Then came the first haunting whistle of a diesel locomotive, signalling doom for the coal industry. The fiery

Manicured garden with fountain. Coal trestle dock in background. Both are now gone.

destruction of the Lakeview Hotel sealed the town's fate. With no employment prospects, Jackfish residents packed up and left. The descent from bustling hub to ghost town was swift. By 1963, everyone was gone.

Strolling the empty beach today one still finds scattered patches of Pennsylvania coal ground by the waves. The remains of the enormous coal dock are visible in the water. Near the tracks, several houses slowly succumb to the encroaching forest, their sagging doors swinging slightly in the breeze. Around the remains of the Nicol cabin, blue delphiniums, planted so many years ago, still grow. Regularly, a CPR train rumbles down the same right of way, carved more than a century ago from some of the world's oldest rock. For that fleeting moment, Jackfish returns.

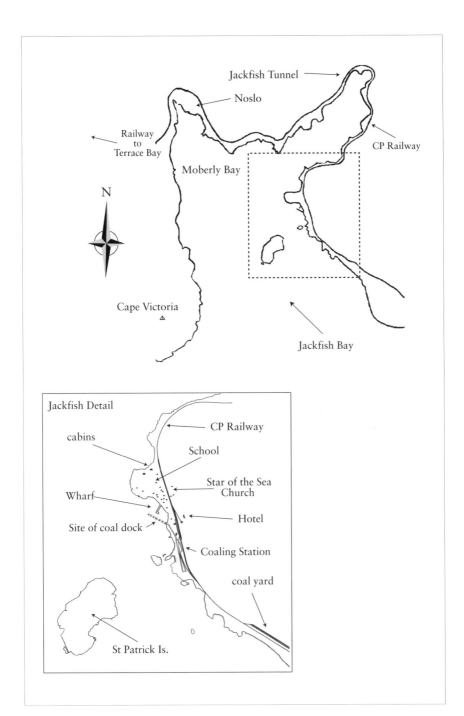

Jackfish Tunnel

Noslo

Railway
to
Terrace Bay

CP Railway

Moberly Bay

N

Cape Victoria

Jackfish Bay

Jackfish Detail

CP Railway

cabins

School

Star of the Sea
Church

Wharf

Hotel

Site of coal dock

Coaling Station

coal yard

St Patrick Is.

NOSLO AND THE LAST SPIKE

"Right here," the man with the close-cropped grey hair and moustache indicated the steel rail between his feet. He looked up at the others who nodded in agreement. Then he reached a tired arm to seize the sledgehammer's handle. Another man pulled a spike out of a bag, and knelt to the rail. One by one, the men took turns driving the spike home.

It was May 16, 1935, at a spot just west of Jackfish Bay. The men were gathered to commemorate the completion of the Montreal to Winnipeg leg of Canada's transcontinental railway, an engineering feat so massive that few people in the 1880s believed it could be accomplished. Some of the celebrants had been young railway construction workers as the same scene was enacted exactly 50 years before.

In 1885, the CPR railway had been completed north of Superior, at an astronomical cost in both dollars and lives. General Manager William Van Horne, one of the driving forces behind the railway, called the unyielding,

Railway navvies working near the Jackfish tunnel. One mile of the route near here had to be blasted from the sheer rock cliffs.

impenetrable rock, and morass of bogs of Superior's North Shore "two hundred miles of engineering impossibilities." (One especially troublesome bog ate seven layers of CPR rails.) The most expensive mile of track, blasted through solid rock near Jackfish, cost $700,000 (in the currency of the 1880s). It was hard, dangerous work, carried out by 12,000 men, 1,500 horses and explosives: dynamite and nitroglycerine. Blasting the right-of-way through North Shore Shield rock caused more than a few disasters. Several unfortunate blasting crews disappeared "in a cloud of pink mist." At one camp, an explosion of nitroglycerine killed every single man.

In *The Last Spike*, Pierre Berton describes the scene in summers: "Throats choked with the dust of shattered rocks, ears ringing with dynamite blasts, arms aching from swinging sledges or toting rails, skin smarting and itching from a hundred insect bites, nostrils assailed by a dozen stenches from horse manure to human sweat..." In the winter, track was sometimes laid on top of snow five feet deep in order to make progress. The men worked in minus 50 Fahrenheit, with winds that "sliced through the thickest garments."

When the last spike was finally driven home in 1935, it seemed the troubles were behind them. Just as they unveiled the historic monument, a CPR train came rumbling down the track. With a blast of his steam whistle, the engineer saluted the men, and their monument to the "National Dream."

New troubles were in store for train conductors like Mugs McCuaig who remembered:

> I had to have a pretty good sense of humour to do the trek I did every day: 300 feet of solid granite rising on one side of you, and 400 feet of that cold, black Lake Superior water below you.... I tell you, I hold a record in the history of the CPR, a record no one has ever beaten or even wants to try and beat: three derailments and one head-on collision in one month, January 1917. There were several times in my day we would derail and go thundering into the bush. Nobody ever got killed on any train I was driving, but I sure picked up more dead and injured men along the tracks than you'd ever believe, by God.

Even after the railway was complete, the Superior stretch was a challenge.

THE SLATE ISLANDS: METEORITES AND MAGIC

On two occasions, NASA scientists scoured the Slate Islands to research an explosion thousands of times more powerful than the atomic bomb that devastated Hiroshima. From the evidence, they concluded that a 30-km-wide (19-mile) asteroid had struck the site of the Slates. When this hurtling space rock hit earth, the instantaneous transfer of energy into raging heat caused the rock to vapourize. Enough dust was tossed into the atmosphere to bring weeks of darkness. A mountain range thrust up, only to be slowly worn down over millions of years by weather and glaciation, finally to be flooded during the formation of Lake Superior. The Slate Islands of today are what remains of the central cone from the original impact crater.

Scientists study meteorite strikes to determine their concentration of minerals (an example is nickel-rich Sudbury). Impact sites also provide information that helps scientists read scars on other planets. The sites also help explain the nature of gravity, the volatility of space and the likelihood of our planet being hit by other meteorites. Each year the earth is bombarded by an estimated 4,500 kgs (10,000 lbs.) of space debris. Small meteorites are of minor consequence. However, the possibility of a "big hit" is of vital concern. We need only look back to the massive comet that struck South America 65 million years ago, to understand the monumental destruction a meteorite could inflict. That comet, a conglomerate of space ice and dirt, caused such environmental chaos that most living things (including dinosaurs) became extinct.

Natural and Human History

Its cosmic creation is only one part of the allure of this island cluster. Crowned by the Slate Islands lighthouse, the cliffs on the south side of Patterson Island are breathtaking. Also on Patterson Island (named for Lieutenant Governor William Patterson of Saskatchewan who leased the island for a time), a fantastical volcanic sculpture garden has been carved near Horace Point: here a bird, there a giant head submerged to its chin. In several places, the island's densely forested shores open up to cobble and gravel beaches. On Golden Slipper Bay, the rocks are awash with a subtle expanse of purple.

Because of the lake's cooling effects, rare arctic and alpine plants thrive here like the narrow-leafed Dryas Drumondii (not found again for another 1,600 kms [1,000 miles] northwest). Another unusual plant, Polygonum

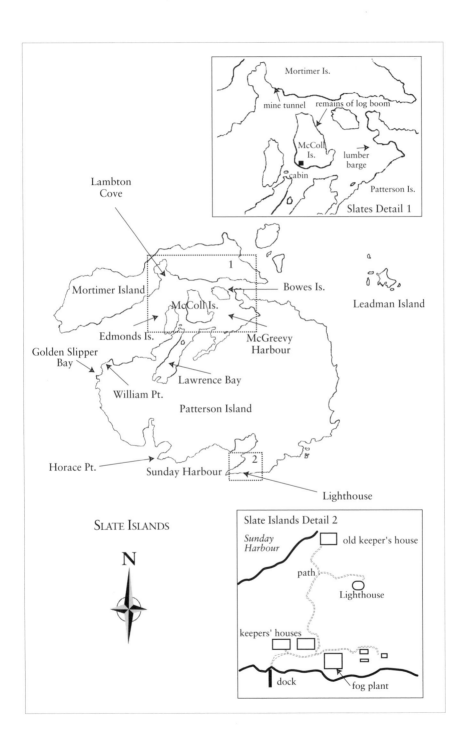

Mortimer Is.

mine tunnel   remains of log boom

McColl
Is.

lumber
barge

cabin

Patterson Is.

Slates Detail 1

Lambton
Cove

Mortimer Island

Bowes Is.

Leadman Island

McColl Is.

Edmonds Is.

McGreevy
Harbour

Golden Slipper
Bay

Lawrence Bay

William Pt.

Patterson Island

Horace Pt.

Sunday Harbour

Lighthouse

SLATE ISLANDS

N

Slate Islands Detail 2

Sunday
Harbour   old keeper's house

path

Lighthouse

keepers' houses

dock   fog plant

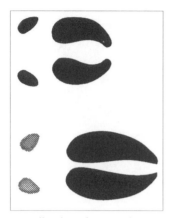

Woodland caribou track (top) and moose track (bottom)

Viviparum, is an Inuit delicacy eaten with seal oil. The Slates are also home to Ontario's largest herd of woodland caribou. At one time, these animals roamed as far as Manitoulin Island on Lake Huron's North Channel, but were forced north as their habitat was disturbed by humans. In 1990, Ministry of Natural Resources officials noticed that many of the 600 caribou were not molting, a strong indication of ill health. Their suspicions proved correct. With a meagre winter food supply, the herd's numbers dwindled to about 100.

Human sites have been found on these remote islands dating to the Terminal Woodland period circa A.D. 1000. In more recent history, the first keeper of the Sunday Harbour lighthouse arrived with his family in 1902. It was a familiar sight to see the keeper's sons rowing to Jackfish in their 5-m (16-ft.) skiff and returning at dusk with a lantern at the bow, throwing light with a reflecting pan. Later, the commercial fishermen built a fishing station on McColl Island. Their cabin has recently been restored as a rustic retreat by the Lions Club.

Signs abound of the miners, loggers and workers who made these island their base: abandoned mine adits; rotting lumber camps; and iron hooks drilled into the rock to attach giant log booms. Before 1935 several companies timbered the Slates. The Pigeon Timber Company followed towing logs from the Little Pic River to the islands for transshipment to the United States. Pigeon also operated a lumber mill at Fort William, so they separated saw logs from pulpwood at the Slates using a "sorting jack" (essentially a raft towed by a small tug that allowed men to separate the logs into two booms).

Jimmy Cross was on the Slates during this era and recalls the scuttling of an old scow in McGreevy Harbour. A steam-operated crane for loading coal onto tugs, barges and the pulpwood-loading machine was mounted on the boat *Mickey Mouse* (named after its operator). Before winter one year, Pigeon Timber Company management requested that all remaining logs be lifted on shore to prevent water damage. During this operation, the crane operator accidentally dropped a number of logs, puncturing the scow's hull and deck. After that, *Mickey Mouse* was retired to McGreevy Harbour and used as an office and dock. The Harbour was also home to 50-60 men who worked the pulpwood-loading machine. This was a boat with a conveyor belt used for lifting logs from the water into freighters for shipment to Detroit mills. Much of the loading crew worked inside the ships, organizing the logs to maximize space. Coal to fuel the boats and loading machine was stored on McColl Island.

In 1985, Ontario established a Natural Environment Provincial Park. The Slate Islands are now a wildlife sanctuary and a haven for kayakers and other boaters, sport fishermen and anyone seeking the remote and the enchanting.

TERRACE BAY: BOOM TOWN MEMORIES

In May 1945, a small group of men trudged along a bumpy road near Black Siding, a CPR flag stop with all of two residents: a section-hand and his wife. Led by Charles Craig, Vice-President of the giant paper manufacturer Kimberly-Clark, the surveyors were searching for an ideal location to build a pulp mill and company town. They found it not far from Black where the pulpwood was plentiful and the Aguasabon River provided water power for the mill and a place to float logs. There was also the railway.

Directly after WWII, there was a hunger for employment, even in blackfly country. The first 100 men arrived by freight train, most with only the clothes on their backs. Skilled tradesmen and labourers, they had come to build a sulphate mill and a town. One worker, Joseph Kennedy, recalled those days,

> I landed here about two o'clock in the morning with two dollars in my pocket. You know, new parka and the old grey Fedora hat of those days after the war. A lot of the people that came were like myself, just out of the armed services. A lot of them were married, working for 60 cents an hour. We all lived in the camps. All the bunkhouses were brought in on flat car. They were made of B.C. fir. Beautiful wood... but you know the winter here—how cold it is.

What happens when a population explodes from 2 to 2,000 in the middle of the back woods? In September 1946, the first ten families moved into their new homes. Groceries were a gravel-truck-ride away in the town of Schreiber. As for water, residents would tie red rags outside their houses and for 25 cents a barrel it would be delivered. A section of the road was an old moose trail that met up with the rail track, and so moose, deer and bear were commonly seen sauntering along. (The Trans-Canada Highway had yet to reach Terrace Bay.)

By the winter of 1947, over a thousand people had flooded in. Attempting to maintain civility and control, the company declared the town and labour camps dry. But nothing could stop the arrival of gamblers and bootleggers, who as a smoke-screen, took on menial jobs. On one occasion, however, the company was glad to have them around.

Every Sunday night it was customary to serve turkey. One day, the stuffed fowl was cooked in the morning, cooled and reheated for supper causing a violent outbreak of food poisoning. 1,000 people were sick at one time! The two in the gravest condition were taken to the two cots in the tiny hospital and given the only intravenous fluids available. Dr. McCausland asked someone go door to door requesting any secreted whiskey. He administered water and castor oil to the rest of the sick, trying to flush out the poison. He also prescribed a tincture of paregoric to calm the stomach, topped off with a few spoonfuls of hooch. Luckily no one died.

Despite a few setbacks, the town grew quickly. The first birth was wildly celebrated by a parade that snaked in and out of homes, accompanied by rifle shots in the air. Within a year, so many babies were born that there was no place to put them. Clothes baskets, boxes and dresser drawers became makeshift bassinets.

Workers, many of them war veterans, poured into Terrace Bay to construct the mill in the 1940s

Within three-and-a-half years of Charles Craig's first visit to Black, more than $23 million (1947 dollars) had been spent to erect the mill and town-site. Another $12.5 million was invested by Ontario Hydro to generate electricity. Things had changed significantly. Schools, a proper hospital, a tourist hotel and all the small-town trimmings were in place. The tote-road that Craig used to discover the mill site was now the main street of the proud company town. The town was renamed Terrace Bay in recognition of the stepped glacial terraces that extend to a height of 99m (331 ft.) above Lake Superior. (For the geological formation of Terrace Bay see Aguasabon River, below.)

AGUASABON RIVER: AN ENGINEERING FEAT

Sometimes the natural flow of things isn't good enough. And the Aguasabon River is a good example. During the retreat of the last glacier from the north shore some 10,000 years ago, melting ice carved this river's passage down to Superior. The massive flow carried large quantities of sed-iment into the newly formed delta. The lake level, as much as 45m (150 ft.) higher than today, lowered in a series of drops creating steps, or terraces, that are the site of today's Terrace Bay. In only a few years, this river was to be irrevocably altered.

In the 1930s, an idea formed in the minds of engineers employed by

This 1850 print shows the terraced beach levels left behind by retreating glacial waters.

Ontario's Hydro-Electric Power Commission (predecessor to Ontario Hydro): "What if we carved some canals to join the Aquasabon with water from the Long Lake basin?" Someone pointed out: "But Long Lake flows away from Superior into James Bay," The first engineer replied, "Precisely, but with a five-mile series of canals, it will flow south into Superior, increasing the flow of water all through the Lakes and especially through Niagara... boosting the power capacity there." With this in place, the engineers built a diversion dam on the Aguasabon River and installed a hydroelectric generating station.

The pulpwood companies working the virgin forests of the Long Lake and Kenogami River basins liked the idea even more. With increased water flow, valuable spruce would become more accessible. Logs could be floated 96 kms (60 miles) through Long Lake and down the Aguasabon to Superior. The giant booms would then be towed to Jackfish or the Slate Islands, loaded on freighters and delivered to hungry pulp and paper mills in Wisconsin. And that's exactly how it happened.

The Aguasabon Gorge is a lovely spot, especially in spring when the Aguasabon River roars over the 30m (100 ft.) drop. It is located on the west end of town, just south of Highway 17.

CASQUE-ISLES HIKING TRAIL

Reversing Tides, Tombolos and Death Valley

The impressive 52.4-km (32.7-mile) Casque-Isles Trail (part of the Voyageur Trail system) begins at the Aguasabon River Gorge and ends at Rossport. Sections can be enjoyed on day hikes, or the full trail can be tackled on an overnight hike. Either is a journey through beautiful scenery and centuries of Superior's human history.

At the long narrow bay known as Kelly's Harbour, west of Terrace Bay, some say an unusual phenomenon can occur called a reversing tide. When wind and wave action are optimal, the waters of Superior rise and surge into the mouths of two creeks, creating a miniature "tidal wave" that heads up river. On the west side of Kelly's Harbour is a "tombolo," which is defined as "a sand or gravel bar connecting an island with the mainland or another island." But expect no sand or gravel here. This is Superior, and this tombolo is composed of boulders the size of cinder blocks.

Soon after the tombolo drops from view, the trail enters Death Valley. Its name refers to the ease with which Ojibwe, perched on the rim of the surrounding hills, could shoot moose and caribou below. After descending

75m (250 ft.) to Nonami Bay, the route climbs to a spectacular view of the off-shore islands, Les Petits Ecrits. At Worthington Beach on Worthington Bay, old Ojibwe red-ochre pictographs can be found inside a small sheltered crevasse. The depictions include a hand, a man, and a circle. North of the pictographs are the cement foundations of buildings constructed for a gold refinery in the 1930s (the ore was crushed and refined at the beach). The mining camp itself lies further west, in a spot where the trail levels out. No buildings remain.

On Mount Gwynne is a brass plaque in memory of Tom McGrath, who was instrumental in creating the trail. Further on, past the point near Abbyon Lookout, watch for a beaver swamp and, at Twin Harbours, look for the old CPR construction dock dating from 1883. From Selim Lookout, the trail passes giant boulders known as "glacial floats," then wanders through Rainbow Falls Provincial Park ending at Rossport.

The Artwork of Les Petits Ecrits

The sun was high when the voyageurs canoed across Worthington Bay on their return trip east. They were approaching a traditional rest area, Les Petits Ecrits, marked by a narrow channel between the mainland and a group of small islands. Their cliff faces, red with feldspar, ran steeply into the water.

After the canoes were beached, the air was quickly spiced with pipe

Passing voyageurs left lichen drawings on the cliffs at Les Petits Ecrits.

smoke. Voyageurs had a unique way of calculating distance. By permitting themselves a five minute smoke break every hour, they kept track, not of the number of miles covered, but of the number of pipes smoked. Pipes finished, the voyageurs resumed their journey.

A newcomer asked about Les Petits Ecrits' pictures, which were hidden in fog on his first trip west. Working with stones and knives, artists had carved away the black and orange lichen leaving the cliffs dancing with figures of fabulous monsters, snakes with wings, animals, men in canoes and warriors with drawn bows. Some of the drawings were freshly carved; others faint and deformed, partially overgrown by creeping lichen. As they paddled, the newcomer's eyes feasted on the sight. Who was the first artist? No one knows, but the tradition is an old one.

SCHREIBER: TENT TOWN TO COMPANY TOWN

It has a lively history, this community set midway between Terrace Bay and Rossport. Its German-sounding name actually originated with a knighted Englishman, while its early residents were overwhelmingly Italian!

The community began humbly as Isbesters Landing, named after a rail-

Schreiber, 1884. Italian immigrants began arriving around the turn of the century.

way construction contractor. The Landing was a supply entrepôt, a tent town for Canadian Pacific Railway's rag-tag assembly of navvies. Goods and materials for the general store and construction sites arrived by barge and were transported inland by mule-drawn carts. The Landing was renamed after Sir Collingwood Schreiber, the engineer who recommend-ed that the Federal government provide the final loan needed to complete the CPR. With the rail line around the Landing still under construction (see Red Rock p.208), it was fitting that this community be honoured by his name.

On November 1, 1885, the first train left Winnipeg bound for Montreal. As it passed through Schreiber, a new era began. Schreiber was designated a CPR home terminal where engines were repaired and services carried out. The backbone of the railway—breakmen, conductors, engineers and fire-men—lived here, and no longer in tents. Frame houses, shops and the first school were built. For a while there was a succession of teachers. Many lasted only a week because the children, unimpressed by the rigours of school attendance, began a successful campaign to drive them away. Finally, in 1891, the students were outsmarted. A teacher was hired on the condition that he not be paid until at the end of semester.

Around the turn of the century the first Italian families arrived in Schreiber. Impressed by the location and its potential, their letters home enticed other families to immigrate. With names such as Spadoni, Figliomeni, Costa and Cebrario, many Schreiber businesses still reflect the Italian influence. Gardens are filled with tomatoes, beans and herbs, and residents carry on many of their Old World traditions, like wine-making. Old-timers recall that during wine-making season in the 1940s, a train would arrive with at least seven cars full of grapes! Even today it is said that when all the basement windows are open during the fermentation period, Schreiber has an aroma distinct from all other North Shore towns.

THE WRECK *GUNILDA* : A MONUMENT TO STUBBORNNESS

Should we laugh at the folly of an immensely wealthy man brought down by his own tight-fisted arrogance? Or weep for the needless loss of a beautiful craft? William Lamont Harkness' greatest pleasure was taking extended cruises aboard his luxurious yacht *Gunilda*. Custom built in Leith, Scotland, the *Gunilda* featured a 60-m (200-ft.) steel hull, richly-appointed cabins and a crew of 21. Entertained by music from a grand piano, this top executive of the Standard Oil Company of Cleveland treated his guests to gourmet meals served on fine china.

The *Gunilda* had sailed around the world before the summer of 1910 when Harkness ordered her into the Great Lakes. The beauty of the North Shore must have appealed to the American tycoon because he returned the following year. All went well until Harkness ordered the yacht master to explore Nipigon Bay. "Perhaps we should hire a local pilot," Captain Corkum suggested. "The bay is poorly charted here."

At first the millionaire grudgingly agreed, but when Corkum said the pilot would cost $15, he thundered "Outrageous!" Nodding dutifully, Corkum began plotting his course. Soon the *Gunilda* was steaming through the Schreiber Channel north of Copper Island, Corkum was alert but relaxed. They slipped past the stunning scenery while stewards took refreshment orders and below them the *Gunilda's* steam engine hummed along contentedly. Everything was perfect until....

The U.S. charts did not include McGarvey Shoal, a hazardous rocky ledge lurking just off Copper Island. When the *Gunilda* struck, the sleek vessel's momentum carried her so far onto the rocks that her graceful bow was left pointing into the air. As tribute to her workmanship, the craft suffered no serious damage and none of her passengers suffered serious injury.

"I'll inform the insurance company," Harkness said to Corkum, "and have them arrange for someone to pull her free." Then he, his family and their guests boarded a yawl to sail for shore, where a train took them to Rossport.

A few days later the tug *James Whalen* arrived from Port Arthur. The captain, an experienced and capable man, was still studying the *Gunilda's* predicament when Harkness demanded, "What do you think?" Worried she might roll over if pulled off, the captain said he wanted backup assistance. Harkness haughtily disagreed. That would cost money.

Cables were run from the tug to the *Gunilda*, and as a precaution, crewmen with axes stood prepared to cut the lines if the yacht should start to sink. The salvage tug began to pull. At first nothing happened. The captain ordered full speed ahead, and this time the *Gunilda* slid slowly off the shoal, listing sharply to starboard. Within moments, she sank, carrying her custom-made silverware, grand piano and million-dollar investment to the bottom. Fortunately the crew had managed to cut the tow-lines, preventing the tug from going under too and allowing the captain to rescue his crew from the bow. It is reported that Harkness cried at the loss. Home in New York, he may have cried again when he discovered that the insurance would cover only $100,000 of the total value.

The luxury yacht Gunilda *foundered on McGarvey shoal due to its owner's stubborness.*

The yacht has remained where she eventually settled, in more than 60m (200 ft.) of icy Superior water. A few items have been recovered, including the top section of the mast, now the flagpole at the Rossport Inn. At least two divers have lost their lives exploring the wreck. Over the years all efforts to raise her have failed and so she remains a submerged monument to one man's short-sighted stubbornness. The wreck is now privately owned, and unauthorized diving is strictly prohibited.

RAINBOW FALLS PROVINCIAL PARK

As the Whitesand (Hewitson) River wends its way south down terraced bedrock to Lake Superior, it creates a series of cascades that toss plumes of mist into the air. At one of the steeper cascades a rainbow often forms, giving the park its name. It is difficult to believe this picturesque location was once called "Maggot River." Back in the early 1800s, when the North West and Hudson's Bay companies were locked in fierce competition for the fur trade, two Nor'Westers were stationed at the firm's outpost. The men remained there all winter in a little hut. No one knows what happened, but both died. By the time voyageurs arrived in the spring, the bodies were blanketed with maggots. When the horrific tale spread along the North Shore, the area became known as Maggot River.

For campers, Whitesand Lake offers hilly terrain, sandy beaches, boating, fishing for small mouth bass and speckled trout and, in mid-summer, water warm enough to swim in: a rarity along the North Shore. Three nature trails provide panoramic views of Whitesand Lake and Lake Superior. Extending from Terrace Bay to Rossport, the 52.4-km (32.7-mile) Casque-Isles trail passes through Rainbow Falls Provincial Park. It offers incredible views of Lake Superior and her islands: cuestas with steep-sided cliffs on their north sides dipping towards gentle southern slopes. (See Casque-Isles trail p.184.)

SELIM

The practice of reversing a fairly common name to produce a unique, more exotic one was employed more than once along the North Shore. Selim is the small community about 16 kms (10 miles) west of Schreiber. Reverse it and it becomes "Miles" in recognition of CPR engineer H. R. Miles. Noslo, the site of the Last Spike ceremony, is simply the familiar Scandinavian name "Olson" written backwards, while Navillus has nothing to do with seafaring. Rather it is the mirror image of Sullivan.

ROSSPORT

Proud residents call their town "the prettiest little harbour on the North Shore." Several names have been attached to the area, including the Ojibwe Bawgawashinge, meaning shallow water over the bar, and MacKay's Harbour, named after Charles MacKay, the first keeper of nearby Battle Island light. When the railroad pushed through, the town became Ross Port in honour of Walter Ross, the contractor responsible for building this section of the route.

In 1884, the CPR built the Rossport Inn to act as both hotel and pay station. Before rail service, Rossport fishermen salt-cured their catches, then stored them for bi-annual shipment by paddlewheeler. In 1896, aiming to increase east-bound fish shipments, the CPR gave station master J.A. Nicol $500 to erect an icehouse and to begin buying fish. Nicol was so successful, he expanded into purchasing commercial fishing licenses. He formed the Nipigon Bay Fish Company in 1903. Packed in ice, fresh fish was loaded aboard CPR cars bound for Canada and U.S. markets. At the height of its commercial fishing, Rossport was home to 350, had 20 fishing tugs,

Rossport as the railway construction camp and fishing village known as MacKay's Harbour, 1885.

and shipped about 375 tons of fish annually via rail.

Rossport remained a fishing centre, even after its fish stocks were devastated by invading sea lamprey in the 1950s. Commercial fishing was replaced by sport fishing. The Rossport Fish Derby, said to be the oldest freshwater fish derby in North America, began in 1937. From the beginning, the event attracted fishermen from all over the continent. However, the awards, for some, failed to live up to the contest's fame. At one postwar derby, a neighbour of President Harry Truman won the grand prize, took one look at the beautiful Banjo rod-and-reel, smiled, and handed it to his guide. The following year, the derby committee loosened the purse strings, and derby winners pocketed a hefty $3,000.

In the 1940s, with construction of a hydro dam and generating station, and the Kimberly-Clark mill in Terrace Bay, thousands of men were brought into the region. During those years, both Terrace Bay and Schreiber were "dry," without liquor outlets or beer parlours. Thirsty workers hitched a ride to the Rossport

Rossport Fish Derby, the oldest continuous freshwater fish derby in North America

Inn where waiters, working on a quota system, encouraged patrons to consume as much alcohol as they could in the shortest possible time. It was not unusual for the hotel to sell 35 cases of beer each hour.

Today Rossport is a quaint village offering good dining and a pleasant view of the surrounding islands. At the town dock are former fishing tugs, now converted into diesel-powered pleasure-craft. Boats can be chartered for cruises through the Rossport Islands.

ROSSPORT ISLANDS

Out from Rossport the islands form an enchanting archipelago. Each island has its own individual history and physical appeal.

Nearby **Nicol Island,** connected by causeway to the mainland, is named for J.A. Nicol, owner of the Nipigon Bay Fish Company and Rossport's long-time CPR station master. Over a century ago, before it became favoured by summer cottagers, Nicol Island served a far less appealing function. Needing to feed thousands of construction crew, the CPR shipped cattle to the mainland where they were herded through shallow waters to Nicol Island. It is said that at the spot where the cattle were butchered (still called Slaughter Dock), the blood-soaked ground still prevents trees from growing.

Whiskey Island also served the CPR construction gangs, but in a slightly different way. It was here various bootleggers stored their illegal whiskey caches.

Battle Island Lighthouse. Spray smashed the lanternroom glass during a 1977 storm.

Battle Island was so-named because of an incident that supposedly occurred in 1885 at the time of the Riel Rebellion. Local Ojibwe were accused of firing on troops marching across the ice on their way to quell the uprising. The soldiers, whose imaginations may have been running wild, claimed the shots came from one of the islands. By firing back, they "did battle with

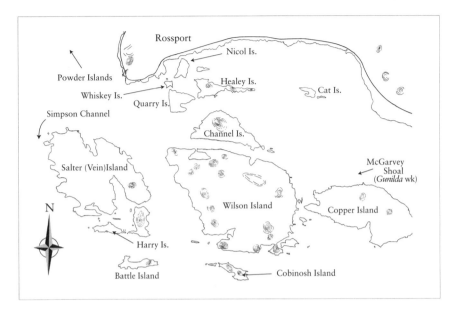

the Indians." It is highly unlikely they were marching this far offshore, but when it came time to name the new lighthouse location, Battle Island was chosen. Set close to the east-west shipping channels, it was meant to guide vessels through the adjacent Simpson Channel. The first lighthouse, a 11-metre-high (36-ft.) wooden structure built in 1877, was replaced in 1911 by the present reinforced concrete tower.

High above the lake, the shining white lighttower and red lanternroom stand out against the massive cliff. The keeper's house is equally brilliant in its new coats of white with red trim. The lighthouse is now fully automated, but Battle Island has been resided in and maintained by former keeper, Bert Saasto.

On a bright blue August day it is a pastoral scene with trees swaying in the breeze and 3-m (10-ft.) waves washing the base of the cliff. But Saasto reminds us what a November 1977 gale with 80 mph winds would have done to the scene:

> The waves from Duluth built to fifty feet high and when they hit the rocks below the light they were strong enough and high enough to wash all the way up the tower. That's about a hundred and twenty feet in all! They smashed the glass right out of the lantern. The storm lasted for three days and nights, and the roar of the storm is deafening. That's what puts the fear of God in you, the sound of the wind and the

A story of soldiers crossing the ice and being shot at from Battle Island gave the island its name.

> waves. You can't get away from it. You almost panic and you feel like running, but out there, there's nowhere to run to.

Just such a savage storm may have been responsible for the sinking of the 54-m (181-ft.) *Ontario*, a CPR supply steamer. Headed for Rossport in August 1899, she sank off the eastern tip of Battle Island. While the wreck is scattered in about 3-12m (10-40 ft.) of water, the ship's boiler lies on shore, long forgotten by the metal salvagers who moved it there.

Vein Island, locally known as Salter Island, was once the site of a major sawmill operation. The name Salter supposedly originated when the owner's sons set out fishing nets. Having caught more fish than they could use, the boys asked their father what they should do with the surplus. His reply was "Salt 'er."

Quarry Island looms high and rocky just beyond Whiskey Island. Sandstone was quarried here in the late 1880s and used for buildings in the Thunder Bay area. The remains of steel rails and the old dock facilities are still visible. For a superb view of Rossport and the surrounding islands, take the trail leading from its harbour through thick stands of wild raspberry bushes to the island's summit.

Healey Island bears the name of the first storekeeper in Rossport.

Channel Island's northeast shoreline has been designated an Area of Natural and Scientific Interest (ANSI) for its 1.5-km (.9-mile) stretch of "Rossport Formation" rock. This cliff face is beautifully marked with bands of brick red, pink, grey and black, formed of marine sediment layers 1.34 billion years old.

Powder Island, which is actually two separate islands, was used by the CPR during construction of the railway right-of-way to store the blasting powder needed to reduce inconvenient rock outcroppings to rubble.

PAYS PLAT FIRST NATION

French voyageurs renamed the area Pays Plat, "flat land," from the Ojibwe name *Bagouachi*, "Shallow floor of the lake hereabouts." Around 1775, in an effort to divert furs away from the rival North West Company, the Hudson's Bay Company strategically established a fur trading outpost here. In addition, they started a native commercial fishery.

Even though the band had been recorded as having been at Pays Plat at least since the 1700s, it was not invited to sign the 1850 Robinson-Superior Treaty. The oversight resulted from a report by two members of a Royal Commission sent to Lake Superior to examine the land claims issue.

After a meeting with Lake Superior Chiefs at Fort William, the commissioners defined and recorded five Lake Superior bands: Michipicoten, Pic, Long Lake, Nipigon and Fort William. Pays Plat was not listed. Neither was it invited to the treaty negotiations, perhaps, because it had no elected chief. (Its first chief was elected in 1885.) When the Treaty was signed in 1850, Pays Plat's signature was missing as were those of the Pic River and Long Lake First Nations.

However, in 1852, when the Pic and Long Lake bands learned the government was distributing Treaty annuities, they too began to collect. No one questioned the action. By the 1870s, the bands began collecting as well. All three bands and the government officials eventually came to assume that the bands had been part of the Robinson-Superior Treaty. The Pays Plat reserve was finally established by 1917.

Waiting for treaty payments, Michipicoten Harbour warehouse, 1905.

ST. IGNACE ISLAND: A SOVEREIGN NATION?

Named by missionaries after Ignatius Loyola, founder of the Jesuit order, St. Ignace Island became a commercial fishing camp in the 1860s. The only regular outside contact came from twice-yearly visits by steamers. Each spring paddle-wheelers arrived laden with salt and empty barrels. In autumn, they returned with empty holds to pick up the barrels, now loaded with salt-cured fish.

In the late 1970s, St. Ignace was claimed by a group calling themselves the Nirivian Nation. The name was taken from a Nipigon bicycle shop belonging to the founding Nirivian Grand Admiral Dave "Zeus" Krujzewski (whose banged-up cabin cruiser served as the flagship of the Royal Nirivian Navy). Their flag displayed a pine tree, a sphinx (after the island's rock formations which resemble ranks of small sphinxes), and a mountain (representing the island's 340-m (1,265-ft.) mountain). The ten-member group claimed the 30-km-long (19-mile) island to be a sovereign nation because in the shuffle of Indian and government lands, St. Ignace Island had somehow been overlooked, thus placing it in a kind of legal no man's land. The Nation's aim was to secede from Canada and control the island until the government promised to turn it into a park protected from mining and logging interests (at one point they even bandied about the idea of issuing their own currency—with singer Gordon Lightfoot's portrait on it). Some of St. Ignace's current hiking trails were old logging trails.

PARADISE ISLAND

Step by step, this small island rises until it reaches its maximum height of 15m (50 ft.) above water. We counted at least twelve beach levels on Paradise, each marking one terrace where waves washed ashore during the steady lowering of glacial waters. Paradise Island is unique. The beach is a mix of terra cotta and white gravel. Further in, a lichen heath appears, made up of some mosses and spongy multi-hued "bushes" of lichen the size of cauliflowers. Accented by contorted Bonsai-shaped trees, Paradise almost seems like a manicured park. This "Krumholz" vegetation—wind stunted spruce, birch, balsam fir and jackpine—partly results from the island's location, vulnerable to the full brunt of wind and waves. These gnarled specimens, combined with arctic-alpine grasses, dramatically reflect the severe climate.

Paradise is an enchanting place but its ridges and slowly regenerating vegetation are fragile. Any footstep can cause years of damage so keep to the path that leads across the island.

BOWMAN ISLAND

The narrow neck of this 3-km (1.8-mile) long island with its spectacular cobble and pebble ridges tells of its post-glacial history. As on Paradise Island, each ridge marks a storm line as glacial waters gradually lowered 3,000 to 4,000 years ago. These beaches have several well-defined Pukaskwa pits, mysterious depressions left by early inhabitants of the region (see p.136).

On the southern tip of Bowman stands an old fishing camp used in the

Talbot Island lightkeeper Thomas Lamphier died during the winter of 1869-70 at Talbot Island's "lighthouse of doom," and was buried the following spring on Bowman Island.

early 1880s by rugged men like George Gerow, John Leckie and William Boon. Its white peeling paint, combined with old red shingles poking out from beneath newer ones, and the British flag hoisted by its current owner make this spot a delight. In the early years, when most fishermen returned home to their communities, George Gerow and his family wintered on Bowman. This harsh life must have invigorated him because Gerow fished Superior until the age of 88.

A path from the old building leads past an abandoned fishing skiff to the grave of lightkeeper Thomas Lamphier, marked by a simple white cross. The spelling on the bronze plaque is "Lampshire." In the 1800s, it was common for French speakers to Anglicize their names to avoid discrimination. Lamphier was one of several keepers who died at the notorious "lighthouse of doom" on Talbot Island (see below). For a short time, both Bowman and Paradise Islands were inhabited by caribou. In 1985, six were reintroduced to Bowman but soon wandered off.

Talbot Island: The Lighthouse of Doom

Talbot Island lighthouse had a gruesome record unequalled by any other Great Lakes lighthouse—all three of its keepers died on the job. Only six years after the "lighthouse of doom" was constructed, the government determined the risk to human life far outweighed its importance to shipping. It was abandoned.

The year 1867 marked more than the birth of Canada. It also marked the building of Lake Superior's first lighthouse. In a small but important decision, the brand-new Canadian government extended efforts to bring safety to Great Lakes shipping by erecting a white, wooden tower powered by three kerosene lamps on Talbot Island. Around the middle of December of that first season, keeper Perry closed the lighthouse and headed in an open sailboat for the Hudson's Bay post at the mouth of the Nipigon River. No one knows what went wrong, but the following spring, Perry's badly decayed body was discovered by his abandoned boat at Perry Bay on Sibley Peninsula—nearly 22 kms (14 miles) from his destination.

In an effort to avoid another tragedy the following year, authorities doubled the size of the living quarters to permit the keeper to winter on the island. Thomas Lamphier was hired. The Lamphiers seemed well-suited for the job. Thomas had captained a Hudson's Bay schooner out of Fort William for almost twenty years and his wife, a native woman from the Hudson Bay area, was used to severe winter weather. But fate was unkind.

Not long after freeze-up, Thomas died suddenly. Trapped on the island with her husband's corpse, Mrs. Lamphier had no means of reporting the tragedy. To add to her misery, the ground was frozen solid, preventing her

Bill Schelling inspects Talbot Island lighthouse foundation, c. 1960s.

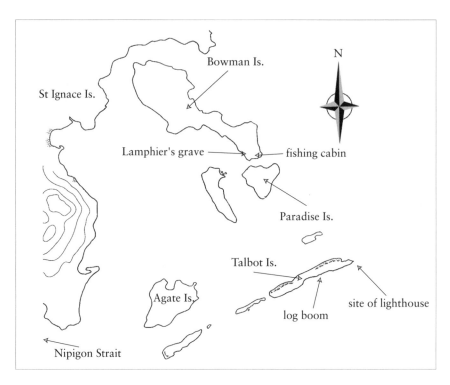

from giving her husband a decent burial. The grieving widow wrapped her husband's body in canvas and set him in a rock crevasse a distance behind the lighthouse.

With the arrival of spring, a passing party of Ojibwe noticed Mrs. Lamphier's frantic signals. They carried her husband's body to nearby Bowman Island and buried him, marking his grave with a simple white cross. When the government supply ship arrived, the crew hardly recognized Mrs. Lamphier. Her raven hair had turned stark white.

At the end of season in the autumn of 1872, the third keeper, Andrew Hynes, extinguished the kerosene lamp for the last time and sealed the lighthouse against the coming storms. Loading provisions and a few possessions in a small boat, he set off in clear weather for Fort William. Conditions soon changed. For a gruelling eighteen days, Hynes struggled in his tiny open craft, travelling a mere 96 kms (60 miles) to the mining community of Silver Islet. He was barely able to identify himself, mumbling details of the torturous journey, before he died.

The government decided to abandon the cursed light, and the wooden hulk remained standing for years. When thick fog rolled in, local fishermen would beat against its sides, sending a hollow echo across the water to aid those caught out on the lake. Some claimed they saw the figure of a woman with long white hair wandering the shore.

Our efforts to locate the foundation were thwarted by the tangled web of trees draped with old man's beard lichen. According to a newspaper article written in 1964, Jim Sigurdson located lath, plaster, hand-forged nails and fireplace bricks about 180m (200 yards) from the south shore and about 450m (500 yards) from the east point. He also located the crevasse he believed Mrs. Lamphier used to store her husband's corpse.

SQUAW HARBOUR

Squaw Harbour was known as CPR Slip in the 1920s. Guests from the CPR lodge in Nipigon came here for fishing expeditions and were billeted in small cabins. After the trout fishing deteriorated, the CPR abandoned the camp. Today, the site is again in use. Liz and Fraser Dougall of Thunder Bay agreed to have the site fixed up and made available for anyone passing through. Local businesses were persuaded to provide building materials for a bunkhouse and Finnish steambath. Inside the bunkhouse, an old table is carved with the names of visitors, and a guest book is thick with their comments. Everyone is welcome but there are two stipulations: the facilities must be left cleaner than on arrival, and the wood supply must be replenished. East across the narrow peninsula, trails extend to the lakeshore and into the interior where the trees hang heavy with old man's beard.

VERT ISLAND

Like Quarry Island, Vert Island served as a source of building materials for local communities, especially Fort William and Port Arthur (now Thunder Bay). The rose-coloured sandstone was transported by rail car to the dock, then loaded onto barges for the journey to the Lakehead. Rusting rail tracks and the old rail beds are still visible, along with remains of the piers and breakwater structures.

LA GRANGE ISLAND

Another sandstone quarry site, La Grange, offers a majestic cliff face carpeted by trees. Locals say the lookout was used as a native spiritual site. Thick stands of white birch along the north shore give the island a surprisingly lush, even tropical appearance.

NIPIGON REGION: DIRTY PLAY IN THE FUR TRADE

In the Nipigon region, competition for control of the fur trade waged for over 200 years. Between 1684 and 1924, eighteen fur trading posts belonging to the French, the British Hudson's Bay Company, Montreal's North West Company and various independent traders tried to out-maneuver one another.

Hoping to cash in on the lucrative fur trade, France attacked the Hudson's Bay Company's five trading posts on Hudson Bay, controlling all but Fort Albany by 1682. Unable to capture this fort, the French decided to neutralize its effectiveness by setting up their own Fort La Maune on Lake Nipigon in order to block furs travelling by river to Fort Albany. So successful was this tactic that France would employ it again in the 1700s.

Stinging from their eviction from Hudson Bay after the Treaty of Utrecht in 1713, France erected three *postes du nord* on Lake Superior. Their main purpose was to block the transportation of furs to Hudson Bay: Michipicoton blocked Moose Factory, Kaministiquia at Thunder Bay blocked York Factory, and another at the mouth of the Nipigon River, Fort Ste. Anne, blocked Albany House.

Over the next 240 years the eighteen rival posts were successful to varying degrees. Some Chief Factors lost sight of their primary goal—making money through trading. Robert Crawford of the Hudson's Bay Company was one such man. To some he was ambitious and forward-thinking; others just called him a fool. Almost as soon as he arrived at Red Rock House at the mouth of Nipigon River in 1870, Crawford initiated sweeping changes. Fuelled by the plan that Red Rock House was to become the western terminus for the future Canadian Pacific Railway—but without first obtaining permission from HBC managers—he authorized (at substantial cost) the construction of new warehouses, a new company store, extensive docks, accommodations for labourers and an impressive house for himself.

Hudson's Bay Company Red Rock House. c. 1882-85.

After a vicious campaign between Nipigon and Port Arthur and Fort William, the CPR chose the twin cities as its terminus. The Hudson's Bay Company was now the reluctant owner of a white elephant. Crawford found himself "transferred" to a post on the Ungava Peninsula in northern Quebec where no railway terminus was conceivable. Red Rock House declined after Crawford's departure. In the 1880s, it had a brief reprieve as the headquarters of the HBC's Lake Superior district. Built in 1859, and abandoned in 1903, parts of the structure subsequently burned. The rest fell into ruin. An archaeological investigation in the 1980s confirmed its location: just after passing the CPR bridge as you head towards the town dock, it is on the right hand side.

THE CREATION OF NIPIGON RIVER AND ITS PICTOGRAPHS

Dots, crosses, moons, a serpent, a thunderbird, bison, and a 10-cm (4") high image of Maymaygweshi adorn the cliff face on the east side of the Nipigon River, midway between Cook Point and the town of Nipigon. They are Ojibwe pictographs depicting their spirit world—although some show a later Christian influence. Unfortunately, the most recent date from the 1940s, and are believed to be grafitti made by lumber barge workers who defaced some of the precious drawings.

Maymaygweshi, "stranger who speaks in a strange language," appears on the rock about 1.5m (5 ft.) above the water, a leaping figure with horns

Pictograph of Maymaygweshi

on his head. The Maymaygweshi are tiny spirits belonging to the underworld of Mishepeshu who rules the water and manifests as either a horned lynx or serpent. Undaunted by stone barriers, these sprites travel regularly by canoe up and down the river between Lake Nipigon and Superior, sometimes taking subterranean passages under and through cliffs and emerging further along the river. Loved by the Ojibwe for their endearing impishness, Maymaygweshi have a special regard for children, especially those who are grieving, lost or despondent.

Ojibwe believe that these playful Maymaygweshi were indirectly responsible for the creation of the Nipigon River. They decided to play a prank on the biggest trickster of all, the giant, Nanaboozho. Paddling up the river one autumn afternoon, Nanaboozho encountered an unexpected mountainous barrier. He was outraged. There was no way he was going to give in to the Maymaygweshi and portage around their newly-created obstacle. Raising his huge tomahawk, he struck a powerful blow, splitting the face of the mountain in two and carving a new river channel. Warmed by all this exertion, he discarded his white rabbit-fur blanket into the water where it turned to stone. Today it is called Split Rock, a favorite location for fishermen to cast their rod.

TOWN OF NIPIGON

Sport-fishing Haven, CPR Sabotage

In the 1860s, "Gentleman Anglers" from all parts of North America and Europe arrived by the steamer load to fish for speckled trout in the 50-km (32-mile) Nipigon River. There were so many that, as early as 1888, there was fear the river might be over-fished. One fisherman lamented that Nipigon had been, "popularized and commericalized... crowding portages with fellow tourists bumping canoes continuously." Sport fishing attracted the rich and the famous (including the Prince of Wales), delivering a steady flow of tourist dollars to Nipigon's hotels and restaurants.

Even more profitable was the construction of three Canadian transcontinental railways in the Nipigon area: the Canadian Pacific in 1883; the

National Transcontinental in 1902; and the Canadian Northern in 1911. Easy rail access may have given a boost to Nipigon's economy, but it also made the community a target....

They looked like tourists and they acted like tourists, but something about them made one Nipigon citizen uneasy. It was March 1915, the first year of the Great War, and all strangers were viewed with suspicion, even in Nipigon, far away from the trenches and gunfire. Two men stepped off the westbound CPR train and, with German accents, asked directions to the famous railway bridge across the Nipigon River. They said they had heard the bridge had been the most difficult bridge to construct along the entire CPR line, and they were anxious to see it for themselves.

After providing directions, the local man alerted police, who watched the strangers carefully inspect the bridge before reboarding a westbound train. The police telegraphed ahead to Port Arthur, where the men were held for questioning. In their luggage, Port Arthur police discovered a long fuse, two loaded revolvers and a complete CPR schedule. The two men, who gave their names as Carl Schmidt and Gustaff Stephens, admitted they each been paid $200 to inspect the bridge for possible sabotage.

So many North American and European sport fishermen flocked to the Nipigon River that by 1888 there were already fears it was overfished.

The Nipigon CPR bridge was almost sabotaged during WWI.

RED ROCK

Farms, Mill Town to Prisoner of War Camp

According to *Red Rock Reflections* a few farmers, mostly Finnish, came to this isolated area in the early 1900s. Wrestling a meagre existence from hay and root crops, they supplemented their seasonal income by cutting firewood. Shopping, mail and banking meant an 8-km (5-mile) walk along the railway tracks to Nipigon. Only when they connected a wagon road to the new Nipigon Highway in the 1920s was their isolation broken.

1936 marked a change. The Lake Sulphite Pulp Company constructed a mill and twenty houses at the site, quickly followed by the CNR which built a spur line to the mill. Red Rock seemed positioned for steady growth. Instead, they got explosive growth. In the dark days of World War II, the British considered it too risky to house captured German soldiers on their soil, since it was possible England would soon be invaded. And so several thousand German officers and men were sent to Canada for the duration of the war.

Constructed in 1940 on the mill's labour campsite, Red Rock, or Camp "R" became home to an eclectic assortment of 1,145 German pris-

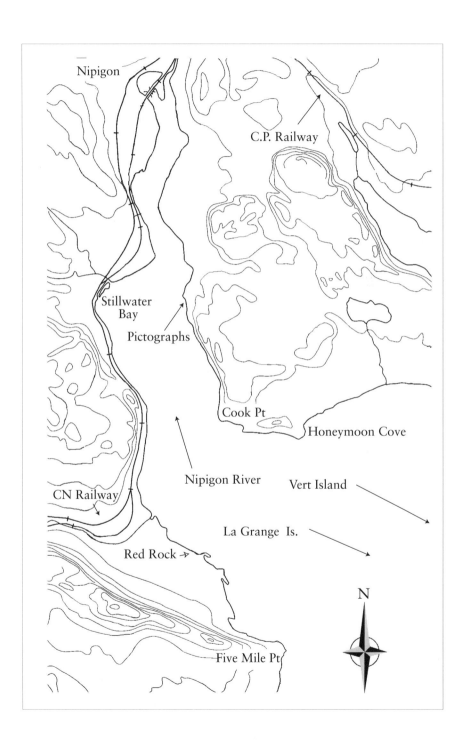

Nipigon

C.P. Railway

Stillwater
Bay

Pictographs

Cook Pt

Honeymoon Cove

Nipigon River

Vert Island

CN Railway

La Grange Is.

Red Rock

Five Mile Pt

N

oners—soldiers, merchant seaman and even a few German Jews. In no time the camp became polarized between Nazi and anti-Nazi sympathizers. The guards, all WWI veterans, were constantly breaking up arguments and fights.

During its short eighteen-month existence, Camp "R" saw several escape attempts. One prisoner dug a tunnel but was informed on by one of the other inmates. A second was more successful, reaching the United States before being caught. Another attempt resulted in one of two escapees being shot. In October 1941 the camp was closed and the prisoners sent to other locations.

For a short time in the early 1940s, the Lake Sulphite and Paper Company was in receivership. However by the middle of the decade Red Rock was again prospering. One hundred new houses were built and wages rose to 63 cents an hour. The St. Lawrence Corporation took over the mill in the 1950s ushering in a boom era. Having weathered many ups and downs, the community celebrated its long heritage with a new marina completed in 1994, and the Land of the Nipigon Trail System linking Red Rock to Nipigon with 21 kms (13 miles) of scenic trails.

RED ROCK: THE END OF THE LONG MARCH

William Van Horne feared few challenges and fewer men. More than anyone, he was responsible for the successful completion of the trans-con-

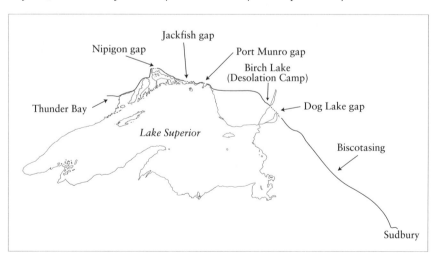

tinental Canadian Pacific Railway which helped to bind Canada into one country. It was not easy. Because of the exorbitant cost, Ottawa was under great pressure to abandon the project. Support came in an unlikely guise. Métis leader Louis Riel was threatening rebellion in the Northwest. The Canadian Government needed to dispatch troops swiftly to quash the uprising. But how? Van Horne saw his opportunity: he promised to deliver the troops in eleven days, knowing that if he succeeded, he would get the funds to complete the railway. With no viable alternative, the government accepted Van Horne's offer. There was only one problem: four gaps totalling 137 kms (86 miles) in the line north of Superior.

When the soldiers arrived at the CPR construction camp in the wilds near Dog Lake, they gasped in surprise. Spread before them were long tables straining under the weight of salmon, lobster, beef, vegetables and fruit of every description, along with fresh bread, deep pies, rich cakes and steaming pots of tea and coffee. Such a feast would be remarkable in the dining halls of Ottawa, Montreal or Toronto, but here? north of Lake Superior? "Maybe we should be building a railroad instead of fighting rebels," one soldier quipped, carving his way through a slice of roast beef

Exhausted and frost-bitten, soldiers fell in their tracks as they trekked across the unfinished sections of the CPR on their way to quell the second Riel Rebellion, 1885

as thick as his thumb. It was to be the last good meal these men from Canada's eastern provinces would enjoy before entering on the most torturous adventure of their lives.

It was 1885 and the soldiers were on their way to face Riel's militia at Fort Qu'Appelle. Left behind were wives and sweethearts and the cheers of good luck from the several small towns that had marked their passage with brass bands and bunting. Unknown to them, ahead lay massive gaps in the vaunted CPR which would have to be crossed in open sleds or on foot in temperatures as low as 35 degrees Fahrenheit below zero.

The day following the banquet, the soldiers traversed the Dog Lake Gap. It was no picnic crossing unbridged ravines, and uneven terrain. They stumbled over stumps, fallen trees, massive granite boulders and through snow drifts as deep as a man was tall. Only when the exhausted troops finally arrived at Magpie Camp did they get any food, but instead of lobster and roast beef, they were fed a railway construction worker's diet: salt pork, molasses, dry bread and tea. "At least the worst is over," one soldier commented. He was wrong. In some ways, the worst was yet to come. At their next stop, "Desolation Camp," one regiment had to wait 17 hours for a train, in minus thirty-five degree temperatures. Sleeping was out of the question, as they might have frozen to death.

Where the rails (some laid directly on hard-packed snow) had been completed, the troops crammed into open flat-cars, bundled in greatcoats against the biting winds. At each break in the line, they had to disembark and manoeuvre themselves, their weapons, packs, horses and artillery, the best way possible. Over some open passages they rode in sleighs, over others they trudged. Men literally marched in their sleep, waking only when they fell into drifts or through thin ice. Just when they thought they had endured the worst they found themselves faced with a twenty-mile stretch between Port Munroe and McKellar Harbour across the glare ice of Lake Superior. They suffered terribly from frostbite caused by the piercing winds, along with blistered skin from the glaring sun. Those who travelled at night were caught in a wild blizzard, and it was all the officers could do to keep the men from drifting away to their deaths.

Although the final gap between Nipigon and Red Rock was only ten miles, pelting rain turned the ice into six inches of thick slush. For the entire journey, the troops had to wade arm in arm to keep one another standing. At Red Rock they boarded the enclosed railcars for the last leg to Winnipeg, some fell on the floor and slept, unable even to pull themselves onto the seats. Nothing they would face at Fort Qu'Appelle would be as brutal and unforgiving as the trials experienced along Superior's North Shore.

However, their horrendous experience did prove the strategic value of a trans-continental railroad and hurried the completion of John A. Macdonald's "National Dream." (For building the railway see Noslo p.176.)

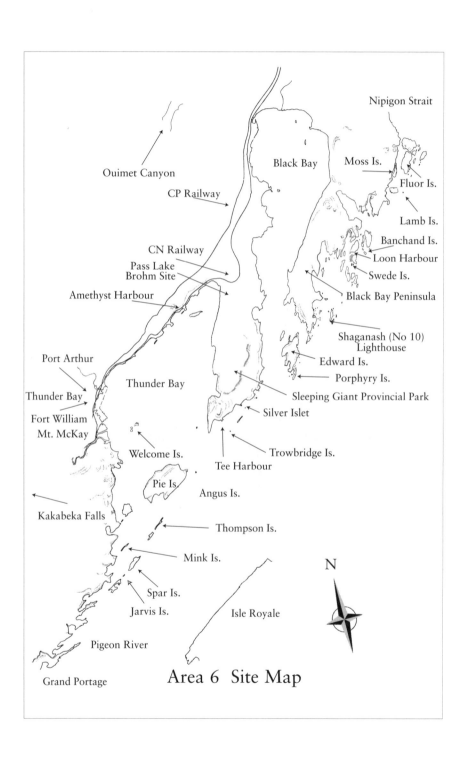

Nipigon Strait

Ouimet Canyon

CP Railway

Black Bay

Moss Is.

Fluor Is.

Lamb Is.

Banchand Is.

CN Railway

Loon Harbour

Pass Lake
Brohm Site

Swede Is.

Amethyst Harbour

Black Bay Peninsula

Shaganash (No 10)
Lighthouse

Port Arthur

Edward Is.

Thunder Bay

Porphyry Is.

Thunder Bay

Sleeping Giant Provincial Park

Fort William
Mt. McKay

Silver Islet

Welcome Is.

Trowbridge Is.

Tee Harbour

Pie Is.

Angus Is.

Kakabeka Falls

Thompson Is.

Mink Is.

N

Spar Is.

Jarvis Is.

Isle Royale

Pigeon River

Grand Portage

Area 6 Site Map

6

AREA SIX: NIPIGON STRAIT TO PIGEON RIVER

MOSS ISLAND: THE COFFIN SHIP *NEEBING*

For years sailors have joked that the *Neebing*'s hull, built in 1892, was so badly rusted that it was held together by layers of paint. Their sarcasm may have been closer to the truth than they thought.

In September 1937, the *Neebing* was being used as a gravel carrier. Lashed together with the barge *Coteau,* the vessels were caught in a storm north of Moss Island. About 240m (800 ft.) from the island, giant waves hammered the steamship. Listing, she banged into the barge and began to sink.

Men aboard the *Coteau* cut the barge free and urged the steamer's crew to abandon ship. Most did, but the ship sank so quickly that some were trapped below deck. Art Bassett was one of the lucky ones: the water pouring in was so powerful, Bassett was thrown out the galley skylight like a shot from a cannon. He landed safely in the water alongside the *Coteau* just as the *Neebing* slipped beneath the surface, taking five men and the captain with her. Only one body was recovered.

The wreckage of the 60-m (193-ft.) steamship lies about 0.4 kms (1/4-mile) off the northern tip of Moss Island in 18-30m (60-100 ft.) of water.

FLUOR ISLAND

During the 1880s a native commercial fishery operated out of Fluor with 38 men and 19 small boats, a dock, cabins and a large storehouse.

Fluor Island off Nipigon Bay from the West, in John Bigby's Shoe and The Canoe, *1850*

Puff Island

From the northeast the island looks like a puff pastry that has been dropped into Lake Superior. On closer inspection, Puff is far from soft, its steep cliff faces are cut in sharp vertical funnels. In 1985, the northern portion of the island was declared a Provincial Nature Reserve.

Willard Island

In a 1988 thunderstorm, lightning started a small fire that smouldered for weeks before turning into a high blaze that consumed most of the island's timber. Fires like these are natural, even necessary, in northern forests. Eventually, the vegetation will return, but for several years, Willard Island will show only patchy tufts of green on its mostly bare surface.

Lamb Island Lighthouse

The lightkeeper's residence sits four-square on its rocky site, shining white and trimmed with red. The well-beaten path to the steel lighttower once led to a wooden tower and dwelling that was built in 1877. A nearby pile of rubble is all that is left of this historic building, demolished in 1961.

The path to the shore continues along a wooded, mossy trail offering a wonderful view across to Fluor Island.

Throughout the twenty-year tenure of lightkeeper Charlie McDonald, tourists would make a point of stopping by to purchase his beautiful agates and to hear him spin yarns. Storytelling was definitely his strong point; housekeeping was not. When a visiting American noticed several pots and pans in the water near the dock, he offered to bring them up to the house. "Oh, don't be doing that!" McDonald replied, "they need to soak for about another week."

BANCHARD ISLAND

Superior's relentless wind and waves have sculpted many island shorelines. On Banchard, a large hole has been worn right through a point of rock, and the water's roar is amplified as it passes through this open throat. A tall rocky flowerpot is another of nature's whimsical creations.

Lamb Island lighthouse built in 1877, demolished in 1961

LOON HARBOUR AND SURROUNDING ISLANDS

Between Lasher, Borden and Spain Islands, Loon Harbour has been described as a lake within a lake. Surrounded by low-lying islands, the harbour is a quiet refuge where the cry of loons echoes through the morning mist. Not far away lies proof of Superior's stronger character. Spain Island is littered with a rusting boiler and crumbling ribs of a pulpwood loader used by the Russell Timber Company. The loader (a scow with a conveyor belt) was used by Walter Russell's company to load logs from the Black Bay Peninsula onto ships in the early part of the century. It was abandoned on Spain Island once the site was obsolete.

SHAGANASH LIGHTHOUSE

The Shaganash lighthouse is not on Shaganash Island. Rather it is located on nearby Island #10. Behind the small lighttower, the beach is covered with tiny volcanic rocks of muted purple, pink and blue, and flecked with agates. The foundation of the keeper's house and the old dock cribs can still be seen.

Painting of Black Bay by William Armstrong.

According to William W. Warren, the name Shaganash is an Ojibwe word for English-speaking whites. In the 1850's, he wrote that a party of Lake Superior Ojibwe travelled to Quebec to fight on the side of Montcalm against the British on the Plains of Abraham: "According to the late noted British interpreter, John Baptiste Cadotte, the name by which the Ojibwe now know the British, *Shaug-un-aush*, was derived from the circumstance of their sudden and almost unaccountable appearance, on that memorable morning on the heights of Abraham It is little changed from the original word *Saug-aush-e* which signifies 'to appear from the clouds.'"

The word *Wa-mit-ig-oshe* was a reference to the French. John Baptiste Cadotte interpreted it as being "derived from *wa-wa*, to wave, and *metig*, wood or stick, and meant literally, people or 'men of the waving stick'" because the French came with priests "who waved the Cross over their heads whenever they landed at an Indian village."

BLACK BAY PENINSULA AND BLACK BAY

To the lonely voyageurs, the twin rounded hills rising above the timbered shoreline were known as *les mamelles,* more commonly referred to on maps as The Paps.

To fishermen, Black Bay represents the largest herring spawning ground on Lake Superior, extending from George Point south to Magnet Island. Just before the start of World War II, Roy Maki and Frank Dampier launched a herring fishery from their camp on Squaw Bay. At war's end, their small enterprise expanded dramatically thanks to the return of younger fishermen and later, to the introduction of trawlers. During the 1960s and 1970s, more than half of all caught herring came from Black Bay. The herring fishery is still going strong despite a significant drop in fish stocks since 1988.

Just north of Ham Point, an unusual peatland extends inland for 5 kms (3 miles). While most peat bogs are caused by poor drainage, the bog on Black Bay was caused by high humidity and thick fog. Rare plants thrive in the bog which also supports a large number of moose. In April and May, the northern end of Black Bay is the most important migration staging ground for waterfowl on Lake Superior. About 2,000 hectares is Crown land, protected from development and unauthorized access.

EDWARD ISLAND

The western half of this 600-hectare (1,500-acre) island is a provincial park, including Osler Bay, Edward Harbour and Horseshoe Cove. Geologists and rock hounds have a field day studying the volcanic and sedimentary rock around the dense northern Boreal forest. Many of the specimens are located in ancient volcanic flows and basalt sheets, or near more recently-formed cobble beaches.

Successful silver mining in the 1870s on nearby Silver Islet meant that Edward Island was subjected to a great deal of optimistic drilling. It is estimated that 10,000 boxes were filled with core samples before the prospectors gave up. The drilling has left a dangerous legacy of open holes among the trees near the shore. One careless step could plunge a curious hiker down an abandoned shaft. Extreme caution is advised.

PORPHYRY ISLAND LIGHTHOUSE AND EMILY DICK

"Some snow flurries all day. Emily scrubbed the floors and is making pies for tomorrow's guzzle." That's how Andrew Dick, lightkeeper at Point Porphyry from 1877-1912, described Christmas Eve 1900, in his diary. Dick was in his seventies and a widower with ten children when he began to keep a record of turn-of-the-century lighthouse life.

After the death of her mother in 1884, eighteen-year-old Emily had assumed the domestic responsibilities. It is clear from her father's entries that she had time for little else on this tiny isolated island.

> January 3 - Emily hauling wood with the dogs. About three loads.
> January 16 - Emily mending fish nets.
> January 17 - Cut some wood. Emily got two loads home with the dogs.
>   She is gone for a bag of wheat to the boat house.
> January 19 - Emily cleaned out the hen-house and put some gravel in it.
> January 22 - Emily baked bread today.

As time went on, the aging keeper became more cranky, complaining about the weather, about his isolation and even about Emily's cooking. On Christmas Day, 1903 he wrote, "Beef and rooster, green peas and pie with soup. Rooster not cooked enough."

Emily was not the oldest child. An elder sister, Agnes, presumably suffered a physical ailment and was rarely mentioned in the diary. The Christmas Day, 1901 entry merely states, "There is one person less in this house since last Christmas. Agnes, the oldest of the family, is gone over to the majority. Fine and mild all day. Emily not able to kill a chicken for dinner. Christmas, but no presents."

Dick kept the Porphyry Point light for thirty-five years. Upon retirement at age 82, in 1912, he was awarded a small pension and a service medal from George V. He died five years later.

The old wooden lighthouse was torn down in the early 1960s and replaced by a modern structure. The entire island has been declared a provincial park in order to protect rare plant species. It has also been designated an Environmentally

Lightkeeper and widower Andrew dick's diary reveals the harsh life suffered by he and his ten children on Porphery Island 1877-1912.

Sensitive Area. In recent years, the Porphyry keeper's house was rented by artist Maureen Robertson. She created a colourful, almost playful space, in sharp contrast with the atmosphere described by Andrew Dick. Each year, Robertson concentrated on adding her artistic touches to another area of the lighthouse grounds. Her centerpiece was a "park" consisting of two 1950s cars painted purple and pink. While cleaning up the island, the artist found several mounds in the woods that were clearly graves. The site was confirmed as the Dick family graveyard by the son of a former keeper. There is no record of the burials but one of them is surely Agnes who died Christmas Day, 1901.

No more is known of Emily. At the time of her father's retirement, she would have been around thirty years old.

OUIMET CANYON PROVINCIAL PARK

Inland from Black Bay and north from Highway 17 is a monumental scar of the glacial ages. Aeons ago, this awe-inspiring landscape was created by fire and ice: fire in the form of molten rock that spewed from the

Dramatic Ouimet Canyon

earth's interior to form a huge horizontal cake of rock called a sill; and ice in the form of mountainous glaciers that scraped their way through the region. The immense weight of the ice crushed and cracked the sill. As the last glacier retreated, the massive volume of meltwater carved out Ouimet Canyon.

It is a spectacular 100m (333 ft.) drop to the canyon floor which is strewn with giant boulders broken off from the walls. Beneath the rocks, ice can stay all year and at least three species of plants, normally found only in the Arctic, are hidden among the boulders. Some columns of rock, resisting erosion and the shattering effects of frost, stand in solitary splendour, like the one known as the Indian Head, which is found along the canyon's west wall near the second lookout area.

A short, 1-km (0.6-mile) walking trail leads from the parking lot to the two viewing platforms. If visiting this spectacular sight, stay on the marked trails. Venturing off may bring the sudden, unguarded edge of a sheer cliff alarmingly near. No camping facilities are available.

PASS LAKE AND THE DANISH EXPERIMENT

The Provincial Paper Company's timber rights had expired in Sibley and McTavish Townships. Why not open it to hard-working Danish farmers? The man presenting this idea was J. H. Keefer, local member of the Ontario Legislature. Keefer was responding to a request made by a group of Danes who wanted the land to be offered exclusively to Danish immigrants.

In 1924, Keefer guided the Homestead Act through the Legislature. Under the Act, Danish homesteaders could acquire 160 acres of land at $0.50 an acre, for $20 down and $20 dollars in each of the next three years. In return, the Danes would erect a house and barn, and agree to clear and cultivate two acres of land each year for the first three years. If, after three years, the land was cleared and the $80 paid, the settler would receive title.

Almost fifty settlers took advantage of the deal. Some were families, but many were single men more interested in cutting the wood than in farming. The community, the only one of its kind in Ontario, became known as Pass Lake. They cut and sold everything in sight—pulpwood, saw logs, lumber, firewood, railway ties and fence posts. When the best wood was gone, many sold and returned to Port Arthur or Denmark. Those who stayed to farm faced many challenges, especially forest fires. Despite the setbacks, the farmers persevered, and by 1930, Pass Lake was shipping cream and potatoes to the Lakehead. A few farmers grew strawberries with impressive results. In 1935, they shipped about 70,000 quarts of the luscious fruit.

The end of World War II brought an influx of immigrants to Canada, including young Danes attracted by the cheap land and the Danish culture at Pass Lake. In the twenty years since it was a pioneer settlement, the community had changed considerably. Most of the land had been cleared, churches and a community centre had been built and growing tourism to the North Shore had created a mini-boom. Today, Pass Lake still reflects its Danish roots.

THE BROHM SITE: SUPERIOR'S FIRST PEOPLE

Danish farmer, Jorgen Brohm, had been struggling for years to clear his fields of unwanted stones. Suddenly something caught his eye: a pointed stone, very unlike the usual rounded ones found on the beaches. Kneeling, he saw that it was flat, roughly oval, and sharpened to a knife-edged point. It must be an arrowhead. He found more and more, and after assembling an impressive collection, Brohm contacted officials at Port Arthur. Would they be interested in examining his finds and their original location?

He did not have to ask twice. In 1950, a team of archaeologists connected the arrowheads with the Plano Indian culture. The Plano were the earliest known humans on Lake Superior. They came 7-9,000 years ago following the retreat of the glaciers. Scientists have deduced that the site was likely a killing ground. At that time, it would have been an ideal spot to ambush herds of migrating caribou because high levels of water could have created a narrow strip of land connecting the southern part of Sibley Peninsula with the mainland. As one of the earliest Plano sites excavated in the upper Great Lakes, the Brohm Site was studied intensively through 1950-70.

SLEEPING GIANT PROVINCIAL PARK

The Park Creation

Motivated by the fear that logging would again lay waste to the Sibley Peninsula as it had during the 1920s, citizens of Port Arthur and Fort William began a campaign in the early 1940s to completely ban future operations. The loggers had not had an easy time with the region's rugged topography which had, as a report at the time put it, "every conceivable kind of precipice, canyon, gully, pothole, hogsback etc. present." The group's determined efforts were rewarded when Sleeping Giant Provincial Park was established in 1944. Today, the precipices and canyons that once thwarted loggers provide some of the most incredible scenery on the North Shore.

SLEEPING GIANT

The Forces of Time and Spirit

The Park's extraordinary formations and vistas were drafted by time, erosion, and the powerful Ojibwe manitous whose spirits imbue the region. Some of their finest work is in the immense sheer cliff scarp known as Sleeping Giant. Seen in profile from the western shore of Thunder Bay, and the southern tip of Sibley Peninsula, Sleeping Giant resembles a man with arms folded across his chest as though in a deep sleep.

Geologists compare the cliff's formation to making a layer cake. Over 1.7 billion years ago, the region was submerged under water. For millions of years, silt filtered to the ocean floor, slowly building up layers of sedimentary rock. Today, this ancient rock is the base of Sleeping Giant. The next major layer, another band of sedimentary rock, is 1.3 billion years old. Mostly quartz sandstone, red dolostone and red shale, the red colour leads geologists to believe there was oxygen in the earth's atmosphere at the time that the rocks were deposited. Visitors will most commonly find these formations on the peninsula's outcroppings.

The top layer, visible on the top portion of Sleeping Giant, formed about 1.1 billion years ago when the continent was splitting apart in the Midcontinent Rift. Volcanoes erupted, and molten magma squeezed up through the sedimentary layers, cooling into a dark, hard fine-grained stone called diabase, which protected the softer layers below. Having made the cake, the wind, rain, and glacial activity needed millions of years to scrape

CPR steamship Manitoba *passing Sleeping Giant*

out the final touches. The result is Sleeping Giant, a magnificent site with the highest vertical cliffs in Ontario, towering 250m (833 ft.) above the water.

With a head, Adam's apple, knees, legs and crossed arms, Sleeping Giant looks remarkably human; it is a marvel that random forces would create such a shape. To the Ojibwe there is nothing random about Sleeping Giant. He has the figure of a man because he is Nanaboozho. Nanaboozho is an Ojibwe manitou, the Ojibwe's teacher, who brought fire and the pipe to mortals, and who gained the protection of the Thunderbirds. Half human and half manitou, Nanaboozho was the spirit with whom humans could most easily identify. His quick temper, blunders and follies were a constant source of stories. (For the story see Sleeping Giant below; for more about Nanaboozho, see Gargantua p.75.)

THE SEA LION

Another manifestation of the Ojibwe spirit world can also be found in the park. The *Sea Lion Trail* leads to a "wall" of rock jutting into the lake, with a tunnel cut through it by waves. Stronger than the surrounding rock,

Sea Lion, c. 1904. Note group posing at top right

it is the remains of a strong volcanic diabase dike that has resisted erosion. Around the turn of the twentieth century, the rock was said to resemble a giant lion sitting on its haunches. While it is still impressive, the head has since broken off.

To the Ojibwe, the Sea Lion was Mishepeshu, the Great Horned Lynx. Mishepeshu was a terrifying underworld manitou who lurked under the water, stirring up white water and drowning people. He was the cause of so much fear that his name was only spoken aloud in winter, when he was safely trapped beneath the ice. To appease Mishepeshu, Ojibwe left offerings of tobacco and food near the "Sea Lion". Another interpretation suggests the Sea Lion is Nanaboozho's faithful pet, Moo-oos (the Little Moose). In a fit of rage, after Moo-oos had misbehaved, Nanaboozho supposedly turned his pet into stone to await forgiveness in eternity. *The Sea Lion is located on Perry Bay, just northwest of the Silver Islet community.*

SLEEPING GIANT PROVINCIAL PARK TRAILS

The *Sea Lion Trail* is one of 19 trails in Sleeping Giant Provincial Park. Each has a distinct character, length, and level of difficulty. All are fascinating.

The *Piney Woods Nature Trail* winds through 175-year-old red and white pine, some of the last softwood timber on the North Shore. Red and white pine used to blanket much of the area, until it was logged in the nineteenth century.

In contrast, the *Sibley Creek Nature Trail* leads to a marshy area filled with beaver dams and lodges. Watch carefully and you might see a moose emerge from the forest to drink in the shallow waters.

The *Thunder Bay Bogs Nature Trail* is a short loop leading to a small lake that is rimmed with ancient peat beds. The shoreline actually floats on the watertable beneath your feet.

There are over 80 kms (50 miles) of trails. Several have designated campsites for weary backpackers. The *Kabeyun Trail* offers spectacular vistas, coves and beaches on the west coast of the peninsula. *Gardner Lake Trail* follows part of an old logging road and is a favourite for anyone wanting to spot moose. For those in search of exotic plants, *Middlebrun Bay Trail* has ankle-deep mosses, arctic plants and orchids, two varieties of which are Ontario's rarest. (The park contains thirty recorded orchid species.)

The trails provide many opportunities to view wildlife: osprey, bald eagles, moose, martin, fisher, deer, timber wolves, bears and "Cross foxes." From 1909-44, Ernest Cross raised silver foxes, some of which escaped and bred with wild red foxes, creating this hybrid.

SLEEPING GIANT: THE TRAGIC STORY OF NANABOOZHO AND SILVER

The giant, Nanaboozho, led the Ojibwe people Anishnaabe to the shores of *Anishnaabe Chi Gaming* (The Ojibwe's Ocean) where they would be safe and secure. One day while sitting on a rock near shore, Nanaboozho scratched the earth and uncovered a large vein of pure *shuniah*, silver: a metal he knew the white man craved.

Gathering his chieftains around him, Nanaboozho warned, "This must always be a secret among us. If the white man learns of the silver, the Ojibwe will be driven from the land by their greed." The Ojibwe people were forbidden to fight the white man by orders of the Great Spirit. Nanaboozho was also warned not to harm the white man.

Nanaboozho gathered all the silver he could find and buried it on a tiny island. Driven by an obsession with *shuniah*, one chieftain watched where Nanaboozho hid the silver, and returned to dig up enough to fashion

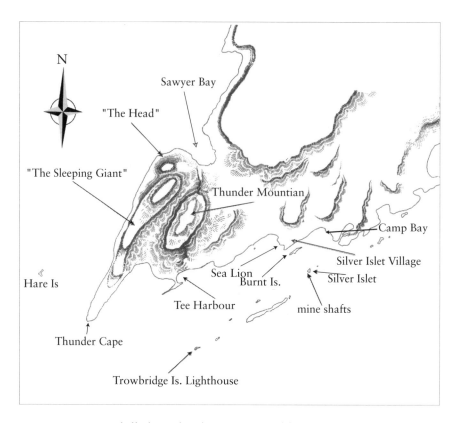

weapons. He was killed in a battle against neighbouring Sioux, and a Sioux warrior seized his weapons. The Sioux knew they were made of *shuniah*, much valued by the white man, and they were certain the metal must be on Ojibwe land around the great lake.

The Sioux devised a plan. If whites learned the Ojibwe territory was rich in *shuniah*, they would drive the Ojibwe off the land. As soon as they found the metal, the whites would take it and leave. Then the Sioux could take over. Putting the plan into action, a Sioux warrior interested two white men in the find and canoed them across the lake. When Nanaboozho saw them approaching, he created a fierce storm that drowned the three men. In doing so, he ignored the orders of the Great Spirit. As punishment, Nanaboozho was cast into stone at the foot of a long peninsula, near the very place he had hidden the silver.

The *shuniah* lay forgotten until two white men stumbled across Canada's richest silver lode near the Sleeping Giant in July, 1868.

THE BATTLE AT SILVER ISLET:

The Bonanza Find

John Morgan had been sent to obtain samples of lead-enriched galena for the Montreal Mining Company. Now he was searching for a place to shield himself from the blast his partner Patrick Hogan was about to detonate. Where to hide? This godforsaken "Island No. 4" was barely 27m (90 ft.) long. When the explosion erupted, Morgan almost didn't hear it because beneath the water, practically within reach of his outstretched hand, lay several nuggets of silver. Within a week, several hundred pounds of silver-rich ore were on board the steamship *Algoma* bound for Montreal, along with detailed descriptions of a silver vein running northwest from Island No. 4 towards the mainland.

The executives in Montreal were very impressed by the samples, less so by the location. An exposed mine site out on Lake Superior? For two years, the company struggled to make the site productive, but it became apparent that the investment would have to be heavy, so the company sold the property to a Major Sibley of Detroit. Sibley knew that in order to succeed, he would need an iron-willed superintendent. He found William B. Frue, spurring him on with the promise of a $25,000 bonus. Frue arrived in 1870, prepared for battle.

The Battle Begins

Frue and his engineers arrived with two horses, machinery, a scow, a raft of timber, provisions and thirty labourers. It was September and the lake was in a surly mood. The men worked eighteen-hour days to build extensive timber breakwaters, foundations and a coffer dam around the vein. Miners managed to extract about seventy tons of ore, no thanks to Superior.

In October, half the breakwater was shredded. They rebuilt it 8-m (26-ft.) wide, twice the original width. Before Christmas, large parts of the cribbing were destroyed, dumping 3,000 tons of rock into the lake. In March, another 75m (250 ft.) was ripped away. As Frue held up the twisted iron bolts, someone quipped, "They might as well have been my wife's hairpins." For the rest of the month, Superior attacked relentlessly, eliminating another 15,000m (50,000 ft.) of timber cribbing.

The first winter was difficult for the wives and families who endured the cold in tents and primitive conditions. It was not until the summer of 1871

Canada's first successful silver mine was on a tiny islet only 27m (90ft.) long.

that the mainland town of Silver Islet Landing was built, along with the harbour's breakwater, basin and wharves. An elegant three-storey house was completed for the President on Camp Bay, and construction began on a jail for drunks and roughnecks. To guide vessels into Silver Islet, the firm installed its own lighthouse and range lights. Frue even organized a library for the single men living in bunkhouses on the Islet. (Because the library was situated in the saloon building, the bartender doubled as librarian.)

As the mining moved underground, a complex grew above: shafthouse, engine house, rock house and pump house (to keep the shaft from flooding). Despite the incredible challenges, the operation at Silver Islet seemed to be progressing. By the end of the summer, the island was surrounded by a breakwater 22m (75 ft.) at the base, with 5-metre-high (18-ft.) bulkheads holding 50,000 tons of rock rubble.

By now the operation employed over 480 men. Originally Frue had hired a group of miners from the Keweenaw Peninsula in Michigan. Later he went further afield, paying the passage for a number of Norwegian and Cornish miners who soon grew dissatisfied and left. A sixty-hour work week, poor conditions, not to mention strict rules—like having their whiskey consumption tallied—were just too much. Frustrated, Frue wrote, "Our last assortment of Cornishmen turned out as troublesome as our Norwegians. Ten of them stole off the day after their arrival. The remainder all struck work after one day underground. As to the reasons offered, they are as many and as opposed to compromise as Quills on a porcupine."

Working conditions were unpleasant, even by mid-nineteenth century standards. Safety measures were virtually non-existent, and miners worked in constant fear that their head candles would ignite trapped pockets of gas. The threat of flooding was ever-present and as the shaft sank deeper and deeper, the terror of being lowered beneath the lake intensified. Only a flimsy wall of wood and stone protected the miners. In one of Superior's frightening assaults, observers watched horrified as mountainous waves crushed the breakwall and crashed into the shaft. Two brave miners entered the shaft to warn others below:

Silver Islet miners worked 1,200 ft. below Lake Superior

Village of Silver Islet formed in a ring around the mainland shore. Inset: mine superintendent William Bell Frue led his miners in a battle against Lake Superior

> We saw to our horror the waves rushing right through the middle of the island between the machinery house and shaft of the mine and boarding house.... We saw two buildings go down before the waves, and as the storm permitted we noticed the breach of water widen more and more while dense clouds of spray shot up against and over the houses, shops, steam-house, threatening to engulf them.... The waves poured over the destroyed breakwater carrying logs and stones upon their crests.

Monthly wages were $68 (minus $14 for room and board). Before leaving the mine after each shift, miners had to submit to body searches, just in case they were hoping to augment their wages with some silver. Anyone who refused the search was fined $10.

Frue left in 1875 and over the next three years, the mine production was disappointing in spite of Frue's very capable replacement, Richard Trethewey. It was only when they brought in a diamond-tipped drill that they struck a new vein (the drill was a first of its kind, improving on European drills used in subway tunnelling).

Superior Succeeds

At that time, Silver Islet was one of the richest silver mines in the world. With breakwalls and cribbing, the 27-m (90-ft.) island had been expanded to ten times its original size. By 1883, one of its shafts reached 375m (1,250 ft.), almost a quarter of a mile deep. Some people worried about nearing 1,300 feet in the 13th year of operation. To them the events of 1883-84 were inevitable.

As winter approached, the mine superintendent noted there was only enough coal to last until March 1st. Without fuel, the pumps could not operate, and without the steam pumps in operation, the mine would flood.

Not to worry. The steam freighter *H. B. Tuttle* was on its way with 1,000 tons of coal, more than enough to hold Superior's waters at bay until spring. But the *Tuttle* did not arrive. The lake froze early and the boat was locked in ice somewhere off Houghton, Michigan. Miners frantically fed wood into the pump boilers. They even began dismantling wooden buildings. But it was not enough. Within weeks the mine flooded and had to be abandoned.

Silver Islet store during the town's heyday

In its 13 years of operation, the Silver Islet Mine had shipped more than $3,000,000 worth of ore, $1,300,000 in its first three years alone. The mine spawned a vibrant community that continues as a summer community to this day. The general store now includes a tearoom. Many of the "camps" or cottages, along the waterfront date back to the mine era. Even the old jail has been converted. At the Islet, remnants of the building foundations, mine shafts, and breakwalls still lie under the frigid water.

From time to time, reminders of the Silver Islet mine era are uncovered, some more poignant than others. When the old freight shed was torn down a hundred years after the closing of the mine, wreckers found a sealed shipping crate. Inside was the small tombstone of a miner's child who had likely died during a typhus epidemic. Perhaps the miner had been unable to pay for the tombstone when it arrived. The tranquil cemetery is gradually returning to nature, in among trees at the far end of The Avenue.

The island is privately owned. Trespassing is prohibited... and Silver Islet residents make it their business to notice transgressors! (Much of the information for this story was gathered from Elinor Barr's *Silver Islet: Striking it Rich on Lake Superior*.)

SURPRISE LAKE

Not far from Superior's shore lies a favourite spot where generations of Silver Islet residents have come to swim and picnic. According to folklore, the lake was bottomless. Its inky black water indicated that it was cupped in the crater of an extinct volcano. Whatever its origins, the lake was known for its huge sturgeon. It is said that a century ago, miners released several sturgeon into the lake. Each May, their giant offspring flaunt their size and then disappear until the next year. According to legend, as many as thirteen of these fish have been counted, ranging up to 5m (16 ft.) long.

Tee Harbour fishing station sprawled along the shore

Women with 80-lb. sturgeon, Tee Harbour

TEE HARBOUR: A FISHING PARADISE

Scandinavians have long been attracted to the North Shore. Danes populated Pass Lake, Swedes were found in lumber camps near Nipigon, and Norwegian and Cornish miners were lured to the Silver Islet Mine. The first Finns and Swedish-speaking people from Finland came to the North Shore in the 1880s; a second wave came shortly after the Bolshevik Revolution of 1917. Well-adapted to northern living, they sought jobs in mining, lumbering and fishing. Two of their fishing communities were at Tee Harbour, on the southeast shore of the Sibley Peninsula, and at Sawyer Bay.

From Tee Harbour, the Ericksons, the Aijalas and the Westerbacks fished for herring, whitefish and trout. At first they fished in open sailboats, later in converted lifeboats with cabins and engines. Until 1943, Tee Harbour was a cozy clutter of shanties, docks and drying reels. Then the residents decided to float all the buildings to Camp Bay at Silver Islet where road access would make it easier to transport their catch to the Lakehead. A few cabin foundations can still be seen on the south side of Tee Harbour.

TROWBRIDGE ISLAND LIGHT AND THE WRECK OF THE *THEANO*

A scant 24 kms (15 miles) from Thunder Bay and sheltered by nearby Sibley Peninsula, Trowbridge Island, its attractive light station and unusual dwelling house appear peaceful and safe. But as the story of the shipwreck *Theano* suggests, appearances can be deceiving.

The *Theano*, one of four steamers originally built for salt-water service, was purchased by Algoma Steel to carry iron ore from the Lakehead to the Sault, and steel rails back. That day in November 1906, she was heavily laden with rails when a gale blew up. The waves tossed the steamer like a cork, and the snow was so heavy that the crew could barely see. Pushed almost a mile off the shipping channel, by the time the *Theano*'s captain saw Trowbridge Island, it was too late. The ship was stuck fast. The crew waited two hours, but when the *Theano* began filling with water they launched the two lifeboats. In the churning seas, the boats became separated. One sailor would later write:

> The trip across Thunder Bay was the most terrible I have ever experienced. One minute it seemed that we were 20 feet below the surface and next we would be on the crest of a gigantic wave with the bow of our boat pointing downwards. Again and again waves would break over us drenching every man to the skin. At times it was impossible to see the men in the opposite end of the boat.... Numbed, exhausted and almost overcome by exposure we arrived in Port Arthur about eleven o'clock. I am sure we could not have survived another six hours.

Safe, there was no rejoicing while the crew on the second boat was lost. They later learned that the others had been picked up by a tug near Hare Island. Another tug set off the next day to inspect Trowbridge Island where the captain had reported the *Theano* had gone down. But there was nothing to be found. Much later, a depth sounder located the wreck at 108m (360 ft.) off nearby Marvin Island.

It was not until 1924 that a lighthouse was installed on Trowbridge. Today, all Great Lakes lighthouses are automated. While most have had their original lenses replaced by solar powered light bulbs, Trowbridge is among the few to have retained its original Fresnel lens (though it is not currently in use). Complaints from fishermen and others that the beam from Trowbridge's solar-powered light is insufficient may lead to the old Fresnel lens being used once again.

Freighter Theano *wrecked near Trowbridge Island in 1906. Eighteen years later, in 1924, a lighthouse was finally installed on the Island*

THUNDER CAPE: LAND OF THE THUNDERBIRDS

Imagine the earth as an island wedged between two spirit realms. Above, the sky cosmos is ruled by *Animikeek*, Thunderbirds, and below, the water underworld is ruled by the horned lynx/sea serpent, Mishepeshu. The two worlds meet at the earthly plane. Thunderbirds protect humans; they are the grandfathers. These giant spirit eagles shoot lightning from their eyes to kill the cruel underworld manitou Mishepeshu, who as lord of the waters, is feared by humans. The sounds of thunder are their voices. When the *Animikeek* are about to attack Mishepeshu, thunder is used as a warning for anyone to get off the lake. Sometimes the young Thunderbirds behave like excited children, which together with their lack of skill at flying and throwing strikes, can inflict injury and havoc on humans.

According to the Ojibwe, the region around Thunder Bay is spiritually charged. For it is here that the Thunderbirds come to hatch their young atop Thunder Cape at Sleeping Giant, and Mount McKay, which towers over the city of Thunder Bay. Down below, where waves smash against the rocks, we are reminded that Lake Superior belongs to Mishepeshu. The mythic relationship between the Thunderbird and the Mishepeshu, these two powerful, opposing Spirits, represents the forces of balance, and the interdependence of this fluid world.

Thunder Cape painting by William Armstrong

In 1873, Catherine Moodie Vickers, daughter of early Canadian author, Susannah Moodie, watched as the Thunderbirds and Mishepeshu unleashed their power at Thunder Cape:

> ...the vivid flashes of lightning lighting up the mountains on each side...; then from all sides of us ribbons of fire ran up the sky in all shapes, more like rockets and fire works, whilst the thunder leaped from mountain to mountain in a continued roar, like nothing I ever heard before, and followed by a low growl.... If I were an artist I would choose Thunder Bay in a storm as the grandest representation of the end of the world.

AMETHYST HARBOUR

It was a clear, pleasant day in 1910 when Robert Ruttan entered Amethyst Harbour. With its bays, white birch and 80-foot cliff, it was an ideal location for a summer colony. Ruttan purchased a large piece of property extending from Amethyst Harbour around the peninsula to North Bay, and divided it into over sixty lots. There was no shortage of buyers. The Van

Baileys, a family of six, started out by squeezing into two tents: the "living tent" with a wooden floor, stove and table, and the "sleeping tent" with beds made of chickenwire and straw mattresses placed on the ground. Eventually they built a summer cottage by hauling supplies in over the winter ice.

1920s group at Trails End, Amethyst Harbour

Summer days were filled with fishing, swimming, hiking and games of croquet. Children would sometimes raft out into the lake to flag down barges and lumber tugs, hoping a sympathetic cook might offer freshly baked bread or pie. It was especially fun to roll a piano to the beach for sing songs and wiener roasts. Sports Day, dances, garden parties, an annual fishing derby, and the very competitive Port Arthur vs. Fort William campers' baseball match were also part of Amethyst Harbour traditions. Eight decades later, many of the cottages still have their rustic charm and campers are still using the ball field and tennis courts at The Ruttan Memorial Park. *(The harbour was either named for a small nearby amethyst mine which operated around the 1860s, or by the CNR blasting gang who discovered amethyst imbedded in the rock.)*

THUNDER BAY'S TWIN TOWNS: PORT ARTHUR AND FORT WILLIAM

Port Arthur: Humble Beginnings

One of Colonel Garnet Wolseley's enlisted men quietly asked, "Does the Colonel really think the Prince will be flattered by having his name attached to this God-forsaken place?" His companion just smiled. Newly-named Prince Arthur's Landing consisted of blackened tree stumps and a few crude buildings, many scorched by a brush fire that had swept the area the week before. Its population of about 300 was mostly rag-tag silver prospectors.

Wolseley camp at Prince Arthur's Landing, 1870. Painting by William Armstrong.

It was May 1870. Colonel Wolseley and his 1,200 soldiers had been sent west to provide a military presence at Red River, Manitoba. The soldiers had been forced to disembark their steamer and land by small boat because the water in the harbour was barely three feet deep. Wolseley's first task was to reinforce the area against a possible Fenian attack from the U.S. Earlier that year, the Irish-led, anti-British movement had already launched small raids into Quebec. After mounting guns, Wolseley prepared his troops for the rigorous portages they would meet along the way to Red River. When the soldiers finally left, there were more than a few puzzled residents in this desolate community with its grand-sounding name.

By the late 1870s, booming mining operations at nearby Silver Islet had transformed the Landing into a lively community. Miners poured in expecting a good time and so much of the town's early growth was based on one product: liquor. "Water Street was filled with saloons," recalled one resident around 1876. "Every other place was a saloon, except where there were two together." Fortunately for those with more diverse needs, scattered among the saloons were general stores, dry goods merchants, bakers, jewellers, and even a photography studio operated by a nephew of poet Alfred Lord Tennyson.

Battles in Railway Land

From the beginning, the little town was spirited, and not solely because of the whiskey. Its feistiness partly derived from the will not to be overshadowed by its neighbour, Fort William. When, in 1875, Fort William hosted the official sod turning for the Canadian Pacific Railway's Lake Superior terminus, Prince Arthur's Landing residents feared their community might languish into a forgotten backwater. They mobilized quickly, raising funds to build a spur line to Westfort, where it connected with the main rail line soon to lead all the way to Winnipeg. In 1876, when the first train on the The Prince Arthur's Landing & Kaministiquia Railroad arrived at the Landing, everyone gathered to cheer. The more exuberant fired guns into the air. Six years later when the main line railway was completed from Winnipeg in 1882, the residents of Port Arthur had secured their role as one half of the Lakehead terminal for grain shipments from the west.

Prince Arthur's Landing (which now had twenty-nine bars and six liquor stores serving a population of 1,200) began to rethink its name, which sounded like a stopping place for steamers. Suggestions came forward but it was CPR General Manager William Van Horne's preference for Port Arthur that carried the most weight. Whatever Van Horne wanted, Van Horne got. The name Port Arthur was adopted in 1883, the same year the CPR completed a grain elevator here. Trains streamed in from the west, and, in the first year, 858 ships loaded at Port Arthur before heading east. Unfortunately, the town soon faced a new problem.

Port Arthur was stung when the local silver boom collapsed. In late 1889, to offset falling revenues, town officials demanded $15,000 in unpaid property taxes from the CPR. Failing to collect, they seized a CPR locomotive and several cars, some of which were full of grain. Van Horne did

Early Port Arthur when it was one bar after another

The first transcontinental train arrived in Port Arthur, June 30, 1882

not like being forced to settle the account, and was further incensed when the bailiff insisted on charging the CPR interest. The town council eventually agreed to forego the interest and to exempt any further CPR improvements from taxation, on the condition that Port Arthur handle all incoming package freight and passengers. Not one to be "railroaded," Van Horne refused to bend to strong-arm tactics. Port Arthur's determination to increase its business with the CPR was fueled by the continued rivalry with Fort William. Even though the Canadian Northern Railway made Port Arthur its terminal point in 1902, the spunky Port Arthur always seemed to be playing "catch-up" with its older rival.

FORT WILLIAM: THE NORTH WEST COMPANY'S GREAT RENDEZVOUS

Before Fort William was erected by the North West Company, two earlier French posts had been set up in 1683 and 1717, along the Kaministiquia River, an important fur route. This location was subsequently abandoned in favour of Grand Portage, which was closer to the Pigeon River, a more favourable western route. Grand Portage remained the centre of operations for Lake Superior's French traders, and later for the North West Company, until after the American Revolution. The newly-drawn international border placed Grand Portage in U.S. territory. Threatened with having duties imposed on their trade goods, the Nor'Westers relocated to the northernmost branch of the Kaministiquia

River near the site of the earlier French posts. They named the new post Fort William, after their esteemed chief director, William McGillivray.

The interior headquarters of the North West Company, Fort William became the site of the annual Great Rendezvous, held in July each year. "Wintering partners" from the interior canoed to the fort with their furs to meet up with the partners from Montreal. The brigades of voyageurs, guides, interpreters, and clerks arrived from Montreal with trade goods such as pots, utensils, spices, clothing and tools. The Great Rendezvous, however, was much more than a business transaction. It was a time for celebration. Freed from the social confines of home, the men let loose. The air filled with the sounds of bagpipes, fiddles, and rum-soaked voices singing sentimental songs of heather and brae.

The revelry, impromptu races and wild dancing were centred in the 18-m (60-ft.) long Great Hall. Here the men dined on buffalo tongue and hump, smoked lake trout and whitefish, roasted venison

Feasting, dancing and impromptu races were all a part of the Great Rendezvous

and beaver tail, stuffed duck and goose, topped off with rich confectioneries brought all the way from Montreal. Their cups overflowed with port and Portuguese wines, whiskies from Canada and Scotland, and amber rum by the hogshead. As one visitor later recounted: "It was the time to settle annual accounts. For the trappers who had lived eight long cruelly cold months in the Canadian bush, it meant a round of feasting, drinking carelessly, dancing with the 'don't care girls,' and playing games of chance with their fur-money with ferocious abandon." Think of it: up to 2,000 visitors crowded together in this remote post at the head of Lake Superior at a time when the entire population of York—soon to become Toronto—numbered fewer than 500.

Two thousand people descended on fort William during the mid-July Great Rendezvous

The fort was an elaborate complex including: the Great Hall, sleeping quarters, a fur warehouse, powder magazine, workshops, a place where canoes were outfitted, and another that sold liquor, bread, pork and butter. There was also a counting house, and buildings for the carpenter, cooper, tin smith, blacksmith, physician, and clerk. Visitors were each given a complimentary loaf of white bread, a half-pound of butter and a gill of rum which they consumed at the saloon, affectionately known as "The Canteen Slop". If they became unruly, they were carted off to jail, usually accompanied by their half-pound of butter, which accounts for the jail's nickname, *le pot au beurre*, "The Butter Tub."

Fun aside, as competition between fur companies heated up, the Nor'westers at Fort William found themselves in trouble.

Attack on Fort William

In 1816, Fort William was invaded. Not by nearby Americans still embittered after the War of 1812, but by the North West Company's rival, the Hudson's Bay Company, led by Lord Selkirk. The attack was retaliation for events that took place hundreds of miles away.

Lord Selkirk had obtained a grant on the Red River (in what is now Manitoba), giving him rights to an area twice the size of England. He promised to create a major colony by settling one thousand families within ten years. The NWC was strongly opposed, fearing it would be cut off from its important western trade corridor and its vital pemmican supply. The company found its best allies among the Métis who feared losing their lands to Selkirk's settlers. In June 1816, tensions exploded.

Semple, the colony's governor, and his men marched into Seven Oaks at the Red River Settlement to intercept Métis who were delivering pemmican for the North West Company. One popular version of events claimed Semple seized the bridle of a Métis' horse. Shots were fired by the Métis and 21 men (including Semple) were killed. Six others escaped into the woods. Later Selkirk was told that the armed Métis had been spurred on by members of the North West Company at Fort William.

Enough was enough. Selkirk's assembled a group of Swiss mercenaries, a handful of native guides and eighty soldiers. He planned to attack Fort William, capture the NWC leaders, and take them back to Montreal for trial. Selkirk succeeded in the first part of his task. In a surprise attack, he seized the fort and ordered his men to escort several NWC men to Montreal. Among the prisoners were William McGillivray, Simon Fraser and Alexander Mackenzie. Selkirk remained at Fort William, a place he described as "an asylum for banditti and murderers."

Then, en route to Montreal, disaster struck. One of Superior's notorious gales drove the convoy onto Maple Island, drowning a number of men (see p.26). When the party finally reached Montreal, Selkirk's men found little sympathy. Selkirk was defeated in one court battle after another. Two years after his raid on Fort William, he returned to England. Suffering from tuberculosis, bankrupt from legal fees, his reputation tarnished, Selkirk died in 1820. The very next year, the inconceivable happened: his beloved Hudson's Bay Company merged with his greatest enemy, the North West Company.

Fort William began to decline, although fur trading continued for another sixty years. In 1889-90, the CPR relocated their main operation to a piece of land beside the fort. As the railway expanded, the old historic buildings were demolished one by one to make way for tracks or new structures. The last to fall was the stone-walled store in 1902.

This marked the end of one era, but signalled Fort William's debut as a major commercial and transportation centre. Soon about 500 men were employed at the new rail facilities and a construction boom followed. Serving as a railway terminal for the main line at the Lakehead, Fort William and Port Arthur received their civic charters in 1907. Fort William was prepared for anything....it thought.

THE NUDISTS OF 1908

Doukhabor Sons of Freedom under house arrest after their nude march through Fort William

New Year's Day, 1908. Queen Victoria was dead but her strong influence on morals and modesty lived on. Naked people do not show themselves in a public place. Besides, it was January!

The ten nudists who paraded down the main street were among eighty members of the Doukhobor Sons of Freedom planning to winter in Fort William before continuing their search for the "Promised Land." Deeply religious, they believed in the rejection of all worldly goods, including clothing.

Launching the New Year in Fort William *sans habilles* earned the group two months' house arrest, which in turn, attracted large numbers of onlookers, eager to glimpse a display of public nudity. Avoiding deportation to Russia, the sect members were eventually placed on a train to Yorkton, Saskatchewan where the first nudist parade had taken place in 1903. It was perhaps better equipped to deal with mid-winter nudity.

As labourers were needed to work in the growing rail and harbour facilities, more immigrants flooded into Fort William. In 1909, their "foreign ideas" and CPR management clashed with explosive results....

THE GREAT STRIKE: WILD WEST IN FORT WILLIAM

The waterfront was a babble of languages. Two freight handlers gossiped in Slavic, another called to his friends in Finnish and the words of a Ukrainian folk song drifted over the warehouse. This was Fort William in 1906, when over a thousand immigrant labourers—Italian, Greek, Croatian and Hungarian, and only a smattering of English and French—

toiled in the CPR freight sheds. Most had never intended to work in Fort William. Arriving from northern and eastern Europe, they had dreamed of homesteading on the Prairies, not working in a gritty freight yard.

But workers go where there are jobs and in the early 1900s there were jobs in Fort William. These men brought a cosmopolitan flavour to the Lakehead. They also brought their socialist traditions, openly objecting to discrimination and unfair labour practice.

Bosses brushed aside small concerns which escalated into bigger problems, and the workers became militant. As the largest work force in the region, why should their power not match their size? When the CPR ignored demands for higher wages and fair treatment, the workers went on strike. At one protest, shots were fired in an effort to control the workers, and strike breakers were brought in to replace those who refused to return to work. A settlement was reached, but worker resentment continued to simmer. On August 9, 1909 it exploded.

More than 700 workers walked off the job. Word spread among local police that the strikers were planning violence. When the police tried to search the strikers for concealed weapons, shots rang out. No one was injured and only one man was arrested, but the CPR

Troops were brought in to subdue the freight handlers' strike

had had enough. Five days later, a group of thirty sullen men arrived from Winnipeg and checked into the CPR boarding house. Management called them "Special Constables." The strikers called them armed thugs, sent to quell the strike by force.

The labour leaders passed the word to the constables: "Stay inside or be shot." When the defiant men emerged, a gun battle broke out. For two hours, bullets and gunsmoke, shattered windows and frightened horses turned Fort William into a Wild West town.

At battle's end, eleven CPR constables and several strike-breakers lay seriously wounded. The following day, Royal Canadian Mounted Rifles and the 96th Regiment of Militia took control of the city and disarmed the strikers. The military presented the city with a bill for $3,345 (most of

The heart of the twin cities

which went to the CPR for their transportation). The freight handlers were later awarded a 2 cent raise per hour, hiking their pay from 18.5 cents to 20.5 cents a day, 23.5 cents for night work. One CPR constable died from his wounds and six strikers were sentenced to jail. The worst strike in Fort William's history was over.

Fort William settled into a long period of peaceful growth, sparked only by the continuing rivalry with its next-door neighbour. On January 1, 1970 that competition ended when Fort William and Port Arthur (each with a population of about 50,000) were amalgamated into the city of Thunder Bay. The Ojibwe had called the region *Animikie*, "Thunder" which the voyageurs translated into *Baie de tonnerre*, "Thunder Bay."

To revive the community's proud heritage, the old Fort was meticulously reconstructed 14 kms (9 miles) upriver from its original site. Old Fort William, with its 42 historic buildings, is a marvellous recreation of the post in the early 1800s, and has become one of the Lakehead's premiere attractions. Standing by the water, it isn't hard to imagine the voyageurs putting on a last burst of speed as they came around the final bend in the river.

While Thunder Bay's harbour is still fringed with grain elevators, it is hard to grasp the quantity of wheat that once passed through here. It is estimated that the   Saskatchewan Wheat Pool Elevator No. 7 stored enough grain to make a loaf of bread for every person in North America! Shipments through Thunder Bay have markedly declined, yet a thriving dry dock (capable of accommodating ships up to 225 metres (750 ft.) in length) is still repairing the big lake vessels. The heart of Thunder Bay remains a port town at the edge of a shining freshwater sea.

MOUNT MCKAY, "THUNDER MOUNTAIN"

Mount McKay towers 300m (1,000 ft.) above the city of Thunder Bay. When the summit is shrouded in clouds, and thunder rumbles through the fresh spring air, the *Animikeek*, or Thunderbirds, have returned home (see Thunder Cape p.235). To the Fort William First Nation living around the mountain's base, the *Animikeek* are the protectors of the Ojibwe people, who call the mountain *Anamikiewakchu*, "Thunder Mountain."

The lookout at 150m (500 ft.) offers visitors a panoramic view. But be warned. To climb higher is to dare the Thunderbirds' wrath. Nearby stands a large white cross commemorating those native people who lost their lives in the two World Wars.

Voting for Chief of the Mission Band on Mount McKay, 1933

KAMINISTIQUIA RIVER: THE DINOSAUR MYSTERY

The drama of the discovery was lost alongside the launch of the first minesweeper to be built locally for service in the Great War. On Saturday June 28, 1918, a group of men were excavating the north bank of the Kaministiquia River in preparation for the minesweeper's launch. Suddenly there was a stir of excitement. 12m (40 ft.) below the surface was a massive skull, several large bones, a copper spearhead and a cedar log. "What would have had a head that big?" someone asked. Everyone exchanged puzzled glances. According to Joseph Mauro's *Thunder Bay: A History*, the relics were placed under lock and key in the minesweeper plant, where they were examined the following day by Peter McKellar. The respected local historian quickly reached his conclusion: "It is most likely the remains of a giant dinosaurus which lived before the glacial period back in the dim recesses of time."

After photographing them, McKellar had the bones displayed at the Fort William Public Library and sent the pictures to the Geological Society in Ottawa. But apparently, the launch of a new minesweeper was more eventful than the discovery of a million year old dinosaur. No one in Fort William kept copies of the photographs, and when the Geological Society requested the actual bones for closer study, they were sent off without debate. Even the media seemed more amused than intrigued. "That dinosaur whose bones were found has been buried there for over a million years, they say," commented the *Times Journal*, its tongue set firmly in its editorial cheek. "We hadn't even a suspicion anything was as dead as that in Fort William."

It took until November for the Geological Society to deliver their opinion. One specimen, the scientists declared, came from a buffalo or some kind of domestic cattle. The rest of the bones were the remains of a horse. The spearhead was of prehistoric Indian make. There it was. The Fort William "dinosaurus" had been reduced to one part buffalo and twelve parts horse. Future discoveries received even less local attention. In 1913, several copper tools were located 12m (40 ft.) below Stanley Street. In 1926, chisels and adzes were found buried under Mountain Avenue, and in the 1930s, while excavating a sewer, workers uncovered the remains of a well-preserved coniferous forest at the same 40-ft. depth. Where are the artifacts today? And did anyone photograph the ancient forest? No one knows.

In the 1960s, a local historian realized that the buffalo and horse remains

Wolseley Expedition portaging around Kakabeka Falls

might have been several thousand years old, making them immensely important. How else to explain their depth beneath the surface? But his inquiries to the Geological Society produced little more than a casual shrug. Nothing remained in the Society's possession—no skull, no bones, no spearhead, no pictures. The mystery remains.

KAKABEKA FALLS: THE STORY OF GREEN MANTLE

The falls and gorge were carved by a turbulent torrent of glacial melt-waters leaving what the Ojibwe called *kah-kah-pee-kah*, "sheer cliff." The power of this waterfall tumbling 39m (128 ft.) over slate cliffs, evokes the folkloric story of young Green Mantle, daughter of Ojibwe Chief Ogama Eagle, who saved her people from the Sioux.

Captured by the notorious Sioux Chief Ogama Dog, Green Mantle was taken to Dog Mountain. By imprisoning her within a circle of tepees, the Sioux planned to slaughter the Ojibwe who tried to rescue her. The situation seemed hopeless for Green Mantle until a manitou came to Ogama Dog in a dream and advised him to attack the Ojibwe camped along the Kaministiquia River rather than to wait. The spirit promised it would be a glorious victory, all the more triumphant if Green Mantle were to lead the

Sioux warriors into battle. The vision was irresistible. Terrified, Green Mantle was forced to paddle in front of the throng of armed warriors to attack her own people.

The Sioux struggled to keep up with the athletic girl, who ignored portages and expertly manoeuvred her canoe through the roughest white-water. It was an exhausting trip. Suddenly, as the water churned wildly, Green Mantle overturned her canoe and struggled for shore. Her timing was crucial. The Sioux were so focused on recapturing their prisoner that none realized how quickly the water had gained momentum. As Green Mantle ran to her village she could hear the screams of the Sioux warriors plummeting to their deaths over Kakabeka Falls. Today, the green mist in the cascades is said to be a reminder of this heroic young woman.

For early travellers, portaging around the thunderous falls was unavoid-able When viewing the falls meant an overnight canoe journey from Fort William, Catherine Moodie Vickers wrote to her mother Susanna Moodie in August 1873:

> There before us was the most glorious sight a mortal eye could see. Gilded and burnished by the morning sun, the great current of water came rushing down almost two hundred feet... one pure torrent of snow-white foam.... As it reaches the rapids below it breaks over the rocks which, from the quantity of iron in the neighbourhood, are bright red. The water in a glass is the colour of brandy or sherry wine so you may imagine what it is when the sun shines on those stones. As we walked, we were in the loveliest rainbow—the stones, the trees, every-thing gloriously coloured with it.

The falls, dubbed the "Niagara of the North", are dramatically different today due to the construction of a hydro-electric power station. *Kakabeka Falls Provincial Park has camping and picnic areas, beaches along the river, hiking trails including the historic 2-km (1.25-mile) Mountain Portage Trail, plus walkways and viewing platforms on either side of the gorge.*

ANGUS ISLAND AND THE DISAPPEARING MINE SHAFT

It's not a large island, barely a kilometre in length and so narrow you can toss a stone into the lake from virtually anywhere. Little vegetation grows on this rocky shoal just east of Pie Island. So how could anyone lose a mine shaft? Early reports mention an underwater silver vein near the shore and a mine that was opened on Angus Island around 1878. Yet no mining records exist. And search as one may, there is no shaft. Did Lake Superior fill it in? Were the reports erroneous? Or perhaps a light station building was built over the shaft?

The Angus Island light was an important navigational aid for the heavy traffic entering Thunder Bay harbour. The lighthouse was erected in 1905 after the wreck of the *Monkshaven*, the first of three "cursed" sister ships (the *Monkshaven*, *Leafield* and *Theano*) that met their fate around Thunder Bay. The foundations of the former lightkeeper's dwelling and other buildings may still conceal the mysterious mine shaft.

Angus Island Lighthouse, 1921

MONKSHAVEN, LEAFIELD AND THEANO: THE DOOMED SISTERS

Saltwater sailors have been known to snub Great Lakes ships and their crews, as though the only true challenges are found on the high seas. Perhaps they should consider three ships, all sturdy saltwater ore and freight carriers, all brought down by Superior's notorious November gales. The British-built *Monkshaven*, *Theano* and *Leafield* were purchased by Algoma Steel in the early 1900s. Within eight years, all had succumbed to the great "Kitche Gummi."

The *Monkshaven* was the first to go in one of Superior's most notorious storms. At the end of three terrible days in November 1905, at least fourteen ships were lost leaving wreckage strewn around the lake. After battling their way across the lake with a cargo of steel rails, the men aboard the *Monkshaven* may well have believed they were no longer in danger. They were bobbing like a cork, but they knew they were not far from Thunder Bay. Suddenly Angus Island loomed out of the snow, dead ahead. One monstrous wave lifted the vessel high in the air, impaling it on a rocky outcropping, which cut through the steel hull as though it were a can of stew.

Crewmembers leaped onto shore. Behind them, the *Monkshaven* filled with water. There they were, 21 ill-clad men, stranded on a pile of rocks in high winds and sub-freezing temperatures. For three days and nights the

Monkshaven aground on Angus Island

men huddled beneath a crude shelter of boards and branches. Their doomed ship towered above them, rolling and groaning with the force of every wave. No one dared to board her. Two of the men went nearly mad with the cold, noise, wind and hunger. All of them were convinced they would die from exposure.

On the fourth day, the winds abated enough for them to board the vessel to retrieve clothing, food, and most importantly, the yawl. Thirteen of the crewmembers sailed the yawl into the shipping channel where they were rescued by a passing freighter. The remaining eight were taken off Angus Island later that day. For many years, the grounded *Monkshaven* sat on the island until she was cut up for scrap.

In a near repetition of her sister ship's fate, the *Theano* went down a year later. (*See Trowbridge Island.*)

Seven years after the *Theano* was lost, the *Leafield*'s turn came, but more than the ship was lost. Every one of her eighteen crewmembers vanished without a trace. The *Leafield* was fighting her way west towards the Lakehead when one of Superior's most infamous storms broke.

The great four-day blizzard was still raging when the liner *Huronic* arrived at the Sault, tons of ice clinging to her superstructure and shell-shocked passengers huddled in their cabins. The captain and helmsman were in bad shape because the pilot house had been destroyed leaving them exposed to the elements.

The captain reported that he had seen the *Leafield* in difficulty off Angus Island, the same rock that had claimed the *Monkshaven*. Another captain whose vessel had been following the *Leafield* into Fort William reported seeing the struggling ship hit by a gigantic wave. When the seas settled, the *Leafield* simply disappeared. No flotsam, no slick, no boats, no lifejackets.

A salvage tug failed to find evidence of the ship, and nothing ever turned up to explain the *Leafield*'s fate or that of her crew. Like others before her and so many after, the *Leafield* seems to have vanished through "a hole in the lake." (For another harrowing *Leafield* story see p.xxxiv).

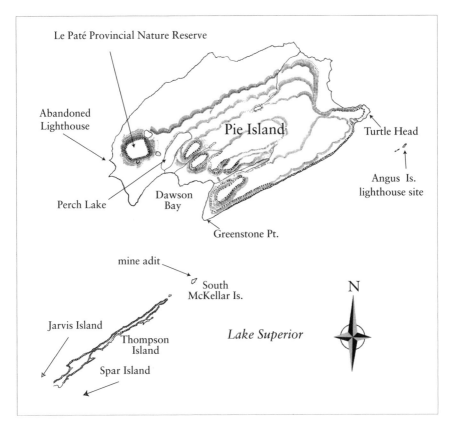

PIE ISLAND: A MERMAID SIGHTING?

A 1782 incident on *Isle Paté*, Pie Island, so haunted the voyageur, Venant St. Germain, that nearly thirty years later he stood before the Judges of the Court of King's Bench in Montreal, swearing a deposition of what he had seen.

Returning from Grand Portage with three other voyageurs and an elderly native woman, the group stopped on Pie Island to make camp. As the sun touched the horizon, St. Germain left to set fishing nets. Something in the water drew his attention. As he advanced, he saw a distinctly human form bobbing in the waves. It is not known how close St. Germain got to the "animal" (as he called it) but he studied the apparition for about four minutes. The torso was that of a seven or eight year old child, one arm oddly extended in the air, the other resting on its hip. Its eyes were

Majestic Pie Island

"extremely brilliant, head small but handsomely shaped, the mouth pro-portionate to the rest of the face, the complexion of a brownish hue." By now the others had joined St. Germain. All were mesmerized by this crea-ture who stared back at them with a mixture of unease and curiosity.

St. Germain never used the word mermaid. That came later in 1824 when the *Canadian Magazine* reprinted his deposition and claimed the tes-timony proved the existence of mermaids on Superior. St. Germain ended his deposition with one final note about another employee of the North West Company who had spotted a similar creature on Pie Island. The judges wrote: "the frequent appearance of this extraordinary animal on the spot has given rise to the superstitious belief among the Indians that the God of the Waters had fixed upon this site for his residence...." St. Germain's encounter with a *Nebaunaubaewuk* is similar to many alleged sightings of the Ojibwe's underwater manitou, Mishepeshu. Unfortunately, the opinion of St. Germain's native passenger is not recorded. Ojibwe believed that *Nebaunaubaewuk* and *Nebaunaubaequaewuk*, Mermaids and Mermen, inhabited the Ojibwe Spirit world. Mermaids would lure and kid-nap mortals into the watery depths. Eventually these captives would accept their destiny, and be transformed into half-human, half-fish beings.

Pie Island also exhibits evidence of another manitou....

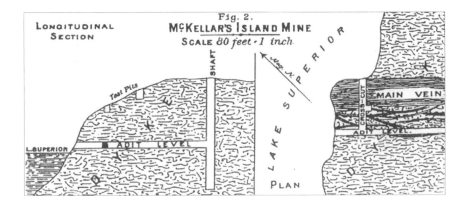

THE MINING ISLANDS

Pie, South McKellar, Thompson, Spar and Jarvis

High above the water, visible for over 16 kms (10 miles), is the "Peeping Squaw", a large stone profile, named for the giant Nanaboozho's wife. Legend maintains that she and Nanaboozho, after travelling many exhausting miles, decided to take advantage of their great size by leaping to their destination. She fell short and landed on Pie Island. Here she remains, waiting in vain for her mate to rise from his slumber on nearby Sleeping Giant (see p.222).

Dramatic **Pie Island** is distinguished by *Le Paté*, a towering steep-sided round mesa that appeared to the voyageurs like a French patty. The island measures 5 by 10 kms (3 by 6 miles) making it the largest of the offshore chain of islands south of Thunder Bay. On a map, they look like a handful of stones tossed in a line by a giant's hand. For many years, these islands shone like silver in the eyes of investors and speculators.

In the early 1870s, an Ojibwe woman caused a frenzy on Pie amid the excitement surrounding the nearby Silver Islet Mine. Finding a rich piece of silver ore, she showed it to friends but refused to reveal its source until offered $20 by visiting Americans.

She was never able to fulfill her promise to take them to the site, for within days she was dead. (Many Ojibwe refused to show Europeans copper and silver sites, believing that revealing these locations brought bad luck, sickness, or even death.) The group went to the island anyway and found more than one silver vein. But did they find the right one? By 1875 an 18-m (60-ft.) shaft had been sunk. Investment money poured in, enough to finance the construction of an enormous 60-m (200-ft.) dock, a large two-storey administration building, boarding houses, a laboratory, and a smelting operation.

Later that year, a 45-kg (100-lb.) sample of ore was refined into a scant three 3-kg (7-lb.) bars. That was the last of the refined silver from the island. Low-grade ore continued to be mined and piled in small mountains, awaiting the purchase of a crusher for refining, but the crusher never arrived.

Over the years, the Pie Island silver mine was bought and then sold by investors who poured money into drilling and ventilation equipment; steam pumps for removing seeping water; and never-ending repairs. Yet the mother lode was never found. By the summer of 1882, with the money drying up, the miners walked off the job after "a misunderstanding with the company in reference to their pay." *(Dock cribs can still be seen in Dawson Bay on the south end of the island. A trail leads into Perch Lake. North of Keefer Point, there is a small abandoned lighthouse somewhat obscured by bush along the west shore.)*

South McKellar Island carries the name of one of the most prominent families in Thunder Bay. Miners, businessmen and historians, the McKellar name pops up constantly in the community's records. Donald, John and Peter, sons of prospector Duncan McKellar, began mining the island for silver in 1869. They did recover some silver but not enough for a profitable operation. In 1882, Peter put in an adit (a horizontal tunnel), and a cross cut shaft. Again the quantity of silver was negligible.

However, South McKellar boasted other mineral riches, including deposits of barium sulphate, an ingredient in paint. For two years beginning in 1886, miners hacked out the highest grade barite in North America, shipping it to Cincinnati where it fetched $5 a ton. When the contract expired, so did mining on South McKellar Island. Today, two abandoned adit entrances can be seen on the north tip of the island.

Thompson Island attracted attention when the Montreal Mining Company—the firm that prematurely sold its rights to Silver Islet—first investigated a vein of silver in 1853. Twenty years later, it reopened the site, dug an adit, a cross-cut (a tunnel running perpendicular to the vein) and a shaft 39m (130 ft.) deep. With little of value found, the mine was soon abandoned. (There are some very old features known as Pukaskwa Pits on the island (see p.136).

Spar Island, unlike others in the chain, was developed as a mine site long before the roaring success of Silver Islet. According to Scott McWilliam's paper *The Island Mines*, as early as 1846, the island was mined for copper, although promising silver specimens convinced the operators to switch their operation. At this time there were no Sault locks, and so any kind of mining was difficult and expensive. A firebrick for a steam boiler, 5 cents in Toronto, cost 25 cents by the time it arrived at Thunder Bay. An early freeze-up meant hay for the horses never arrived. Owners had to substitute bread to feed the animals.

Since Spar Island's silver mine produced only limited quantities of low-grade ore, when the shafts flooded with water faster than the men could remove it, the decision to close the mine was an easy one. The entire island has been designated Crown Land, and no further mining has taken place.

Jarvis Island may always be remembered as the place where the mine owners managed to convert a year's production valued at $117.34 into $150,000 in cash. Located immediately south of Spar Island, the island boasted a vein of silver ore running in the same northwest direction as the vein on profitable Silver Islet. In 1870, the Ontario Mineral Lands Company recovered $117.34 worth of ore from a shallow, 3.6-m (12-ft.) shaft. The following year they sank the shaft deeper and recovered a few more samples. Thanks to the frenzy surrounding the Silver Islet ore, they were able to sell the mine to English and American investors for $150,000.

The new owners drilled three mine shafts, one 48m (160 ft.) deep, and built new accommodations for the miners. However, the company failed in 1872 and the mine sat idle for fourteen years.

In 1886, one of the new owners, Arthur McEwen, had to return to Port Arthur when Superior's ice was melting. It was a precarious journey. Laying down a plank, he walked its length to spread his weight over the thinning ice, then repeated the manoeuvre for almost 40 kms (25 miles). In spite of falling into the lake several times, McEwan was too excited about his mine's prospects to care. But yet again, in spite of small volumes of rich ore, the operation on Jarvis Island was not profitable. By the time the mine was abandoned in 1888, the shaft was 104m (346 ft.) deep. There seems little doubt that Jarvis Island held some rich reserves, but the operation was plagued by too much water and too little money.

PIGEON RIVER: ROUTE TO THE WEST

Canada/U.S. Border

The Ojibwe knew Pigeon River as the beginning of the river route to the west, to a region more vast and abundant than any explorers could imagine. Explorer and fur trader, Pierre de Varennes, Sieur de la Vérendrye was

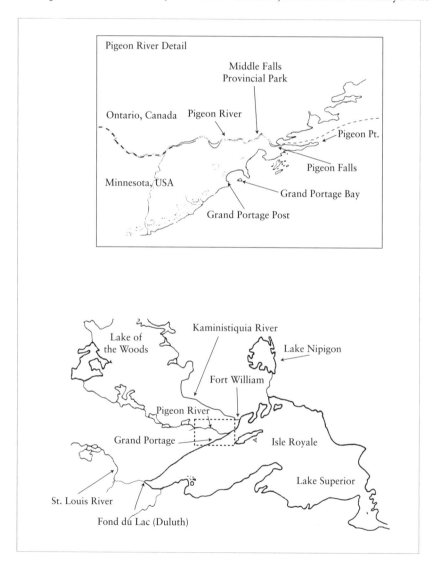

counting on it. La Vérendrye's goal was to find the fabled saltwater sea in the continent's interior, said to lead to the Pacific Ocean. In 1731, he landed with three of his sons and a retinue of over 50 at Grand Portage Bay. La Vérendrye was not able to proceed that year, but his party began the trek up the Pigeon River. They used a 14.4 km (9-mile) portage to circumvent a torturous 20-mile series of falls and rapids (the elevation of Pigeon River drops almost 700 ft. in twenty miles). This "Grand Portage" was subsequently used by inland canoe brigades for many years. After completing the Grand Portage, travellers heading inland would follow a chain of lakes and rivers to Rainy Lake, Lake of the Woods, Lake Winnipeg and on to Athabasca and the northwest.

Back in 1731, La Vérendrye and his party had set up a small encampment in the protected Grand Portage Bay, ten miles southwest of the mouth of the Pigeon River. At the end of the Seven Years War in 1763, the French relinquished their claim to the continent's interior, and the British took possession. In 1768, British trader John Erskine drafted an order for the construction of a barracks at the same location. (Attached to the order he added: "I need two pretty slave girls from nine to sixteen years old. Have the goodness to ask the Gentleman to procure two for me." This was a routine request, no doubt filled as commonly as a requisition for flour and bedding materials.)

With the merging of independent traders into the North West Company between 1779-83, Grand Portage became their inland headquarters. It was at this stockaded post that wintering partners from the Northwest, and the voyageurs from Montreal first began their annual July rendezvous to exchange goods and pelts. But politics soon got in the way of commerce.

The American Revolution brought the United States independence. With it, came a new border through the Great Lakes and through the heart of Lake Superior's fur trade country. Dividing the territory was not an easy task. At the time, this lucrative land was largely an unknown hinterland. For assistance they turned to a 1755 map that later became known as "Mitchell's Map." John Mitchell's map of North America gave them what they needed: a line marking the voyageur route from Superior to Lake of the Woods by way of a river that travelled through Long Lake. The Pigeon River thus came to mark the international border. The British were loath to leave Grand Portage until, around the turn of the century, they were threatened by U.S. customs officials wanting to impose duties on their furs. In 1801, the NWC began building Fort William (see p.240) at a spot near the mouth of the Kaministiquia River (in present-day Thunder Bay).

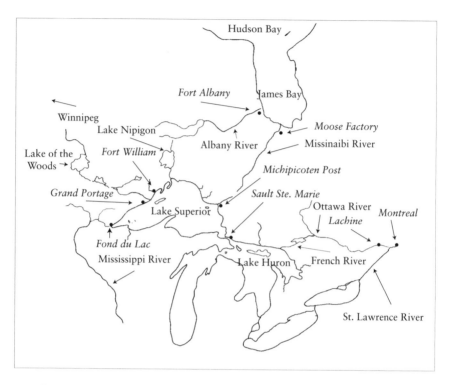

All seemed well until 1822, when the international border commission set out to define the border more clearly. They were plagued by inaccuracies from early sources such as Mitchell's Map and its depiction of mysterious Long Lake. Since the border was meant to follow the old voyageur route to Lake of the Woods, negotiators had to decide which river connected to the fictitious Long Lake: the St. Louis River route, the Pigeon River route, or the Kaministiquia route further north (see map p.258). The commission sought the help of Mitchell's Map, only to discover that it had been lost. Fierce debate ensued. Each side wanted the river route that gave them the most land, the Americans desiring Kaministiquia, and the British the more southerly St. Louis. It was not until 1842, twenty years later, that the Webster-Ashburton Treaty designated the Pigeon River route as the international boundary.

Over a century later, in 1917, Canadian and American neighbours on both sides of the border felt the lack of a bridge across the Pigeon River. When both Federal governments refused to construct one, locals from both sides chose to build their own. Though Washington and Ottawa disapproved, the citizens went ahead with the project and soon were using "The

Outlaw Bridge." Much later, the two countries jointly funded a new official bridge and The Outlaw Bridge entered the folklore of Superior's North Shore. Long gone, it is still remembered.

Today the river's history is commemorated on both sides of the international border. At the former Grand Portage post in Minnesota, post buildings have been reconstructed as part of Grand Portage National Monument. The monument also includes the famous portage trail, and the site of Fort Charlotte, a former inland depot for the canoe brigades. On the Ontario side, Middle Falls Provincial Park offers hiking trails along sections of the falls and cascades which had been such an obstacle to the canoe brigades.

PICTURE CREDITS

Archives of Ontario: 229, 239, 263
Baldwin Room, Metro Toronto Reference Library: 140, 216
Ron Brown Collection: 126
Peal Bussineau: 36
Canadian Pacific Archives: x, xxvii, 191(top), 206, 240, 268
Canal Park Marine Museum Collection, Duluth: 23
Mary Lou Covello: 237
Lee Fletcher: 134
Historic Sites and Monuments, Canadian Coast Guard Collection: 107, 113, 116
Hudson's Bay Company Archives, Provincial Archives of Manitoba:130
Charles Humber Collection, Heirloom Publishing: 157
Huronia Museum: xxxvii, 17, 235
Pat Johnston: 114, 115, 117, 119
Lake Superior Provincial Park: 32, 35, 57, 58, 68, 72, 73, 91(top)
Lynx Images Collection: xviii, xxxii, 29, 34, 44, 64, 198, 254
Metro Toronto Reference Library: xxiii, xxviii, xxxix,10, 13 ,25, 26, 42, 55, 29,138,157,162, 163, 168, 170, 183, 189, 199, 214, 219, 238, 241, 242, 249, 255
Michipicoten Heritage Committee: 62, 84, 85, 87 ,91(bottom), 93 ,95, 97, 99, 196
Dan Miles: 48, 49, 50
National Archives of Canada: xx, xxi, xii, xiv, xxxiv ,6, 30, 103, 104, 122, 143, 176, 185, 194 ,203, 205, 209, 211, 215, 223, 236, 251, 261
National Gallery of Canada, Ottawa: 60
Lyle Nicol: 173, 174(top and bottom)
Notman Photographic Archives, McCord Museum of Canadian History, Montreal: 153
Ontario Paper Company: 156
Parry Sound Public Library: xxxvi
Mort Purvis: 106, 108, 111
Pukaskwa National Park: 133, 141, 144, 148, 149
Rossport Historical Society: 191(bottom)
Sault Ste. Marie Museum: 2, 39, 40
Sault Ste. Marie Canal, National Historic Site: 8
Schreiber Public Library and Archives: 186
Sleeping Giant Provincial Park: 220

State Historical Society of Wisonsin, Iconographic Collection: xvii, 25, 76
Terrace Bay Public Library, Local History Collection: 182
Thunder Bay Historical Museum Society: xxiv, xxxv, 165, 192, 205, 224, 228, 230, 231, 244, 245, 246, 247, 252, 277
Toronto Dominion Bank Archives: 159
John Westerback: xxix, 232, 233

Excerpt from A.J.M. Smith's "The Lonely Land" is from *The Classic Shade Selected Poems*, McClelland and Stewart Inc., The Canadian Publishers: 53

Miners at Silver Islet

SELECTED BIBLIOGRAPHY

Agassiz, Louis and Cabot, J. Elliot. *Lake Superior*. Boston: Gould, Kendall & Lincoln, 1850.

Barr, Elinor. *Silver Islet: Striking It Rich*. Natural Heritage/Natural History Inc., 1988.

Barry, James. *Old Forts of the Great Lakes*. Lansing: Thunder Bay Press, 1994.

_____. *Ships Of The Great Lakes*. Holt, Michigan: Thunder Bay Press, 1996.

Bayliss, Joseph & Estelle. *River of Destiny: The Saint Marys*. Detroit: Wayne University Press, 1955.

Berton, Pierre. *The Last Spike: The Great Railway 1881-1885*. Toronto: McClelland and Stewart, 1971.

Bigsby, John J. *The Shoe and the Canoe*. Vol. II. London: Chapman & Hall, 1850.

Bogue, Margaret Beattie and Virginia Palmer. *Around the Shores of Lake Superior: A Guide to Historic Sites*. Madison: The University of Wisconsin Press, 1979.

Boultbee, Jean. *Pic. Pulp and People: A History of the Marathon District*. Township of Marathon, 1981.

Butts, Ed. *Pirates and Outlaws of Canada 1610-1932*. Toronto: Double Day Canada Ltd., 1984.

Capp. E.H. *Annals of Sault Sainte Marie*. Sault Star Press, 1904.

Conway, Thor & Julie. *Spirits on Stone: The Agawa Pictographs*. San Luis Obispo, California: Heritage Discoveries, 1990.

Dahl, Bonnie. *The Superior Way: A Cruising Guide to Lake Superior*. Ashland: Inland Sea Press, 1983.

Danziger, Edmund Jefferson. *The Chippewas of Lake Superior*. University of Oklahoma Press, 1978.

Dean, Pauline. *Sagas of Superior: The Island Sea*. Manitouwadge, Ontario: Great Spirit Writers, 1992.

Dorson, Richard M. *Bloodstoppers and Bearwalkers*. Cambridge, Massachusetts: Harvard University Press, 1952.

Drew, Wayland and Litteljohn, Bruce. *The Haunted Shore*. Gage Publishing Limited, 1975.

Driben, Paul. *Aboriginal Cultures of Ontario*. Ontario Ministry of Citizenship and Culture, 1987.

Fowle, Otto. *Sault Ste. Marie and it's Great Waterway*. New York: G.P. Putnam's Sons, 1925.

Gutsche, Andrea. *Alone in the Night: Lighthouses of Georgian Bay,*

Manitoulin Island and the North Channel. Toronto: Lynx Images Inc., 1996.

_____. *The North Channel and St. Marys River: A Guide to the History.* Lynx Images Inc., 1997.

Hornbeck Tanner, Helen. *Atlas of Great Lakes Indian History.* University of Oklahoma Press, 1986.

Johnston, Basil. *The Manitous: The Supernatural World of the Ojibway.* New York: HarperCollins, 1995.

Kelso, John. *Our Living Heritage: The Glory of Nipigon.* Echo Bay: Mill Creek.

Longstreth, T. Morris. *The Lake Superior Country.* Toronto: McClelland and Stewart, 1924.

Lund, Duane. *The North Shore of Lake Superior: Yesterday and Today.* Staples, Minnesota: Nordell Graphic Communications, 1993.

Marcella, Jeanne, ed. *A History of Jackfish.* Terrace Bay: Terrace Bay Public Library, 1986.

Mauro, Joseph. *Thunder Bay: A History.* Thunder Bay, Ontario: City of Thunder Bay, 1981.

Ministry of Northern Development and Mines, Ontario. *ROCK Ontario.* Sudbury: Ontario Ministry of Northern Development and Mines, 1994.

Mount, Graeme. *The Border at Sault Ste. Marie.* Toronto: Dundern Press, 1995.

Newman, Peter C. *Company of Adventurers.* Vol. 1. Markham: Viking/Penguin Books Canada Ltd., 1985.

_____. *Caesars of the Wilderness (Company of Adventurers,* Vol. 2.) Markham: Viking/Penguin Books Canada Ltd., 1987.

Nute, Grace Lee. *Lake Superior.* Indianapolis: Bobbs-Merrill, 1944.

Osborne, Brian. *The Sault Ste. Marie Canal.* Ottawa: National Historic Parks and Sites Branch, Parks Canada, 1986.

Pye, E.G. *Roadside Geology of Ontario: North Shore of Lake Superior.* Rock On Series 2. Sudbury: Ontario Ministry of Northern Development and Mines, 1997.

Schmaltz, Peter S. *The Ojibwa of Southern Ontario.* Toronto: University of Toronto Press, 1991.

Smith, Philip. *Harvest from the Rock*: A History of Mining in Ontario. Toronto: MacMillan of Canada, 1986.

Smith, Theresa S. *The Island of the Anishnaabeg.* Moscow, Idaho: University of Idaho Press, 1995.

Steer, Don. *Superior's East Shore: Mamainse To Garantua.* Don Steer, 1995.

Turcott, Agnes. *Land of the Big Goose: History of Wawa and Michipicoten Area*. Dryden, Ontario: Alec Wilson Publications, 1982.

Valley of Tree and Water: Recollections of Goulais River. Goulais River: DAK General Services, 1978.

Warren, William W. *History of the Ojibway Nation*. Minneapolis: Ross & Haines Inc., 1970.

Waters, Thomas F. *The Superior North Shore: A Natural History of Lake Superior's Northern Lands and Waters*. Minneapolis: University of Minnesota Press, 1987.

Wolff, Julius. *Shipwrecks of Lake Superior*. Duluth, Lake Superior Marine Museum, 1979.

Articles, Reports and Pamphlets

Ackerman, Paul W. "Lake Superior Dive Chart." Chicago: Midwest Explorers League, 1987.

Ministry of Natural Resources, "A Chronology of Man in Lake Superior Provincial Park."

Carruthers, P.J. "Rock Structures of Lake Superior." 1979.

Colemen, Margaret. Federal Heritage Buildings Review Office Building Report 88-143, "Davieaux Island and Quebec Harbour."

Conway, Thor. "Archeology in North East Ontario: Searching For Our Past." Ministry of Culture and Recreation.

Dawson, K.C.A. "The Pukaskwa Religious Stone Features of Lake Superior." Victoria, B.C.: British Columbia Museum, 1979.

"Diary of My Father, Soren Lassen." Michipicoten Township Public Library, 1890.

MacDonald, Bill ed. "Emanations of Silver Islet." Porphyry Press, 1995.

MacDonald, Graham. "East of Superior: A History of the Lake Superior Provincial Park Region." Ontario Ministry of Natural Resources, Wawa District Office, 1974.

_____. "The Saulteur—Ojibwa Fishery at Sault Ste. Marie 1640-1920." Thesis for the University of Waterloo, 1978.

Kershaw, William. "Agawa Rock Indian Pictographs: Background Document for Naturalist Staff." Lake Superior Provincial Park.

MacMillan, Colin. "The Discovery of the Pukaskwa Pits." *Wanikan*, Feb. 1986.

Marsh, John. "The Human History of the Pukaskwa National Park Area 1650-1975," 1976.

Mattie, Joan. Federal Heritage Building Review Office Report 90-206, "Otter Island Light."

_____. Federal Heritage Building Review Office Report 88 141 and 88-

144, "Angus Island Lightstation and Lamb Island Lightstation."

"Environmental Sensitivity Atlas For Lake Superior's Canadian Shoreline."
Toronto: Environment Canada, Conservation and Protection
Branch, 1993.

McKenzie, P. "Inspection Report, Michipicoten River Post, Michipicoten
District, 1892." Hudson's Bay Company Archives.

McWilliams, Scott. "The Island Mines." Scott McWilliams, 1988.

Morrison, Johanna & Kaireen. "Michipicoten Memories." Wawa:
Michipicoten Heritage Committee, June 1992.

Morrison, Johanna. "Focus on Superior East Regional Assessment
Project," May 1991.

Mountain, James. "The Inhospitable Shore: An Historical Resource of
Neys Provincial Park." Ministry of Natural Resources, Parks
Division, Historical Sites Branch.

Phemister, Martha. Federal Heritage Buildings Review Office: Building
Report: 90-194, "Ile Parisienne Lightstation."

"Robinson Treaty." Ottawa: Queen's Printer and Controller of Stationery,
1957.

Sundland, Judi."A Visit To Rossport, Ontario, Canada." Rossport
Historical Society.

Simons, David. "Sibley Provincial Park History." Sibley Provincial Park,
1971.

Shchepanek, M.J. "The Early History of the Michipicoten Post Sites."
Ottawa, National Museum of Canada.

Surtees, Robert. "Treaty Research Report: The Robinson Treaties".
Treaties and Historical Research Centre, Indian and Northern
Affairs, 1986.

Vosper, Rick. "Logging in: Lake Superior Provincial Park." Ministry of
Natural Resources, May 1984.

_____. "Transportation and Associated Communities: Lake Superior
Provincial Park." Ministry of Natural Resources, May 1984.

_____. "Artistic Response To: Lake Superior Provincial Park."
Ministry of Natural Resources, May 1984.

_____. "Tourism in Lake Superior Provincial Park." Ministry of
Natural Resources, May 1984.

_____."Development of Lake Superior Provincial Park." Ministry of
Natural Resources, May 1984.

Weiler, John. "Michipicoten: Hudson's Bay Company Post." Historical
Sites Branch, Report 3, December 1973.

Wright, J.V. "An Archeological Survey Along the North Shore of Lake Superior." Ottawa: Dept. of Northern Affairs and National Resources, N. 3, March 1963.

Young, Marilyn. "Red Rock Reflections." Red Rock Public Library Board, 1995.

Journals

"Early Transportation on the Upper Lakes." *Freshwater: A Journal of the Great Lakes Marine History*. V.2, No. 2, Fall 1987

Goodier, John L. "Fisherman and their Trade on Canadian Lake Superior: One Hundred Years." *Inland Seas*. Vol. 45, 1990.

"Kidakiminan (Our Land)." *Ontario Indian*. 1984

"Lake Superior Ojibway Land." *Ontario Indian*. July, 1978.

Temporary timber trestle over the Pic River

INDEX

Trawlers at Port Arthur dock, 1910

ACKNOWLEDGEMENTS

This book could not have been compiled without the generous assistance of the following individuals. While many have contributed to the project, any errors or omissions found in the text are ours alone.

We would like to extend a special thanks to those who helped in researching areas that encompassed many sites, and those who graciously allowed us to draw on their published material: Carol Dersch, Sam Helmer-Vosper, and Rick Vosper at Lake Superior Provincial Park; Robin Heron Promaine at Pukaskwa National Park; Johanna Morrison Rowe (Michipicoten and Wawa); Don Steer (Superior's East Shore); and Elinor Barr (Silver Islet).

Our gratitude goes to all others who helped in our research, fact-checking and picture gathering:

Greg Agawa, Shawn Allaire, Gary Babcock, Lynn Banks, Ned & Shelagh Basher, Olav Bjornaa, Brad Buck, Bob Burns, Linda & Michael Burtch, Pearl Bussineau, Dennis Carter-Edwards, Dan Couchie, Mary Lou Covello, Brenda and Jimmy Cross, Kenn Cutts, Maureen Dampier, Lucy DelGuidice, Gerald Demers, Wayland Drew, Jim Dyson, Tom Farnquist, Lee Fletcher, Sally Gibson, Protheus Goodchild, Kennedy Gordon, Mike Hailstone, G.S. Halter, Carolyn Harrington, Fred Howe, Gail Jackson, Pat Johnston, Linda and Terry Kearns, Sheila Kretz-Greco, Ted Leahy, Fern Lecours, Kevin Leveque, Bill MacDonald, David and Joanna MacDougall, Jeanne Marcella, Donna Martin, Marty Mascarin, Bruce McCuaig, Judy McGonigal, Angus McLeod, Donna Mikeluck, Dan Miles, Blair Mills, Ethel Mole, Mike Moore, Paul Morra, Jean Morrison, Michael Morrow, Mike Murphy, Susan Myers, Mike Neveau, Lyle Nicol, Nancy Parish, Shawn Patterson, Phillip Pelletier, Mort Purvis, Bill Ross, Brian Ross, Maureen Robertson, Louise Robillard, Peter and Kevin Robinson, Joe Tom Sayers, John Scott, Mike Scott, Cam Snell, Bruce Strapp, Merritt Strum, Judi Sunland, Dave "Just remember, the waves get bigger with every beer" Thomas, K.R. Thomson, Tory Tronrud, Jason Van Slack, Jake Vander Wal, and John Westerback.

Research and Supporting Institutions:
Algoma Central Railway Inc.
Archives of Ontario
Art Gallery of Algoma

The Original Bug Shirt Co.
Marathon Heritage Committee
Marathon Public Library
Metropolitan Toronto Reference Library
Ministry of Natural Resourses
Michipicoten Township Public Library
National Archives of Canada
Red Rock Public Library
Sault Ste. Marie Canal National Historic Site
Sault Ste. Marie Museum
Sault Ste. Marie Public Library
Schreiber Heritage Committee
Schreiber Public Library and Archives
Terrace Bay Public Library
Thunder Bay Historical Museum Society
Thunder Bay Public Library

The deepest thanks go to our indefatigable editor, Barbara D. Chisholm; to Deb Wise Harris and her red pen; to R.W. Chisholm; John Reynolds for his spirited work; Janet Looker for maps and support; and to baby Benjamin "Bean" Gutsche Harlton for sleeping when he was supposed to.

Tug James Whalen, *Port Arthur*

Lake Superior Human Time line

7-9000 years ago The Plano enter the region after the retreat of the last glacier
c.5000-500 BC   Shield Archaic culture, ancient copper miners
c.500BC-AD500   Laurel Culture
c.AD 900-1650   Terminal Woodland culture
1619-22 Etienne Brûlé reaches the Sault and reports an inland sea beyond
1632   Samuel de Champlain's map shows Lake Superior and the *Sault de Gaston* (Sault rapids)
1641   Jesuits Charles Raymbault and Isaac Jogues visit the Sault, renaming the rapids Sault Ste. Marie
1659   Pierre Esprit Radisson and Médard Chouart, Sieur des Groseilliers travel to Lake Superior. They return to Montreal the following year with pelts, and are fined for trading without a licence.
1662   Iroquois try to invade Superior country, but are defeated by the Ojibwe and others at Point Iroquois.
1668   Jacques Marquette establishes a Jesuit mission at Sault Ste. Marie (then moves on the following year, and is replaced by Claude Dablon)
1670   Charles II of England grant charter to the Hudson's Bay Company for all territory draining into Hudson Bay
1671   François Daumont, Sieur de Saint Lusson claims all territory west of Montreal for Louis XIV of France
1682   Hudson's Bay Company lose 4 of its 5 forts on Hudson Bay to the French
1683   Daniel Greysolon, Sieur du Lhut builds first post on the Kaministiquia River near present Thunder Bay
1696   English recapture HBC forts for a short time then lose them again.
1713   Treaty of Utrecht - France relinquishes claim to Hudson Bay
1716   French institute *les postes du nord* on Superior's north shore
1735   Louis Denis, Sieur de la Ronde builds a decked ship at Point aux Pins for his copper explorations.
1756   The Seven Years' War begins between Britain and France (called the French and Indian War in North America)
1763   The Treaty of Paris — French territories in Canada ceded to Britain.
1768   Montreal merchants trading in the "North West" outside of the HBC's Rupertsland. Grand Portage post established.
1768-1803 NWC posts established at Sault Ste. Marie, Michipicoten, Pic River, Pays Plat, Nipigon, and Fort William.
1770   Alexander Henry explores for copper on south shore and Michipicoten, and has a sloop and barge built at Point aux Pins in 1772.
1783   North West Company emerges after several previous partnership agreements. Competition with The HBC for the interior is fierce.
1797-8   NWC builds a canoe canal and lock to bypass the St. Marys Rapids
1798   Some NWC members break away and form the competing XY Company
1803   NWC headquarters moved from Grand Portage to Fort William after Grand Portage becomes U.S. territory
1804   NWC and XY Co. merge after NWC's Simon McTavish dies

1804-21 NWC shipping more furs than HBC, but fierce competition and over-
trapping strain both companies

1811   Lord Selkirk, a major HBC shareholder creates a settlement at Red River.

1812   War of 1812 between U.S. and Britain begins

1814   American troops burn NWC post at Sault Ste. Marie and destroy lock.
Treaty of Ghent defines border between Canada and the U.S.

1816   Seven Oaks massacre of Red River settlers. Lord Selkirk descends on
Fort William with Swiss mercenaries and arrests NWC partners he
accused of complicity in the massacre.

1821   HBC and NWC merge under the HBC name, ending years of feuding

1834-5 American Fur Co. has extensive fur trading and fishing operations on
Lake Superior

1839   HBC begins (short-lived) commercial fishery to compete with AFC.

1841   Upper Canada becomes Canada West; Lower Canada, Canada East

1842   Webster-Ashburton Treaty, British/American border set at Pigeon River.
Giant copper boulder found on South Shore sets off a staking rush
around Superior. Increases pressure for a lock to be constructed.

1845   Steam propeller *Independence* is first steamer on Superior after being
portaged around Sault rapids

1848   Louis Agassiz's scientific expedition around Superior

1849   Raid at Pointe aux Mines

1850   Robinson-Superior Treaty signed

1855   American shipping canal and lock opened at the Sault.

1866   Fenian raids into Canada

1867   Canadian Confederation

1868   Silver discovered at Silver Islet

1870   Red River Rebellion. Colonel Garnet Wolseley leads expedition west.
Americans block one of the expedition's boats at Sault locks. Increases
demand for a Canadian lock and canal.

1870s   Settlers flooding west

1884   CP's three passenger steamers, the *Alberta, Algoma*, and *Athasbasca* built

1880s   Grain elevators built at Fort William and Port Arthur

1880s-1930s Booth Fisheries Co. dominates commercial fishing on Lake Superior

1885   Northwest Rebellion. CPR completed around Superior's North Shore.

1887   CPR's "Soo Line from Sudbury to the Sault opens, ends winter isolation.
Construction begins on Canadian canal

1893   Around 12,000 pass through American Sault locks. Most of cargo is iron
ore, also coal, copper, flour, grain, lumber and salt

1895   Canadian Sault lock officially opened

1890s   Francis Clergue founds industries, including the Algoma Central Railway

c.1900 Already fears of some overfishing

1905   Bad year of storms on Lake Superior with terrible loss of ships and life

1913   Great Storm of 1913

1934   Purvis fishery begins at former Booth station at Quebec Harbour

1946-8 Arrival of ship-to-shore radio and radar on Lake Superior

1960   Highway 17, part of the Trans-Canada completed around Superior's
North Shore

GHOSTS OF THE BAY

The Forgotten History of Georgian Bay
Guide Book and Video

The 90-minute film leads viewers on an expedition to the haunting vestiges of Georgian Bay's past (now an eerie world of shipwrecks, ghost towns, fishing camps, lumber villages, and native sites). The Bay's story comes alive through archival film, photographs, character voices, and stunning underwater cinematography.

Bring the book along on your own journey, and transform your experience of Georgian Bay. The 300-page book includes 140 sites, 50 maps, and fascinating archival photographs.

ISBN 0-9698427-1-6   Book/Video
ISBN 0-9698427-0-8   Video
ISBN 0-9698427-3-2   Book

THE NORTH CHANNEL AND ST. MARY'S RIVER

A Guide to the History

For centuries, Lake Huron's North Channel and the St. Mary's River (leading to Lake Superior) have provided an essential passageway, first for native peoples and then for successive waves of Europeans. The footprints of natives, explorers, missionaries and fur traders, soldiers and settlers, entrepreneurs and scoundrels are ever visible. Brimming with stories, folklore and eccentric frontier characters, the book pulls you through a fascinating history of this region. Over 125 sites, maps and archival photographs highlight shipwrecks, abandoned forts, frontier towns and hidden places.

ISBN 1-894073-00-2

ALONE IN THE NIGHT

Lighthouses of Georgian Bay, Manitoulin Island and the North Channel
Book and Video

Lighthouses capture the imagination with their fascinating stories and forgotten memories. Together the book and 72-minute video take you on a compelling journey to the lighthouses of Georgian Bay, Manitoulin Island, and the North Channel, and return you to a time when the Great Lakes were the lifeblood of the country. *Alone in the Night* traces the evolution of lightkeeping, revealing the heroic and the scandalous, the gritty and the routine aspects of this remarkable chapter of Canada's marine heritage.

Discover the over 50 lighthouse sites through stories, photographs, and maps.

ISBN 0-9698427-4-0   Book/Video
ISBN 0-9698427-5-9   Video
ISBN 0-9698427-6-7   Book

ABOUT LYNX IMAGES

Lynx Images is a partnership of Russell Floren, Andrea Gutsche, and Barbara Chisholm. Together they have created a unique company that combines filmmaking and book publishing to explore and document vanishing pieces of Canadian history. The company's Great Lakes focus has generated several best-selling titles: *Ghosts of the Bay: the Forgotten History of Georgian Bay; Alone in the Night: Lighthouses of Georgian Bay, Manitoulin Island and the North Channel*; and *The North Channel and St. Mary's River: A Guide to the History*. The past is brought alive through juxtaposing historical photographs and rare archival footage with sites as they appear today—ghost towns, shipwrecks—sites abandoned by time. Next to be released is the book and film package, *Mysterious Islands: Forgotten Tales of the Great Lakes*, a culmination of five years of extensive Great Lakes research.

LYNX IMAGES
P.O. BOX 5961, STATION A
TORONTO, ONTARIO
CANADA, M5W 1P4
WEB SITE: HTTP//WWW.LYNXIMAGES.COM

Rough seas on the Canadian Leader. *Andrea Gutsche and Russell Floren film* Superior: Under the Shadow of the Gods *with Capt. Randy Smith.*

Photograph by Barbara Chisholm